A HARDY CHRONOLOGY

MACMILLAN AUTHOR CHRONOLOGIES

General Editor: Norman Page, Professor of Modern English
Literature, University of Nottingham

Reginald Berry
A POPE CHRONOLOGY

Edward Bishop
A VIRGINIA WOOLF CHRONOLOGY

Timothy Hands
A GEORGE ELIOT CHRONOLOGY
A HARDY CHRONOLOGY

Harold Orel
A KIPLING CHRONOLOGY

Norman Page
A BYRON CHRONOLOGY
A DICKENS CHRONOLOGY
A DR JOHNSON CHRONOLOGY
AN OSCAR WILDE CHRONOLOGY

F. B. Pinion
A WORDSWORTH CHRONOLOGY
A TENNYSON CHRONOLOGY

R. C. Terry
A TROLLOPE CHRONOLOGY

A Hardy Chronology

TIMOTHY HANDS

First published by
MACMILLAN PRESS LTD
Houndmills, Basingstoke, Hampshire RG21 6XS
and London
Companies and representatives
throughout the world

ISBN 0–333–45914–8

A catalogue record for this book is available
from the British Library.

This book is printed on paper suitable for recycling and
made from fully managed and sustained forest sources.

Transferred to digital printing 2000

Printed in Great Britain by
Antony Rowe Ltd, Chippenham,Wiltshire

For Judith and Peter

Contents

General Editor's Preface

Most biographies are ill adapted to serve as works of reference – not surprisingly so, since the biographer is likely to regard his function as the devising of a continuous and readable narrative, with excursions into interpretation and speculation, rather than a bald recital of facts. There are times, however, when anyone reading for business or pleasure needs to check a point quickly or to obtain a rapid overview of part of an author's life or career; and at such moments turning over the pages of a biography can be a time-consuming and frustrating occupation. The present series of volumes aims at providing a means whereby the chronological facts of an author's life and career, rather than needing to be prised out of the narrative in which they are (if they appear at all) securely embedded, can be seen at a glance. Moreover, whereas biographies are often, and quite understandably, vague over matters of fact (since it makes for tediousness to be forever enumerating details of dates and places), a chronology can be precise whenever it is possible to be precise.

Thanks to the survival, sometimes in very large quantities, of letters, diaries, notebooks and other documents, as well as to thoroughly researched biographies and bibliographies, this material now exists in abundance for many major authors. In the case of, for example, Dickens, we can often ascertain what he was doing in each month and week, and almost on each day, of his prodigiously active working life; and the student of, say, *David Copperfield* is likely to find it fascinating as well as useful to know just when Dickens was at work on each part of that novel, what other literary enterprises he was engaged in at the same time, whom he was meeting, what places he was visiting, and what were the relevant circumstances of his personal and professional life. Such a chronology is not, of course, a substitute for a biography; but its arrangement, in combination with its index, makes it a much more convenient tool for this kind of purpose; and it may be acceptable as a form of 'alternative' biography, with its own distinctive advantages as well as its obvious limitations.

Since information relating to an author's early years is usually scanty and chronologically imprecise, the opening section of some volumes in this series groups together the years of childhood and adolescence. Thereafter each year, and usually each month, is dealt with separately. Information not readily assignable to a specific month or day is given as a general note under the relevant year or month. The first entry for each month carries an indication of the day of the week, so that when necessary this can be readily calculated for other dates. Each volume also contains a bibliography of the principal sources of information. In the chronology itself, the sources of many of the more specific items, including quotations, are identified, in order that the reader who wishes to do so may consult the original contexts.

NORMAN PAGE

Preface

Hardy was in favour of chronologies (two he recommended to Gosse in October 1904 have been used in this publication), but fundamentally opposed to literary biography – especially when the subject was himself. 'Lives of poets are a mistake', Sir George Douglas suggested to Hardy in the summer of 1923, and he cannot have been surprised by the agreement he elicited. Accordingly, Hardy decided, in Robert Gittings' phrase, to erect a barrier against biography. He did his best to ensure that only such papers as he wished to survive did so, and, in *The Life of Thomas Hardy*, a selectively accurate autobiography posing as the work of his second wife Florence, attempted a pre-emptive biographical first strike.

Wherever possible, *A Hardy Chronology* aims to tell the story of Hardy's life using Hardy's own words, principally those of the *Life* and, by kind permission of the Oxford University Press, of the recently published *Collected Letters*. But, especially for the earlier years, where Hardy's attempts at repressing significant biographical details or misrepresenting the importance of certain events or relationships were particularly wide-ranging, this method can be only partially satisfactory. Selective use has therefore been made of the markings Hardy made in books preserved in his library at the Dorset County Museum, which form a kind of irregular diary of his life, and which are particularly informative about the earlier years. From Hardy's Prayer Book, for example, has been included under 11 September 1864 the revealing entry 'Doubt' – a dated marking which Hardy erased so deeply that it has eluded all his major biographers. In addition quotations have occasionally been added from biographies other than Hardy's own, the purpose being to help the reader appreciate the significance of events and personages (such as the character of his mother, the engagement to Eliza Nicholls, or the death of Florence Henniker) which Hardy was at best unable to assess neutrally and at worse anxious to suppress. The chief source for such quotations has been what is now generally considered the standard study, Michael Millgate's *Thomas Hardy: A Biography*.

An additional consideration peculiar to this volume, as compared with others in the same series, is that of bulk. Hardy wrote extensively, in more than one genre, in a life of more than eighty-seven years lived at a time of exceptional change and many great events. Selectiveness has therefore been essential. In general, this survey includes only the first editions of Hardy's prose fiction, and subsequent editions which have textual or biographical importance. Poems dated by Hardy (and caution needs always to be exercised before accepting any such dating) have been included under that date. Where date of composition is known, and date of first appearance (if published prior to inclusion in one of Hardy's eight volumes of poetry), this information too has been added. Further bibliographical information can be found in R. L. Purdy's standard *Thomas Hardy: A Bibliographical Study*, whilst the third volume of Samuel Hynes's edition of Hardy's *Complete Poetical Works* offers a useful 'Complete Chronological List of Dated Poems'.

This series does not aim to provide broad cross-references to the historical events and cultural productions of the period: the reader who wants such enlightenment can read this volume in tandem with a work such as S. H. Steinberg's *Historical Tables*. But a number of background works – including both the chronologies recommended by Hardy – have been consulted, and details from them have been added on a necessarily subjective basis. The principle has been to pay particular attention to personages and events in which Hardy took special interest, such as the Boer and First World Wars.

A question mark indicates reason for caution before confidently assigning the event mentioned to the date shown. A singular verb without subject always implies Hardy himself as the subject of the sentence (as in 'Finishes manuscript of *Far from the Madding Crowd*'), whilst a similarly subjectless plural verb implies Hardy's spouse as the joint subject. The unrelated personal pronouns to which this compressed sentence structure occasionally gives rise should cause the reader only the most momentary difficulty.

I am grateful to Jennie Barbour for scrutiny of the typescript; Catherine Hands for the index; the General Editor, Norman Page, for his characteristic helpfulness; and the copy-editor, Graham Eyre, for his detailed attention to the typescript.

List of Abbreviations

DNB	*Dictionary of National Biography*
ELG (later ELH)	Emma Lavinia Gifford, Hardy's first wife
FEH	Florence Emily Hardy, née Dugdale, Hardy's second wife
Friends of a Lifetime	Viola Meynell (ed.), *Friends of a Lifetime: Letters to Sydney Carlyle Cockerell* (London, 1940)
Letters	*Collected Letters of Thomas Hardy*, ed. Richard Little Purdy and Michael Millgate, 7 vols (Oxford, 1978–88)
Life	'Florence Emily Hardy', *The Life of Thomas Hardy* (London, 1962)
Millgate	Michael Millgate, *Thomas Hardy: A Biography* (Oxford, 1982)
Personal Notebooks	*The Personal Notebooks of Thomas Hardy*, ed. Richard H. Taylor (London, 1978)
Purdy	Richard Little Purdy, *Thomas Hardy: A Bibliographical Study* (London, 1954)
TH	Thomas Hardy

A Hardy Chronology

Early Years (1840–61)

1840   (2 June) Born at Higher Bockhampton, in the parish of Stinsford, near Dorchester, at 8 a.m. At first thrown aside as dead, but saved by the observation and slap of the midwife. TH described his father, Thomas Hardy the Second, by profession a mason-*cum*-builder, as unpossessed of 'the tradesman's soul' (*Life*, p. 21), whilst his mother, a cook before her marriage, was presented as of 'unusual ability and judgement, and an energy that might have carried her to incalculable issues' (*Life*, p. 8). The marriage was thus not entirely either equal or equable, its solemnisation (22 Dec 1839) having been precipitated by TH's conception some weeks previously. Possibly born prematurely, TH suffered much physical weakness in his early years, and was not expected to survive. Of the more idyllic circumstantial physical surroundings of the family home, the early poem 'Domicilium' gives a full impression.

(5 July) Baptised by the vicar of Stinsford, Arthur Shirley.

In the same year (10 Feb) Queen Victoria married Albert of Saxe-Coburg.

1841   (23 Dec) Birth of TH's sister Mary, physically more robust and temperamentally slightly less troubled, with whom he subsequently develops a close relationship, based on much childhood companionship.

In same year, rejection by Parliament of the Chartist petition causes increased civil unrest. Peel's budget modifies the sliding scale in order to encourage the import of corn.

1843   The Stinsford churchwardens, probably at Shirley's suggestion, decide to make no further payment to the church choir from parish revenue, signalling the end of a body with which the Hardy family has been associated for many years, and which TH is imaginatively to commemorate for many more.

1

Some time between 1843 and 1846 Jemima Hardy becomes dangerously ill following a miscarriage, and after her recovery she becomes far more determined. Whatever the effect of his mother's illness on TH, it apparently does little to stunt his intellectual development: both he and Jemima claimed that he was able to read at the age of three.

?1844   Given a toy concertina in this or the next year, TH is soon afterwards introduced to the violin, and to involvement in the secular activities to which the Stinsford string band could still enthusiastically contribute. His enduring sensitivity to music and interest in its performance thus become rooted early and strong.

1845   Peel's 'Free Trade' budget abolishes all export duties, and reduces or abolishes duties on many imports. TH 'had a little wooden sword, which his father had made for him, and this he dipped into the blood of a pig which had just been killed, and brandished it as he walked about the garden exclaiming: "Free Trade or blood!"' (*Life*, p. 21).

Increased consciousness of working-class conditions seen in the publication of Engels' *The Condition of the Working Classes in England* and Disraeli's *Sybil, or the Two Nations*.

1846   Impressed by, though not of course conscious of the significance of, demonstrations for the repeal of the Corn Laws, to which Royal Assent is given on 26 June. Dorset generally regarded at this time as 'a poor, backward, and somewhat uncouth corner of the kingdom' (Millgate, p. 32), with many examples, well known to TH's parents, of acute agrarian poverty. TH almost certainly attends the wedding at Stinsford in this year of his cousin George, and the Hardy family help provide music for the ensuing merrymaking. The alcoholic character of such occasions – a partial relief from the miseries of widespread rural deprivation – impresses the young child considerably.

1847   Following the introduction of a standard gauge in 1846, railways in Britain develop rapidly. The railway arrives in Dorchester, 'the orally transmitted ditties of centuries being slain at a stroke by the London comic songs that were introduced' (*Life*, p. 20). Michael Millgate comments further on the significance of the railway's arrival: 'Hardy, in fact, was born just in time to catch a last glimpse of that English rural life which, especially in so conservative a county, had existed largely undisturbed from medieval times' (p. 35).

Presented in this year with a copy of *The Rites and Worship of the Jews*, but the family cannot afford to satisfy TH's appetite for further books. Childhood favourites which TH later particularly recalled include Dryden's translation of the *Aeneid*, Johnson's *Rasselas*, and a translation of Bernardin de Saint-Pierre's *Paul et Virginie*.

1848 Enters the parish National School, represented by TH as being the brainchild of Julia Augusta Martin, the wife of the local landlord, though in fact it probably owed its existence as much to the energy of the Stinsford vicar. TH the first pupil to enter the school's new building, which is recalled in 'He Revisits His First School'. Away from the almost exclusively adult and largely feminine world of his home, TH forms the first of an extensive series of attractions to members – especially the more unattainable – of the opposite sex, in this case a fellow pupil, Fanny Hurden. In the light of his later literary career, TH's education must be viewed as having a dual base: his formal schooling, and his exposure at home to a culture steeped in folklore, folk music, and the more vital and primary aspects of story-telling. 'Hardy was – to an extraordinary degree – a child of the oral tradition, and perhaps, in England, that tradition's last and greatest product' (Millgate, p. 37).

1849 (Autumn) Absent from school for several weeks, accompanying his mother on a visit to her sister in Hertfordshire, and thereby gaining his first glimpse of London and its expanding suburbs. TH's attractive aunt, Martha, and her talented but restless husband, John Sharpe, impress the young boy greatly: they may well influence the subsequent presentation of Bathsheba and Troy in *Far from the Madding Crowd*.

1850 (23 April) Death of Wordsworth, following which Tennyson (who publishes *In Memoriam* this year) becomes Poet Laureate.

(2 July) Death of Peel.

(Sep) Jemima decides to send TH to a Nonconformist school in Dorchester, its chief attraction being the excellent teacher, Isaac Last. The move endears the Hardy family neither to their vicar, nor, more particularly, to Julia Augusta Martin, who has grown inordinately fond of the boy, while TH for his part has grown 'more attached than he cared to own . . . his feeling for her was almost that of a lover' (*Life*,

p. 19). TH's father loses the estate business as a consequence, while TH later recalled his emotional encounter with Mrs Martin at a Harvest Supper.

In the same month the Roman Catholic hierarchy in Britain is re-established, whilst the judgement of the Privy Council in the Gorham Case leads H. E. Manning and many others to Rome.

(Nov) TH witnesses burnings of effigies of the Pope and Cardinal Wiseman during No Popery riots in Dorchester: 'The sight to young Hardy was most lurid, and he never forgot it' (*Life*, p. 21). A fuller experience of the manifold everyday workings of the county town begins to become an important by-product of the change in schooling.

1851   Birth in March of TH's cousin Tryphena and in August of his brother Henry.

The Great Exhibition serves as an expression of Britain's industrialism, economic growth and international dominance.

(19 Dec) Death of Turner.

1852   Begins Latin under Last's tuition, continuing with some success. Also wins local approval as a violinist of enthusiasm and sensitivity. Around this time, becomes an instructor in the Stinsford Sunday School, one among many signs of youthful ecclesiastical aspirations: 'As a child, to be a parson had been his dream' (*Life*, p. 376). Attraction towards local girls proves however a strong – and also abiding – rival interest, whilst his family's consistent Liberal political sympathies find expression when TH helps to draw through the streets the carriage of Dorchester's victorious Liberal candidate in the July election.

(14 Sep) Death of the Duke of Wellington.

1853   Moves with Last to the latter's new independent academy. In the following three years TH makes rapid intellectual strides, as well as building up physical strength.

1854   Fordington, a suburb of Dorchester, suffers a cholera epidemic, victims being cared for by the vicar, the Revd Henry Moule, father of TH's future friend Horace, and a partial model for Mr Clare in *Tess*.

Britain (28 Mar) and France (27 Mar) declare war on Russia, leading to the Crimean campaign.

1855 Good progress under Last rewarded by the prize of Beza's *Novum Testamentum.*
    Courbet organises a Pavillon du Réalisme at the Paris World Fair.
(31 Mar) Death of Charlotte Brontë.

1856 TH's confession that he had been 'a child till he was sixteen, a youth till he was five-and-twenty, and a young man till he was nearly fifty' (*Life*, p. 32), hints at adolescent emotional development in this year. His unrequited love for a local farmer's daughter, Louisa Harding, recalled in the poems 'Louie' and 'To Louisa in the Lane', dates from roughly this time. Leaves Last's academy, becoming apprenticed on 11 July to the architect John Hicks at 39 South Street, Dorchester. Academic education furthered in the ensuing period by a programme of self-study at home, including a course in Greek; conversation with a fellow apprentice, Henry Robert Bastow; and visits to the school kept next door to Hicks's office by the poet and philologist William Barnes. Finds himself drawn into three separate existences, 'the professional life, the scholar's life, and the rustic life' (*Life*, p. 32). The beginning of a fourth life, that of the published author, is perhaps marked by an article entitled 'The Town Clocks' in the *Dorset County Chronicle* for 17 January, which may represent the skit to which the *Life* refers (p. 33). Also assists in the preparation of articles for the same paper, giving details of church restorations by Hicks. Dorchester itself provides TH with several abiding amusements this year: a belated commemoration on 30 June of the ending of the Crimean War, later to suggest celebration scenes in *The Mayor of Casterbridge*, and the hanging of Martha Browne, which TH vividly recalled almost seventy years later. The Hardy family completed with the birth (2 Sep) of TH's sister Kate.

1857 (Jan) Death of TH's grandmother Mary Hardy, a cottage companion since his birth. She is recalled in the early poem 'Domicilium', written some time between this year and 1860, and is commemorated in the later poem 'One We Knew'.
    On close terms by this year with Horace Moule, son of the vicar of Fordington, and around this time becomes increasingly well known to other members of the Moule family. 'In Horace Moule, Hardy recognized for the first time a model of what he himself most deeply wished to become, and his contact with the Moule brothers and with the life of Fordington vicarage both exacerbated his sense of in-

feriority and incited his ambition for self-improvement' (Millgate, p. 68).

(12 June) Birth of Elgar.

George Eliot commences her fictional career this year with serial publication of *Scenes of Clerical Life*.

1858 Purchases a copy of the *Iliad*. Also lent by Horace Moule G.A. Mantell's *The Wonders of Geology*, a book much disapproved of by Moule's father.

Some early literary activity – including lost essays on Lamb and Tennyson and several poems, perhaps including 'Domicilium' – in this and the next year. TH very secretive about these projects, perhaps showing nobody the finished results.

Frith exhibits his painting *Derby Day*, later much admired by TH.

1859 Publication of J. S. Mill's *On Liberty*, which TH claimed ke knew almost by heart in 1865; and of Darwin's *Origin of Species*, of which he says he was 'amongst the earliest acclaimers' (*Life*, p. 153).

1860 Kept on by Hicks as a paid assistant. Hardy's architectural interests seem to have remained largely ecclesiastical, and several designs and sketches from this early period survive.

Purchases a copy of Griesbach's Greek New Testament, probably as a result of a heated dispute over the merits of paedobaptism. The dispute also brings him into closer contact with a Baptist minister, Frederick Perkins, the model for Woodwell in *A Laodicean*, and with members of his family.

Somewhere around this year, begins to show an interest in the Evangelical movement, probably as a result of a Revival affecting Dorchester in the early months of this year.

Later in the year Bastow emigrates to Australia, and TH's friendship with him declines. TH, his bookishness undiminished, begins to find more time for the company of other like-minded friends, especially Hooper Tolbort and the older Horace Moule, who serves as a kind of mentor to the younger pair. 'Horace Moule's impact upon Hardy was immense. He was handsome, charming, cultivated, scholarly, thoroughly at home in the glamorous worlds of the ancient universities and of literary London' (Millgate, p. 67).

1861 (11 Apr) Some form of Evangelical conversion experience, indicated by a Bible marking of unusual particularity. Subsequently purchases various religious books, and commences a methodical programme of Bible study.

(2 June) TH's twenty-first birthday.

(14 Dec) Death of Prince Albert.

1862

February

8 (Sat) Marks in his Prayer Book against Tate and Brady Psalm 43 the lines

> Why then cast down, my soul? and why
> So much oppress'd with anxious care?
> On God, thy God, for aid rely,
> Who will thy ruin'd state repair.

There is some evidence that a proposal of marriage to a Dorchester shop assistant, Mary Waight, was turned down early this year, and the marking may reflect TH's resulting state of mind.

March

23 (Sun) Enters the date against Habbakuk 2:3: 'For the vision is yet for an appointed time, but at the end it shall speak, and not lie: though it tarry, wait for it; because it will surely come, it will not tarry.'

April

17 (Thurs) Having been advised by Horace Moule against considering a university education, sets out for London, cautiously purchasing a return ticket, but soon finding lodgings at 3 Clarence Place, Kilburn. 'It may be hardly necessary to record . . . that the metropolis into which he . . . plunged at this date differed greatly from the London of even a short time after. It was the London of Dickens and Thackeray' (*Life*, p. 41). Amongst early London experiences are a re-encounter with Julia Augusta Martin and several trips to operas and to fashionable dance halls, drawn on for the poem 'Reminiscences of a Dancing Man'.

May

5   (Mon) Finds employment with the architect Arthur (later Sir Arthur) Blomfield, at 9 St Martin's Place. The genial musical and ecclesiastical practice suits TH well.

11 Attends St Stephen's Church, Paddington, an Evangelical church whose vicar has Dorset connections.

August

7   (Thurs) Visited by Horace Moule, who is delighted by Hooper Tolbort's high success in the exam for the Indian Civil Service. Goes with Moule to the Jesuit church at Farm Street.

17 Reports, in the first of his letters still surviving, to Mary Hardy on his London activities: attendance at St Mary's, Kilburn (a distinctively High Church choice); a trip with Martha Sparks to the International Exhibition; theatre trips; and reading, including Ruskin's *Modern Painters*.

October

Proposed by Blomfield as a member of the Architectural Association. Entertains his father on a visit to London, taking him to Wallace's *Lurline* at Covent Garden, the International Exhibition, and the Thames Tunnel.

31 (Fri) Attends a conversazione of the Architectural Association to hear his name proposed.

1863

The *Life* reports, 'By as early as the end of 1863 he had recommenced to read a great deal, with a growing tendency towards poetry . . . it was suggested to him that he might combine literature with architecture by becoming an art-critic for the press. His preparations for such a course were, however, quickly abandoned' (p. 47). Draws several 'Diagrams shewing Human Passion, Mind, & Character', based on his reading in Fourier. Hears Dickens reading in the spring of this year, and at some stage becomes 'more or less formally engaged' to a lady's maid, Eliza Bright Nicholls (see Millgate, p. 84), an engagement which lasts for four years and provides the basis of the 'She, to Him' sequence of poems. Moves to 16 Westbourne Park Villas, Paddington, where 'Discouragement' (dated 1863–7) is written.

February
19   (Thurs) Further London news sent to Mary Hardy, including details of a competition TH is entering for the design of a country mansion.

March
10   (Tues) Sees the illuminations celebrating the wedding of the Prince of Wales and Princess Alexandra of Denmark.

April
17   (Fri) Attends a conversazione of the Architectural Association to receive the first prize for their Country Mansion Design Competition.
Late this month, pays a brief visit to his sister Mary, now teaching at Denchworth, Berkshire.

May
12   (Tues) Begins to summarise details of painters since the Renaissance in a notebook entitled 'Schools of Painting', perhaps intended as a preparation for a career as an art critic. For text see *Personal Notebooks*, pp. 105–14.
18   Presented by the President of the Royal Institute of British Architects with a silver medal for his essay 'On the Application of Colored [*sic*] Bricks and Terra Cotta to Modern Architecture'.

July
5   (Sun) Receives Communion in Westminster Abbey.

October
1   (Thurs) Buys a shorthand primer – again with a view to some journalistic career – and by Christmas has reached forty words per minute.

November
Present at the laying of a memorial stone at All Saints, New Windsor, a church which he had helped to design. The Crown Princess of Germany's uncertainty as to how to use a trowel subsequently suggests an incident in *The Poor Man and the Lady*.

December
19   (Sat) Advises Mary Hardy to read Thackeray: 'He is considered

to be the greatest novellist [sic] of the day – looking at novel writing of the highest kind as a perfect and truthful representation of actual life – which is no doubt the proper view to take' (*Letters*, I, 5). Thackeray dies four days later.

1864

February
Horace Moule suggests that TH should become London correspondent of a provincial newspaper. All the literary–journalistic schemes of this time seem to have been designed to finance a university education leading to a career in the Church; TH does not seem to have sought a permanent career in journalism.

April
3   (Sun) Visits Brighton.

September
11 (Sun) Pencils the word 'Doubt' against Isaiah 44–5, a marking later heavily erased.

December
24 (Sat) Submits 'How I Built Myself a House' to *Chambers's Journal*.
25 Spends Christmas Day with his family.
26 Visits Puddletown to see the Sparks family.

1865

The *Life* reports, 'By 1865 he had begun to write verses, and by 1866 to send his productions to magazines. . . . He also began turning the Book of Ecclesiastes into Spenserian stanzas, but finding the original unmatchable abandoned the task' (p. 47). This year does indeed see TH set himself up, with characteristically earnest painstakingness, as an author, and especially as a poet. Purchases include Nuttall's *Standard Pronouncing Dictionary*, Walker's *Rhyming Dictionary*, Henry Reed's *Introduction to English Literature* and several volumes of verse. Literary output definitely inclines more towards verse than prose at this time, and reading for pleasure consists almost entirely of verse – especially, in the winter months, Horace. Starts a notebook, 'Studies, Specimens, &c', with carefully transcribed extracts from his poetic reading. Attempts at verse publication are not successful, however, and much early work is later destroyed. The poems which do survive (though their dating is not necessarily reliable) are 'Amabel' (dated 1865) and 'Her Confession' (dated 1865–7). In the summer, reading works by John Stuart Mill (whose *Auguste Comte and Positivism* appears this year), and around this period begins to show interest in the ideas of Comte, annotating a copy of *A General View of Positivism* lent him by Horace Moule. For recreation, visits the National Gallery for twenty minutes each lunch hour, attends Phelps's series of Shakespeare plays at Drury Lane, hears readings by Dickens, and in October begins evening classes in French at King's College, London.

January
1 (Sun) Presented by Horace Moule with *The Thoughts of the Emperor Aurelius Antonius*, a book that he subsequently always keeps by his bedside.

March
18 (Sat) 'How I Built Myself a House' published in *Chambers's Journal*. TH once remarked that the acceptance of the piece determined his career.

June
2 (Fri) 'My 25th birthday. Not very cheerful. Wondered what woman, if any, I should be thinking about in five years' time' (*Life*, p. 50). The note suggests a deterioration in the relationship with Eliza Bright Nicholls, and hints at the depression and loneliness which TH often felt, sometimes with great acuteness, in his London years. He marked the date 1865 against the fourth stanza of Keble's poem for twenty-fourth Sunday after Trinity in *The Christian Year*:

> For if one heart in perfect sympathy
>   Beat with another answering love for love,
> Weak mortals, all entranced, on earth would lie,
>   Nor listen for those purer strains above.

July
2   (Sun) Reading Newman's *Apologia*, Byron's *Childe Harold*, and Thomas Moore's *Lalla Rookh*.
13   Edward Whymper climbs the Matterhorn.

August
23   (Wed) The *Life* records the comment, 'The poetry of a scene varies with the minds of the perceivers. Indeed, it does not lie in the scene at all' (p. 50). Other such perceptions of this year are also recorded in the *Life* in some detail.

September
3   (Sun) Prayer Book marking shows attendance at St James's Church, Paddington. Last church marking for several years, suggesting TH's increasing doubt.

October
18   (Wed) Death of Palmerston, whom TH, at some time since his arrival in London, has seen speak in the House of Commons.
27   Attends Palmerston's funeral in Westminster Abbey.
28   Sends Mary Hardy an account of the Palmerston funeral: 'I think I was never so much impressed with a ceremony in my life before, & I wd not have missed it for anything' (*Life*, p. 53). Also informs her that *Barchester Towers*, which he has recently sent her, is considered the best of Trollope's novels, and asks if he might bring H. A. (probably Henrietta Adams, a friend of Jemima Hardy's) down to visit on Christmas and Boxing Days.

November
12   (Sun) Death of Elizabeth Gaskell.

December
30   (Sat) Birth of Kipling.

1866

TH apparently becomes increasingly indifferent towards Eliza Nicholls this year, and indeed overall the year is a restless and uneasy one. One probable reason for this is a recognition by TH that the impediments to his plans for obtaining university entry are likely to prove insurmountable. In a letter to Mary Hardy he announces his abandonment of this scheme: 'it seems absurd to live on now with such a remote object in view' (*Letters*, I, 7). Poetic enthusiasm and output increase greatly as a result of this decision, whilst the practice of architecture becomes less attractive, not least because of TH's superintendence of the removal of bones from Old St Pancras Churchyard to facilitate a railway cutting. Poems dated this year by TH are 'Hap', 'In Vision I Roamed', 'At a Bridal', 'Postponement', 'A Confession to a Friend in Trouble', 'Her Dilemma', the 'She, to Him' sonnet sequence, 'The Fire at Tranter Sweatley's', 'The Two Men', 'The Ruined Maid', 'Her Definition', 'From Her in the Country', 'A Young Man's Epigram on Existence', 'Dream of the City Shopwoman', and, probably, 'Revulsion'. Publication of Swinburne's *Poems and Ballads*.

March
29 (Thurs) Death of Keble, whose *Christian Year* TH had read and annotated much in the early years of the decade.

June
2 (Sat) Begins a short holiday.
22 Sketches the view from his room in Westbourne Park Villas.

October
Writes 'The Musing Maiden'.

December
26 (Wed) Opening night at Covent Garden of Gilbert à Beckett's pantomime *Ali-Baba and the Forty Thieves*, which runs for a week. TH takes a walk-on part in one performance, a symptom of his growing interest in theatre (especially Shakespeare) and opera during his stay in London.

1867

End of the Eliza Nicholls relationship, perhaps brought about by a brief flirtation with Eliza's sister Jane. 'Neutral Tones', assigned by TH to this year, almost certainly describes the end of the Eliza affair. 'Heiress and Architect' written in Blomfield's office at 8 Adelphi Terrace; 'Her Reproach', '1967', 'To an Actress' and 'A Young Man's

Exhortation' written at 16 Westbourne Park Villas. First entry – a note on former burial customs at Stinsford for musicians in the choir – in the 'Memoranda 1' Notebook.

April

21 (Sun) 'To an Impersonator of Rosalind', a tribute to the actress Mary Scott-Siddons, written.

July

Leaves London to take up a position in the practice of John Hicks, having decided to leave Blomfield's practice partly because of ill health, and partly because 'he constitutionally shrank from the business of social advancement, caring for life as an emotion rather than for life as a science of climbing, in which respect he was quizzed by his acquaintance for his lack of ambition' (*Life*, p. 53). Poems already written (several identified by the *Life*) left behind at Westbourne Park Villas. The *Life* comments, 'He easily fell into the routine that he had followed before, though, with between five and six years superadded of experience as a young man at large in London, it was with very different ideas of things' (p. 56). Also according to the autobiography, it is the contrast between London and provincial existence which encourages TH to begin work on his first novel, *The Poor Man and the Lady*, on which he works for the last five months of the year. Emotional exhaustion, following the end of Eliza Nicholls affair, though unmentioned in the *Life*, is probably also an important factor in the decision to leave London. In the opinion of some, a new emotional problem now sets in: a relationship with TH's cousin Tryphena Sparks, leading to the birth of an illegitimate child in 1868, and the prevention of marriage when it is realised that the lovers are in fact uncle and niece. The beginning this summer of a relationship which may have developed a sexual character and led to the exchange of rings is now generally accepted; the remaining suggestions are not. The relationship lasts until 1870 at the latest, possibly ending considerably earlier.

August

6 (Tues) The Reform Bill passes the House of Lords.
14 Birth of Galsworthy.

October

Returns to London to collect belongings from Westbourne Park Villas.

1868

January

16   (Thurs) Begins making a fair revised copy of *The Poor Man and the Lady*, eventually finished early in June.

February

28   (Fri) Disraeli becomes Prime Minister.

April

Reading Browning (whose *Ring and the Book* begins publication this year) and Thackeray.

June

9   (Tues) Finishes copying *The Poor Man and the Lady*.

17   At work on an uncompleted poem on the Battle of the Nile – 'the war with Napoleon was even then in his mind as material for poetry of some sort' (*Life*, p. 58).

22   Writes a draft, subsequently 'Retty's Phases'.

July

1   (Wed) Probably depressed by his work and prospects, notes down three texts which are 'Cures for despair': Wordsworth's 'Resolution and Independence', J. S. Mill's 'Individuality' in *On Liberty*, and Carlyle's 'Jean Paul Richter' (*Life*, p. 58).

25   Manuscript of *The Poor Man and the Lady* posted, on the recommendation of Horace Moule, to Alexander Macmillan. TH's accompanying letter explains 'That now a days, discussions on the questions of manners, rising in the world, &c (the main incidents of the novel) have grown to be particularly absorbing' (*Letters*, I, 7).

August

12   (Tues) Receives news of Macmillan's likely rejection of *The Poor Man and the Lady*; though the rejection is tempered with encouragement, forestalled whilst further advice is sought, and accompanied by comments from Macmillan's reader John Morley.

26   Takes a day trip with Mary to Lulworth Cove.

September
10 (Thurs) Asks Macmillan if he can offer further news, remarking, 'I have been hunting up matter for another tale, which would consist entirely of rural scenes & humble life; but I have not courage enough to go on with it till something comes of the first' (*Letters*, I, 8).

November
Drafts 'Gallant's Song'.

December
Goes to see Alexander Macmillan in London, who declines to publish an altered version of *The Poor Man* submitted in November, but suggests an approach to Chapman and Hall.
2 (Wed) Gladstone becomes Prime Minister.
8 Sees Chapman, leaving the manuscript of *The Poor Man and the Lady* with him.

1869

'Her Initials', 'Her Father', 'At Waking' and 'The Dawn after the Dance', assigned by TH to this year. 'In St Paul's a While Ago' was originally entitled 'In St Paul's: 1869'.

January
17 (Sun) Moves temporarily to London, awaiting Chapman's reply. Writes date of departure against Psalm 86, which begins, 'Bow down thine ear, O Lord, and hear me: for I am poor, and in misery.'

February
8 (Mon) Chapman and Hall reject *The Poor Man and the Lady*. TH arranges to call on Chapman, seeing Thomas Carlyle there. Chapman agrees to publish the novel if TH will put up £20 as a guarantee against loss.
12 Death of John Hicks.

March
At Chapman's invitation, visits London, seeing Chapman, and meeting the reader of *The Poor Man and the Lady*, George Meredith.

Meredith advises at best postponement of publication, cautioning that the novel's socialistic tone might harm TH's future, and recommends an attempt at a novel with more plot. TH takes the manuscript away from the meeting, returning with it to Bockhampton. There may therefore be a personal background to the Notebook entry '1869. Spring . . . . One of those evenings in the country which make the townsman feel: "I will stay here until I die – I would, that is, if it were not for that thousand pounds I want to make, & that friend I want to envy me"' (*Personal Notebooks*, p. 4).

April
Invited by G. R. Crickmay, a Weymouth architect, to assist him in church restorations. TH's chief concern is the rebuilding of Turnworth Church, where much of his architectural handiwork may still be seen. Soon resides in Weymouth at 3 Wooperton Street, working there on *Desperate Remedies*. 'At a Seaside Town in 1869' and 'Seaside Lovers' recall this period in Weymouth.
15   (Thurs) Reluctant altogether to abandon *The Poor Man*, TH sends off the novel to Smith, Elder, who swiftly reject it.

June
 8   (Tues) Sends off *The Poor Man* to Tinsley Brothers.

July
29   (Thurs) Jane Nicholls, sister of Eliza, marries, thereby ending any hopes TH may have entertained of her hand. The poems 'At Waking', 'Her Initials' and 'The Wind's Prophecy' probably refer to a final renunciation of Jane.

September
Rejected manuscript of *The Poor Man* returned to TH, who always retains a belief in its quality and a resentment at its rejection, subsequently plundering the manuscript for several episodes in his published writings, not least his current project, *Desperate Remedies*.

November
Persuaded by a friend in Crickmay's office, identified in the *Life* – perhaps spuriously – as the model for Edward Springrove in *Desperate Remedies*, to join a quadrille class. 'The Dawn after the Dance' draws on these experiences.
 7   (Sun) Marks part of the text of Psalm 35 in his Prayer Book:

'Lord, how long wilt thou look upon this: O deliver my soul
from the calamities which they bring on me . . . .' Frustrations in
literature and love are the probable cause of this anxiety.

1870

The Education Act this year establishes Board schools, thus increasing the opportunities for TH to find suitable architectural employment. Poems assigned by TH to this year are 'Ditty' and 'In the
Vaulted Way'.

February
Returns from Weymouth to live with his parents, and work in
quieter surroundings on *Desperate Remedies*.
11 (Fri) Crickmay writes to request TH to visit St Juliot in Cornwall
    in connection with the restoration of the church there. Initially
    declines.

March
5   (Sat) Nearly complete manuscript of *Desperate Remedies*
    despatched to Alexander Macmillan.
7   Sets off at 4 a.m. for St Juliot. 'When I Set Out for Lyonnesse'
    provides a retrospect of this departure. Meets on arrival Emma
    Lavinia Gifford, the rector's sister in law – by turns, attractive,
    impulsive, vivacious, eccentric, alluring and fateful. 'A Man
    Was Drawing Near to Me' provides her hypothetical response
    to TH's arrival. After ELH's death, TH's desk calendar remains
    turned to this date.
8   Drawing and measuring in the church.
9   Drives with ELG and Mrs Holder to Boscastle and Tintagel,
    inspecting Penpethy slate quarry, a visit which is the germ of
    the poem 'Green Slates'.
10 Taken by ELG to Beeny Cliff.
11 Leaves St Juliot. Notes 'E.L.G. had struck a light six times in her
    anxiety to call the servants early enough for me' (*Life*, p. 75). Poem
    'At the Word "Farewell"' based on this incident.

April
5   (Tues) Having returned to live in Weymouth in order to work
    on the St Juliot drawings, receives rejection of *Desperate Remed-*

ies, on the grounds of excessive sensationalism, from Macmillan.

7 Tinsley acknowledges receipt of *Desperate Remedies*.

May

Reading Comte, and also, later in the summer, Shakespeare, the Bible, much poetry, Alison's *Europe*, and Bosworth Smith's *Mohamedd and Mohameddanism*. Sees much of Horace Moule. Writes to ELG. Notebook records, 'A sweet face is a page of sadness to a man over 30 – the raw material of a corpse' (*Personal Notebooks*, p. 4).

2 (Mon) Crickmay approves TH's plans for St Juliot.

3 Tinsley suggests that *Desperate Remedies* should not be published without alteration.

5 In response to TH's suggestion, Tinsley states the terms on which he will publish *Desperate Remedies* as it stands.

16 Leaves for London, having abandoned his employment with Crickmay. 'He seems to have passed the days in Town desultorily and dreamily – mostly visiting museums and picture-galleries, and it is not clear what he was waiting for' (*Life*, p. 76). Some work undertaken for Blomfield and for Raphael Brandon, whose offices provide a model for Knight's chambers in *A Pair of Blue Eyes*.

June

2 (Thurs) TH's thirtieth birthday.

9 Death of Dickens.

July

19 (Tues) France declares war on Prussia. TH and Brandon follow the progress of the war with keen interest.

August

8 (Mon) Leaves for Cornwall, becoming reunited with ELG, with whom a correspondence of intimacy has developed. Enjoys a three-week stay of great happiness, including a visit to Tintagel subsequently influential on *The Famous Tragedy of the Queen of Cornwall*, returning to Bockhampton with an understanding that he is betrothed.

14 Attendance at evensong at St Juliot provides the experience on which 'The Young Churchwarden' is based.

18   The French defeated at Gravelotte. TH sees the scene which subsequently inspires 'In Time of "the Breaking of Nations"'.
22   Makes a sketch (preserved in the Dorset County Museum) of Beeny Cliff.

September
25   (Sun) Writes the initials ELG and a series of subsequently erased characters in his Bible against part of Proverbs 14. Several markings of this period indicate the intensity with which he is considering ELG.

October
30   (Sun) Records, 'Mother's notion, & also mine: That a figure stands in our van with an arm uplifted, to knock us back from any pleasant prospect we indulge in as probable' (*Personal Notebooks*, pp. 6–7).

November
16   (Wed) Marking of Revelation 10:11 ('And he said unto me, Thou must prophesy again before many peoples, and nations, and tongues, and kings'), perhaps suggesting a new resolution to proceed with a literary career.

December
Manuscript of *Desperate Remedies*, much of it recopied by ELG, sent off to Tinsley. Terms agreed by the end of this month, though TH considers that Tinsley has unjustifiably readjusted the original agreement.

1871

'The Minute before Meeting' written.

January
28   (Sat) The French sign the armistice ending the Franco–Prussian War.

February
'Some men waste their time in watching their own existence' (*Personal Notebooks*, p. 8).

March
25 (Sat) *Desperate Remedies* published.
30 Returns to Weymouth, again lodging at 3 Wooperton Street, to give further assistance to Crickmay. Projects with which assistance is given probably include work on two Weymouth hospitals, the restoration of Stoke Wake church, extensions to local schools, and alterations to Slape House, Netherbury.

April
1 (Sat) *Desperate Remedies* favourably reviewed in the *Athenaeum*.
13 *Desperate Remedies* favourably reviewed in the *Morning Post*.
22 TH much disappointed by the *Spectator's* response to the novel: 'He remembered, for long years after, how he had read this review as he sat on a stile leading to the eweleaze he had to cross on his way home to Bockhampton. The bitterness of that moment was never forgotten; at the time he wished that he were dead' (*Life*, p. 84).

May
Under the Greenwood Tree completed during the late spring and early summer. Late in the month, pays a brief visit to ELG. 'Love the Monopolist', begun at least as early as this year, refers to a train departure from Launceston, perhaps on this visit.
29 (Mon) 'The most prosaic man becomes a poem when you stand by his grave at his funeral and think of him' (*Personal Notebooks*, p. 10).

June
3 (Sun) Returning from Cornwall, is disappointed to see *Desperate Remedies* remaindered in a shop on Exeter station.
7 Asks Tinsley to include suggested passages from reviews in advertisements for *Desperate Remedies*.

July
Marks the lines in *Macbeth*, 'Things at their worst will cease, or else climb upward / To what they were before'.

August
7 (Mon) Offers *Under the Greenwood Tree* to Macmillan, explaining that the novel's rustic content was partly encouraged by favourable aspects of the reviews of *Desperate Remedies*: 'It is

entirely a story of rural life, & the attempt has been to draw the characters humorously, without caricature' (_Letters_, I, 11).

October

3 (Tues) Asks Tinsley to include an extract from Horace Moule's appreciation of _Desperate Remedies_ in the _Saturday Review_ in future advertisements of the novel.

14 Requests further news of _Under the Greenwood Tree_ from Macmillan. Alexander Macmillan subsequently decides not to proceed with the book, though offering TH some encouragement.

20 Tells Tinsley that he has proceeded some way with a new novel (_A Pair of Blue Eyes_) 'the essence of which is plot, _without crime_' (_Letters_, I, 14).

1872

Moves his lodgings to 1 West Parade, Weymouth. Just before Easter moves to London, lodging at 4 Celbridge Place, Westbourne Park, and assisting the architect T. Roger Smith with the design of new schools.

February

20 (Tues) Asks Tinsley to settle the _Desperate Remedies_ account.

March

19 (Tues) Tinsley finally settles the _Desperate Remedies_ account, and inquires about TH's next novel.

April

8 (Mon) Manuscript of _Under the Greenwood Tree_ sent to Tinsley. 'I wish you to bear in mind that the manner & subject of this story are the points in which the critics of Desperate Remedies were unanimous in saying I was strongest, & that, had I no other reasons, that would be one for going further into this class of writing' (_Letters_, I, 16).

22 Tinsley offers £30 for the copyright. TH signs the agreement the same day, a decision subsequently regretted.

June

Under the Greenwood Tree published early this month.

July

4   (Thurs) Journey up Oxford Street on this day recalled in the poem 'Coming up Oxford Street: Evening'.

27 In response to a suggestion from Tinsley, agrees terms for a serial to run in *Tinsley's Magazine*. Leaves Smith's office at the end of the month.

August

7   (Wed) Sets off from London for Cornwall, having supplied copy for the first instalment of *A Pair of Blue Eyes*. Later in the month, approaches ELG's father with a formal proposal, but is dismissed on social grounds. The poems 'I Rose and Went to Rou'tor Town' and 'Near Lanivet, 1872' reflect something of the resultant tensions.

September

First instalment of *A Pair of Blue Eyes* appears in *Tinsley's Magazine*.

8   (Sun) Reads both lessons at evensong in the restored St Juliot Church.

11 Back in Celbridge Place, but later in the month returns to Dorset in order to facilitate composition of *A Pair of Blue Eyes*, remaining there into the spring, and refusing further employment offered him, on preferential terms, by T. Roger Smith – a clear statement of confidence in the likely success of future literary endeavours.

30 Manuscript of *A Pair of Blue Eyes* up to fo. 163 sent to Tinsley by this date.

October

Informed by Tinsley that as a result of continental reprint rights he will receive an extra £10 for *Under the Greenwood Tree*.

November

29 (Fri) Invited by Caddell Holder to pay a long visit to St Juliot.

30 Invited by Leslie Stephen to contribute a serial to the *Cornhill*.

December

Makes notes on Dorset astrologers and conjurors.

1873

'She', later retitled 'She at His Funeral', dated this year. Publication of Leslie Stephen's *Essays on Free Thinking and Plain Speaking*.

March
12   (Wed) Final chapters of *A Pair of Blue Eyes* sent off to Tinsley.

May
A Pair of Blue Eyes published in volume form, with several alterations from the serial version, in the last week of this month.
 8   (Thurs) Death of J. S. Mill.

June
 9   (Mon) Travels to London with his brother Henry.
15   Lunches and dines with Horace Moule in London, and spends the next days showing his brother the sights of the capital.
18   Asks Tinsley to send a copy of *A Pair of Blue Eyes* to the *Spectator*, where it is reviewed favourably on the 28th.
20   Sets off for Cambridge, staying in Queens' College with Horace Moule.
21   Bids farewell to Moule (his last meeting with him), travelling on to Bath for a holiday with ELG and her friend Anne d'Arville. 'Midnight on Beechen, 187–' recalls an incident on this holiday.

July
 2   (Wed) Returns to Bockhampton, settling down in earnest to the composition of *Far from the Madding Crowd*, substantial elements of which took root in his mind as early as the spring and summer of 1872.

September
23   (Tues) Visits Woodbury Hill Fair, on which the Greenhill Fair of *Far from the Madding Crowd* is subsequently based.
24   Shocked to hear of the suicide of Horace Moule, probably his closest friend ever, whose memory becomes a lifelong devotion.
30   Sends to Leslie Stephen the early part of *Far from the Madding Crowd*.

October
Requested to have *Far from the Madding Crowd* ready for the January number of the *Cornhill*.

November
20   (Thurs) Writes to Smith, Elder about terms for *Far from the Madding Crowd*.

23 Offers another serial to Tinsley, in response to a query from him.
29 Agrees terms for *Far from the Madding Crowd*.
30 Apologises to Tinsley for the unintended discourtesy in transferring to another publisher.

December
4 (Thurs) Asks Smith, Elder to ensure that in the illustrations for *Far from the Madding Crowd* 'the rustics, although *quaint*, may be made to appear *intelligent, & not boorish* at all' (*Letters*, I, 25). Later in the month TH sends sketches of various rustic costumes and buildings to ensure accuracy.
8 Leaves for a few days in London, calling there on Leslie Stephen.
25 Christmas spent with ELG.
31 Returning from Cornwall, opens a copy of the January *Cornhill* on Plymouth Hoe station to find the first instalment of *Far from the Madding Crowd* at the front of the magazine.

1874

Following his introduction to the Stephens, begins to find himself entertained amongst a new class and style of London acquaintance. He is extremely strongly attracted to the illustrator of *Far from the Madding Crowd*, Helen Paterson, whom he subsequently wishes he had married. The episode is remembered in the poem 'The Opportunity (For H. P.)'.

January
The *Spectator* reviews *Far from the Madding Crowd* favourably, even suggesting that it might be by George Eliot. A less public admirer is Julia Augusta Martin, who sends a letter of congratulation.
4 (Sun) Accepts an invitation to spend an evening with Geneviève Smith, wife of the vicar of West Stafford.
6 Thanks Geneviève Smith warmly for the occasion, speaking of himself as 'denied by circumstances until very lately the society of educated womankind, which teaches men what cannot be acquired from books, and is indeed the only antidote to that bearishness which one gets into who lives much alone' (*Letters*, I, 26).

9 Tells Leslie Stephen, 'I have decided to finish it here, which is within a walk of the district in which the incidents are supposed to occur. I find it a great advantage to be actually among the people described at the time of describing them' (*Letters*, I, 27).

February
18 (Wed) Agrees to alterations suggested by Leslie Stephen: 'Perhaps I may have higher aims some day, and be a great stickler for the proper artistic balance of the completed work, but for the present circumstances lead me to wish merely to be considered a good hand at a serial' (*Letters*, I, 28). Disraeli, with the first clear Conservative majority since 1841, replaces Gladstone as Prime Minister.

March
Makes notes on the experiences and habits of mail-coach guards.
4 (Wed) Clarifies his feelings over American copyright in a letter to Smith, Elder.
12 Leslie Stephen admits altering one or two passages in *Far from the Madding Crowd*, for which he blames his own 'prudery'.

April
13 (Mon) Stephen warns that he thinks the cause of Fanny's death is unnecessarily emphasised. He would be glad to omit the baby, and invites TH to discussion and dinner.

July
ELG remarks, 'Your novel seems sometimes like a child all your own & none of me' (*Personal Notebooks*, p. 117). Composition of *Far from the Madding Crowd*, and with it TH's last extended period of residence in his birthplace, come to an end. 'Hardy's departure from Bockhampton, and the world of his rural subject matter, for London, and the world of his publishers, his critics, and his essentially urban audience, represented a sharp break with both the place and the manner of his upbringing' (Millgate, p. 162).

August
Corrects proof for the autumn number of the *Cornhill*.

September
12 (Sat) Sends 'Destiny and a Blue Cloak' to the *New York Times*.

17   Marries ELG at St Peter's, Elgin Avenue, Paddington. ELH later
     records, 'The day we were married was a perfect September
     day – the 17th, 1874 – not brilliant sunshine, but wearing a soft
     sunny, luminousness; just as it should be' (Millgate, p. 163). The
     couple spend their wedding night at Morton's Family and
     Commercial Hotel in Brighton, then honeymoon in France,
     travelling to Paris by way of Dieppe and Rouen. ELH's account
     of the honeymoon is preserved in her 'Diary 1'.

October
4   (Sun) 'Destiny and a Blue Cloak' appears in the *New York Times*.
    Never reprinted by TH.
6   Move into St David's Villa, Hook Road, Surbiton.
9   Asks Smith, Elder to include his name in announcements of the
    book version of *Far from the Madding Crowd*.

November
23 (Mon) *Far from the Madding Crowd* published in two volumes.
24 Asks Tinsley whether he might relinquish the copyright of *Under
    the Greenwood Tree*.

December
Invited by Stephen to provide another story for the *Cornhill*. The *Life*
comments that 'This was the means of urging Hardy into the unfortunate course of hurrying forward a further production before he
was aware of what there had been of value in his previous one:
before learning, that is, not only what had attracted the public, but
what was of true and genuine substance on which to build a career
as a writer with a real literary message' (*Life*, p. 102).

1875

January
Rough draft of the first part of *The Hand of Ethelberta* submitted to
Smith, Elder.
20 (Wed) Declines Tinsley's price of £300 for the copyright of *Under
    the Greenwood Tree*.
23 Death of Kingsley.

March

9   (Tues) George Smith offers TH £700 for the serial and volume publication of *The Hand of Ethelberta*. First chapters submitted this month.

22   Move from Surbiton to lodgings at 18 Newton Road, Westbourne Grove, Paddington.

23   Requested by Leslie Stephen to witness his renunciation of Holy Orders, a sign of the closeness of their friendship, and of TH's personal proximity, through that friendship, to the major theological controversies of the day.

April

Still sufficiently interested in poetic composition to be making out a list of possible future subjects and titles.

May

10   (Mon) Takes part in a deputation to Disraeli in support of a motion for a Select Committee to inquire into copyright law.

11   Visits Oxford, dining in the Mitre as a guest of the undergraduate Shotover Club.

June

8   (Tues) Congratulates R. D. Blackmore on *Lorna Doone* (published in 1875), declaring fellow feeling with him as an observant chronicler of rural – and especially West Country – life.

16   Reading G. H. Lewes's *Life of Goethe*.

18   Visits the Chelsea Hospital on the sixtieth anniversary of the Battle of Waterloo to meet veterans of that battle.

July

12   (Mon) Move briefly to Bournemouth, a stay which the poem 'We Sat at the Window' recalls.

15   Move to Swanage, where TH spends the autumn and winter at work on *The Hand of Ethelberta*. The first instalment, illustrated by George Du Maurier, appears in the *Cornhill* this month.

September

7   (Tues) Take a day trip to the Isle of Wight.

13   Picnic at Corfe Castle with Mary and Kate Hardy, who visit Swanage for a fortnight.

October

24 (Sun) Tells Tinsley that he would welcome the opportunity of a substantial revision of *Under the Greenwood Tree* if ever the opportunity should arise.

November

'The Fire at Tranter Sweatley's', later retitled 'The Bride-Night Fire', appears in the *Gentleman's Magazine*, the first of TH's poems to be published.

4 (Thurs) Asks his American publisher, Henry Holt, for a clear statement of account every six months. Regrets that he cannot enter into an arrangement for a serial with the *Examiner*, chiefly for domestic reasons; 'But I need hardly mention that I am truly gratified by such an invitation from the office of a periodical I so much respect' (*Letters*, I, 41).

28 'I sit under a tree, and feel alone: I think of certain insects around me as magnified by the microscope: creatures like elephants, flying dragons, etc. And I feel I am by no means alone' (*Life*, p. 107).

29 'He has read well that has learnt that there is more to read outside books than in them' (*Life*, p. 107).

1876

January

26 (Wed) Last instalment of *The Hand of Ethelberta* sent off.

March

Move to 7 St Peter Street, Yeovil, Somerset.

5 (Sun) Asks George Smith for advice on how to proceed when authorising translations, also revealing 'I do not wish to attempt any more original writing of any length for a few months, until I can learn the best line to take for the future' (*Letters*, I, 43).

April

3 (Mon) *The Hand of Ethelberta* published in two volumes. Critical reception lukewarm: the *Life* comments 'It was, in fact, thirty years too soon for a Comedy of Society of that kind' (*Life*, p. 108).

May
Spend a fortnight in London before departing at end of month for holiday in Holland and the Rhine. For details see *Life*, p. 110, and ELH's 'Diary 2'.
16   (Tues) Advised by Leslie Stephen not to worry excessively about critical canons, and perhaps to limit reading of critics to Sainte-Beuve and Matthew Arnold.

June
26   (Mon) Notes, 'If it be possible to compress into a sentence all that a man learns between 20 and 40, it is that all things merge in one another – good into evil, generosity into justice, religion into politics, the year into the ages, the world into the universe. With this in view the evolution of species seems but a minute and obvious process in the same movement' (*Life*, p. 111).

July
3   (Mon) Move into Riverside Villa, Sturminster Newton: 'It was their first house and, though small, probably that in which they spent their happiest days' (*Life*, p. 111). This happiness derives not only from marriage, but also from an intimacy with the plenitude and hardships of nature and rural life (reflected in a number of Sturminster poems), and a growing confidence and ambition as an author (as evidenced in the Literary Notebooks, probably started in the first half of this year and kept with autodidactic zeal, and in the ambitious style of *The Return of the Native*, largely written at Sturminster). Such happiness must however be set against a developing frustration at remaining childless. For TH's poetic reflection on the Sturminster years see 'A Two-Years' Idyll'.
15   Charles Kegan Paul's article 'The Wessex Labourer' appears in the *Examiner*, praising the precision of TH's portrayal of the Dorset countryside and its inhabitants.

December
Attends a conference in London on the Eastern question, hearing Gladstone, Shaftesbury, and Trollope.
5   (Tues) Advises Evangeline Smith on a story she has written.
25   Spend Christmas at Bockhampton with ELH, one of several attempts at this time to bring the Hardy and Gifford families closer together.

1877

January
1 (Mon) Queen Victoria proclaimed Empress of India.

February
13 (Tues) Asks John Blackwood to let him know if he should ever require a serial for *Blackwood's*, and offers to let him see part of his present project.

April
12 (Thurs) Following lack of interest by Leslie Stephen, tells Blackwood that he has forwarded the first fifteen chapters of *The Return of the Native* to him for consideration.
26 Thanks Blackwood for sending his criticism of *The Return*.

May
One-volume edition of *The Hand of Ethelberta* published.

June
Again considering the form of a large work on the Napoleonic war. *The Return*, sent again to Leslie Stephen, rejected for publication by him.
16 (Sat) Offers *The Return* to George Bentley for *Temple Bar*.
29 Their maid, discovered the previous evening in an outhouse with her lover, leaves.

July
13 (Fri) Unexplained notebook entry: 'The sudden disappointment of a hope leaves a scar which the ultimate fulfilment of that hope never entirely removes' (*Life*, p. 116). Agrees to provide Nancy Meugens with a story ('The Thieves Who Couldn't Help Sneezing') for *Father Christmas*, December 1877.

August
13 (Mon) 'We hear that Jane, our late servant, is soon to have a baby. Yet never a sign of one is there for us' (*Life*, p. 116).
28 '. . . clouds, mists, and mountains are unimportant beside the wear on a threshold, or the print of a hand' (*Life*, p. 116). Copy for the first two instalments of *The Return* despatched to *Belgravia*.

September
Inquiring into local history with a view to *The Trumpet-Major*.

October
Travels to Bath to meet his father, who is undertaking a cure for rheumatism there.

November
8   (Thurs) Parts, 3, 4 and 5 of *The Return of the Native* posted to Chatto and Windus.
25 Birth of Harley Granville Barker.

December
'The Thieves Who Couldn't Help Sneezing' appears in *Father Christmas*.
22 (Sat) Attends the post mortem of a local boy.

1878

'The Sergeant's Song' written; 'Valenciennes' begun.

January
First instalment of *The Return of the Native* appears in *Belgravia*.

February
8   (Fri) Thanks Arthur Hopkins for contacting him about the illustrations for *The Return*, giving him hints on the characterisation and plot.
20 Sends Hopkins sketches of mummers' costumes and staff.

March
5   (Tues) Attend the Sturminster Literary Institute concert, a performance there later serving as the basis for 'The Maid of Keinton Mandeville'.
18 'End of the Sturminster Newton idyll . . . ' (*Life*, p. 118).
22 Move to 1 Arundel Terrace, Trinity Road, Wandsworth Common. TH's literary activities during the first half of the year here extensive: he writes 'The Impulsive Lady of Croome Castle' and 'An Indiscretion in the Life of an Heiress', and is busy with revisions and proof-reading.

April

6 (Sat) First instalment of 'The Impulsive Lady of Croome Castle', later retitled 'The Duchess of Hamptonshire', appears in *Light*.

22 Records characteristic speculations on seeing beauty in ugliness, and the superiority of beauty of association to beauty of aspect.

30 Applies to the British Museum for a reader's ticket. Reads here on several occasions this summer, many of his researches being recorded in the *Trumpet-Major* Notebook (for text see *Personal Notebooks*, pp. 117–86).

May

9 (Thurs) Sends off to the Boston journal *Literary World*, in response to a request, a slightly aggrandising biographical account of himself.

June

Elected a member of the Savile Club, 'and by degrees fell into line as a London man again' (*Life*, p. 121). As TH probably calculated, the move to London facilitates social engagements, and his circle of acquaintance grows considerably.

4 (Tues) Sends 'An Indiscretion in the Life of an Heiress' to the *New Quarterly Magazine*.

16 Dine with Alexander Macmillan.

21 Regrets having to decline an invitation from the Kegan Pauls, and thanks Kegan Paul for his part in securing TH's election to the Savile Club.

24 Tells Henry Harper that he hopes to have further dealings with his firm.

July

'An Indiscretion in the Life of an Heiress' appears in the *New Quarterly*.

August

3 (Sat) Sees Henry Irving perform at the Lyceum, and drinks champagne in his dressing-room afterwards. Congratulates Arthur Hopkins on the illustration accompanying the August instalment of *The Return*: 'I think Eustacia is charming – she is certainly just what I imagined her to be, & the rebelliousness of her nature is precisely caught . . . ' (*Letters*, I, 59).

31   Begins a ten-day visit to Dorset.

September
27   (Fri) Agrees terms with Smith for publishing *The Return of the Native* in book form.

October
1   (Tues) Asks Chatto and Windus to forward the fee for 'An Indiscretion in the Life of an Heiress'. Sends Smith, Elder a sketch of a map of the setting of *The Return of the Native*, remarking, 'Unity of place is so seldom preserved in novels that a map of the scene of action is as a rule impracticable: but since the present story affords an opportunity of doing so I am of opinion that it would be a desirable novelty . . .' (*Letters*, I, 61).
21   The Irish National Land League founded.
27   At Chelsea Hospital meets a Pensioner who took part in the retreat to Corunna.

November
4   (Mon) *The Return of the Native* published in book form.
28   'Woke before it was light. Felt that I had not enough staying power to hold my own in the world' (*Life*, p. 124). This sentiment probably results from disappointment at the critical reception of *The Return of the Native*.
30   Letter 'Dialect in Novels' appears in the *Athenaeum*.

December
8   (Sun) Sends Smith, Elder extracts from reviews for use in publicising *The Return of the Native*.

1879

'The poem "A January Night. 1879" in *Moments of Vision* relates to an incident of this new year . . . which occurred here at Tooting, where they seemed to begin to feel that "there had past away a glory from the earth". And it was in this house that their troubles began' (*Life*, p. 124). 'The Announcement' may refer to the same experience.

February
1   (Sat) Travels to Dorchester, staying there for a fortnight, noting down several pieces of folklore as reported by his family.

March
17   (Mon) Accepts Walter Besant's invitation to join the Rabelais Club.

April
'The Distracted Young Preacher', later retitled 'The Distracted Preacher', appears in the *New Quarterly*.

May
19   (Mon) Offers Alexander Macmillan *The Trumpet-Major* for *Macmillan's Magazine*.

June
9   (Mon) Offers to send John Blackwood parts of *The Trumpet-Major* to look over with a view to publication.
21   Visits Harrow School.

July
1   (Tues) Copies a phrase of Leslie Stephen's into his notebook: 'The ultimate aim of the poet should be to touch our hearts by showing his own' (*Life*, p. 128). The *Life* comments that this is but one instance of the many influences exerted by Stephen on TH since 1873.
5   Agrees to the offer of £400 for the appearance of *The Trumpet-Major* in *Good Words*.
12   Attends the funeral of the young Louis Napoleon at Chislehurst, Kent.
30   Offers *The Trumpet-Major* to *Lippincott's Magazine* for Amercian serial appearance: 'I may add that it is to be a cheerful, lively story, & is to end happily' (*Letters*, I, 65).

August
Holidays in Dorset for part of this month.
1   (Fri) Tells William Isbister that he can send the first three or four instalments of *The Trumpet-Major* immediately.

September
6   (Sat) Offers American serial rights of *The Trumpet-Major* to the *Atlantic Monthly*.

October
Review of Barnes's *Poems of Rural Life* (the only review written by
TH) appears in the *New Quarterly*.
17   (Fri) Thanks Charles Kegan Paul for the encouraging tone of the
      article about TH (by Alexandra Sutherland Orr) which has
      recently appeared in the *New Quarterly*.

December
Attends the inaugural meeting of the Rabelais Club.

1880

TH's dramatisation of *Far from the Madding Crowd* (undertaken some
time in the previous year) revised by J. Comyns Carr in the spring
and submitted in the summer to the managers of the St James's
Theatre as *The Mistress of the Farm*.

January
First instalment of *The Trumpet-Major* appears in *Good Words*.
28   (Wed) Gladstone forms his second ministry.

February
Meets Matthew Arnold for the first time, discussing style with him.
2   (Mon) Warmly congratulates Frederick Locker on his poem
      'The Old Stone-Mason', comparing it to Wordsworth.
3   Death of the Revd Henry Moule.
11   Congratulates Handley Moule on his funeral sermon: 'I cannot
      refrain from sending you a line to tell you how deeply it has
      affected me' (*Letters*, I, 70).
21   Sends George Du Maurier an idea for a *Punch* cartoon.

March
Call by arrangement on Anne Procter, the first of a long series of
such visits, at which TH frequently encounters Browning. Also lunch
this month with Tennyson, who expresses admiration for *A Pair of
Blue Eyes*. Dinner at several clubs this spring and summer also in-
creases TH's social acquaintance and confidence.

April
'Fellow-Townsmen' appears in the *New Quarterly*.

16 (Fri) Congratulates Harper Brothers on their plan to establish an English edition of *Harper's New Monthly Magazine,* and specifies the terms he would expect for a serial contributed to it.

20 Discusses purchasing land in the Dorchester area with Henry Hardy.

May
3 (Mon) Bradlaugh claims the right to affirm rather than take the oath at the swearing-in of the Commons.

26 Goes to the Derby.

June
4 (Fri) Attempts to get Helen Allingham (née Paterson) to provide the illustrations for *A Laodicean.*

11 Tells Harper Brothers that George Du Maurier has agreed to illustrate *A Laodicean.*

July
Arranges book publication of *The Trumpet-Major* with Smith, Elder.

12 (Mon) Tells J. Henry Harper that Du Maurier would be happy to entertain them both to lunch.

27 Leave for a French holiday.

September
2 (Thurs) Warmly congratulates George Manville Fenn on his 'Nightingale Notes' in the *Graphic* for 24 July.

October
16 (Sat) Begin a week-long visit to Cambridge. 'After the first day or two he felt an indescribable physical weariness, which was really the beginning of the long illness he was to endure' (*Life,* p. 141).

26 *The Trumpet-Major* published. TH afflicted by serious pain which is soon diagnosed as internal bleeding, the cure being either a major operation or several months lying in bed. The latter course adopted.

November
Forced to dictate *A Laodicean* from his bed to ELH.

11 (Thurs) The managers of the St James's Theatre finally reject *The Mistress of the Farm.*

15   Makes light of his illness in a letter to R. R. Bowker, Harper Brothers' London representative.
20   Visited by Tauchnitz regarding a continental edition of *The Trumpet-Major*.

December
First instalment of *A Laodicean* appears in *Harper's New Monthly Magazine*, helping to inaugurate the magazine's European edition.
 3   (Fri) Asks Sir Henry Ponsonby whether he might offer Queen Victoria a copy of *The Trumpet-Major* because of its royal associations.
15   Apologises to Charles Moule for being unable, owing to ill health, to attend the consecration in St Paul's Cathedral of George Evans Moule as Bishop of Mid-China.
22   Death of George Eliot, which sets TH thinking about Positivism.

1881

February
 4. (Fri) Death of Carlyle.
15   Reminds R. R. Bowker (with whom many brief notes are being exchanged at this time) that he has undertaken to provide four revises each month.

March
22   (Tues) Visited by Maggie Macmillan, who reflects the sun into TH's face by the use of a looking-glass.

April
10   (Sun) Leaves the house for the first time since October.
18   Thanks Charles Kegan Paul for his recent article 'Mr. Hardy's Novels', though cautioning him 'I have an opinion that the less people know of a writer's antecedents (till he is dead) the better' (*Letters*, I, 89).
19   Death of Disraeli.
23   Authorises a translation of *The Trumpet-Major* into French by Charles Bernard-Derosne. Drives with ELH and his sister Kate to Badbury Rings, pointing out to them Charborough Park, later to be used as a setting in *Two on a Tower*. Enters into the

'Memoranda ɪ' Notebook details of his conversation with their driver about old post-boy and postilion practices.

May
9 (Mon) Attempting to reconcile a scientific view of life with an emotional and spiritual.

June
22 (Wed) Move to Llanherne, The Avenue, Wimborne, TH having decided that permanent residence in London is good for neither his physical health nor his imaginative creativity.
29 Advises John Antell on the design of a tombstone for his father, John (thought to have been part of the inspiration for the character of Jude).

July
Jots down notes on fictional theory, 'possibly for an article that was never written' (*Life*, p. 150).
29 (Fri) Tells the agency Tillotson and Son the price he would require for a short story.

August
10 (Wed) Agrees terms for a short story ('Benighted Travellers') with Tillotson.
23 Leave Wimborne for a Scottish holiday, including visits to places associated with Walter Scott.

September
Corrects proofs for the book edition of *A Laodicean*. Writes 'What the Shepherd Saw' this autumn.
28 (Wed) Thomas Bailey Aldrich inquires whether TH might write a serial for the *Atlantic Monthly* (the result being *Two on a Tower*).

October
15 (Sat) Letter 'Papers of the Manchester Literary Club' published in the *Spectator*.
20 Regrets having to decline an invitation to dine with Turgenev, 'a writer whose courage in the choice of subject I admire no less than his power in the treatment of it' (*Letters*, ɪ, 94).

November
25   (Fri) *A Laodicean* published in book form.
27   Applies to visit the Royal Observatory for research on the background to *Two on a Tower*.

December
Places *Two on a Tower* with the *Atlantic Monthly*. Attends a ball at Canford Manor, and is gratified that the old mill nearby is not to be pulled down, 'having as great a repugnance to pulling down a mill where (to use his own words) they ground food for the body, as to pulling down a church where they ground food for the soul' (*Life*, p. 151). The *Life* further records, 'Thus ended 1881 with a much brighter atmosphere for the author and his wife than the opening had shown' (p. 151).
5   (Mon) 'What the Shepherd Saw' appears in the *Illustrated London News*.
13   Thanks W. C. Unwin for sending astronomical information.
14   Applauds the critic Alexandra Sutherland Orr for sensing an ambiguity at the end of *A Laodicean*, and draws her attention to the improved nature of the book version of the novel, especially as regards the characterisation of Paula. Inquires whether the Prince of Wales might accept a copy of *The Trumpet-Major* on account of its royal associations.
17   'Benighted Travellers' (later collected as 'The Honourable Laura' in *A Group of Noble Dames*) appears in the *Christmas Leaves* supplement of the *Bolton Weekly Journal*.
29   First performance of Pinero's *The Squire*, which TH hencefoward suspects of having made unfair use of his own dramatisation of *Far from the Madding Crowd*.

1882

'The Levelled Churchyard' written. The Married Woman's Property Act gives married women the right of separate ownership of property of all kinds.

January
2   (Mon) Letters of protest by TH about similarities between *The Squire* and *Far from the Madding Crowd* appear in the *Daily News* and *The Times*.

5 Thanks Alfred Pope and William Black for their advice over *The Squire*, but reports that he will be taking no further action, 'having better work to do in my regular province' (*Letters*, I, 100).
25 Birth of Virginia Woolf (née Stephen).

February
2 (Thurs) Birth of James Joyce.
16 Notes, 'Write a history of human automatism, or impulsion – viz., an account of human action in spite of human knowledge, showing how very far conduct lags behind the knowledge that should really guide it' (*Life*, p. 152).
27 First night of *Far from the Madding Crowd*, J. Comyns Carr's drastic revision of *The Mistress of the Farm*, at the Prince of Wales Theatre, Liverpool.

March
Travel to Liverpool to see the *Far from the Madding Crowd* adaptation.

April
26 (Wed) Attends the funeral of Darwin in Westminster Abbey.
29 Dramatisation of *Far from the Madding Crowd* transfers to the Globe Theatre in London, where it runs for 114 performances.

May
First instalment of *Two on a Tower* appears in the *Atlantic Monthly*.
6 (Sat) The Phoenix Park murders in Dublin.
28 Takes Henry Stevens to a dinner of the Rabelais Club.

July
'A Legend of the Year Eighteen Hundred and Four' (later retitled 'A Tradition of Eighteen Hundred and Four') sent off to Harper Brothers.
22 (Sat) Declines for the time being an invitation from Margaret Oliphant to contribute a sketch of the Dorset labourer to *Longman's Magazine*, though revealing that the project interests him.

August
8 (Tues) Thanks Charles Bernard-Derosne for sending six copies of *Le Trompette-Major*.
12 Asks the advice of Moy Thomas over a bad poem published

under the name Thomas Hardy by a former architectural col-
league of TH's, complaining, 'I seem doomed to squabbles this
year!' (*Letters*, I, 108).

September
Take a short holiday touring adjacent counties, returning to
Wimborne via a visit to William Barnes.

October
Holiday in Paris. *Two on a Tower* appears in book form.

November
25   (Sat) 'A Tradition of Eighteen Hundred and Four' appears in
     Harper's Christmas.
30   Applies to the Duchy of Cornwall for a building-lease for the
     land on which Max Gate is subsequently erected.

December
4   (Mon) Sends Edmund Gosse a copy of *Two on a Tower*, 'in the
     belief that you will perceive, if nobody else does, what I have
     aimed at – to make science, not the mere padding of a romance,
     but the actual vehicle of romance. The execution is hurried, &
     far from what I intended – but it could not be avoided' (*Letters*,
     I, 110).
6   Death of Trollope.
10   Tells Gosse 'We propose to leave Wimborne for good about
     March: the house we are in lies rather too near the Stour level
     for health' (*Letters*, I, 110).
23   Letter supporting the treatment of English authors by Harper
     Brothers appears in the *Athenaeum*.

1883

'He Abjures Love' written.

January
17   (Wed) Tells Anne Procter that reception of *Two on a Tower* has
     been mixed, but that the reading public have shown 'that their
     interest in it is greater than in anything I have done latterly'
     (*Letters*, I, 114).

19 Denies, in a letter to the *St James's Gazette*, that any insult to the Church was intended in making the Bishop a victim in *Two on a Tower*.

February
25 (Sun) 'The Romantic Adventures of a Milkmaid', written this winter, sent to the *Graphic*.

March
'The Three Strangers' appears in *Longman's Magazine*.

April
5 (Thurs) Undertakes to provide a short story ('Our Exploits at West Poley') for Perry Mason and Co.
29 Congratulates Havelock Ellis on his article 'Thomas Hardy's Novels', acknowledging that his heroes come from 'the type to which the great mass of educated modern men of ordinary capacity are assimilating more or less' (*Letters*, I, 118).

May
'In London off and on during May and June, seeing pictures, plays, and friends' (*Life*, p. 159). TH's engagements allow him to meet Browning at least twice.

June
Move from Wimborne to Dorchester: 'This removal to the county town, and later to a spot a little outside it, was a step they often regretted having taken; but the bracing air brought them health and renewed vigour, and in the long run it proved not ill-advised' (*Life*, p. 161).
25 (Mon) Dines at the Savile Club with Gosse. 'The Romantic Adventures of a Milkmaid' appears in the *Graphic*, and 'The Dorsetshire Labourer' in *Longman's Magazine*. TH comments to John Morley, 'Though a Liberal, I have endeavoured to describe the state of things without political bias' (*Letters*, I, 119).

July
22 (Sun) By previous arrangement, takes Gosse to Winterborne Came church to hear Barnes preach, visiting the rectory for tea afterwards.

August
16   (Thurs) TH's obituary notice for T. W. H. Tolbort appears in the
      Dorset County Chronicle.

November
 5   (Mon) 'Our Exploits at West Poley' sent off. Tells Percy Bunting
      in response to an earlier invitation for an article, 'I have been
      looking into the question of the labourer & his vote, & find it to
      be such a purely political subject that I must decline to attempt
      it' (*Letters*, I, 123).
26   Building commences at Max Gate.

December
31   (Mon) Plants trees on the recently acquired Max Gate plot.

1884

At work on *The Mayor of Casterbridge* by this spring, and the greater
part of it completed this year. Writes 'A Countenance'. The *New*
(later *Oxford*) *English Dictionary* begins publication.

January
Part of the month spent in London, meeting Henry James, Gosse,
Hamo Thornycroft and Sir Laurence Alma-Tadema, among others.

March
Contemplating a novel to be called 'Time against Two' (see *Life*,
p. 164).

April
26   (Sat) Sight of four itinerant female musicians in Dorchester
      High Street forms the germ for the poem 'Music in a Snowy
      Street'.

May
'Interlopers at the Knap' appears in the *English Illustrated Magazine*.
13   (Tues) Reads his paper 'Some Romano-British Relics Found at
      Max Gate, Dorchester' to the Dorset Natural History and Anti-
      quarian Field Club. Such excavations partially explain the back-
      ground to *The Mayor of Casterbridge*.

June
Some time spent in this and the following month in London, meeting Burne-Jones, Matthew Arnold, Du Maurier and Henry James.

3   (Tues) Attends a circus at Fordington, one of several circus visits at this time. One resulting experience gives rise to the poem 'Circus-Rider to Ringmaster'.

August
14   (Thurs) Sees a performance of *Othello* by strolling players in Dorchester.

October
18   (Sat) Attends a dinner for the Incorporated Society of Authors given by the Lord Mayor of London.

December
Gladstone's Franchise Bill extends the electorate to 5 million.
31   (Wed) Attends the New Year's Eve bell-ringing at St Peter's Dorchester.

1885

The *Dictionary of National Biography*, edited by Leslie Stephen, begins publication.

March
13   (Fri) Sends ELH an account of his arrival to stay with the Earl and Countess of Portsmouth.
15   'Ancient Earthworks and What Two Enthusiastic Scientists Found Therein', later retitled 'A Tryst at an Ancient Earthwork', appears in the *Detroit Post*.
18   Allows Frederick Macmillan to decide the date at which *The Woodlanders* should begin to appear in *Macmillan's Magazine*.

April
5   (Sun) Compares the narrative techniques of the Bible with those of modern fiction (see *Life*, p. 171).
17   Finishes *The Mayor of Casterbridge*.
19   Notes, 'The business of the poet and novelist is to show the

sorriness underlying the grandest things, and the grandeur underlying the sorriest things' (*Life*, p. 171).

May
16 (Sun) Sends ELH an account of his recent social engagements, including a meeting with Margaret Oliphant, whom he found 'propriety & primness incarnate' (*Letters*, I, 133).
31 Calls on Anne Procter, where he again meets Browning.

June
At the end of the month furniture moved into Max Gate. For a description of the house see *Life*, p. 173.
17 (Wed) Tells Frederic Harrison that he has enjoyed attending his Positivist lectures.
25 Salisbury forms a Conservative ministry following the resignation of Gladstone.
29 Sleep in Max Gate for the first time.

October
17 (Sat) Calls on William Barnes. First instalment of 'A Mere Interlude' appears in the *Bolton Weekly Journal*.

November
17 (Tues) Depressed by difficulties with the plotting of *The Woodlanders*.
20 Sends John Morley his views on the disestablishment of the Church of England, a major issue in the General Election, and good wishes for Morley's success in that election.
27 Asks whether the *Atlantic Monthly* might be interested in publishing *The Woodlanders* in America.

December
31 (Thurs) Records 'the end of the old year . . . finds me sadder than many previous New Year's Eves have done' (*Life*, p. 176).

1886

January
2 (Fri) *The Mayor of Casterbridge* begins publication in the *Graphic* and *Harper's Weekly*. TH notes, 'I fear it will not be so good as I

meant, but after all, it is not improbabilities of incident but improbabilities of character that matter' (*Life*, p. 176).

3 Notes, 'My art is to intensify the expression of things, as is done by Crivelli, Bellini, etc., so that the heart and inner meaning is made vividly visible' (*Life*, p. 177).

21 Suggests to Frederick Macmillan that he might wish to purchase the American serial rights of *The Woodlanders*.

February
1 (Mon) Gladstone forms his third ministry.

March
7 (Sun) Reading proofs of *The Mayor of Casterbridge*. Tells George Smith that he himself may decide whether *The Mayor* appears in two volumes or three (the former subsequently decided on).

April
Much interested in the progress of the Irish Home Rule bill (introduced 8 April), recording, 'I never remember a debate of such absorbing interest as this' (*Life*, p. 177). The *Life* comments on the problem as 'a staring dilemma, of which good policy and good philanthropy were the huge horns' (p. 178).

22 (Thurs) Declines to give a lecture in Cheshire: 'lecturing is not in my way – is, indeed, almost beyond my physical powers' (*Letters*, I, 143).

May
Lodgings taken first at 14 Bedford Place, and later at 28 Upper Bedford Place, both near the British Museum. Many social engagements at the end of this month and throughout the subsequent two, including TH's first encounter with Walter Pater, 'whose manner is that of one carrying weighty ideas without spilling them' (*Life*, p. 180), and meetings with Gosse, Whistler and Henry James, 'who has a ponderously warm manner of saying nothing in infinite sentences' (*Life*, p. 181). Much time this summer spent reading Napoleonic material in the British Museum. First instalment of *The Woodlanders* appears in *Macmillan's Magazine*.

10 (Mon) *The Mayor of Casterbridge* issued in book form. The *Life* comments on the excess of incident in the novel, and attributes it to the pressures of serialisation. (p. 179).

13 Goes to the Houses of Parliament to hear the Irish debate.

June
Asked by Gissing if he may call for advice. Gissing subsequently
sends a letter of fulsome thanks (*Life*, p. 182).
7   (Mon) Tells Robert Louis Stevenson, 'I feel several inches taller
     at the idea of your thinking of dramatizing the *Mayor*, Yes, by
     all means' (*Letters*, I, 146).
28   Gratified by good sales of *The Mayor*.
29   Calls on Leslie Stephen, subsequently noting his acid manner.

July
26   (Mon) Salisbury forms a Conservative ministry.

August
18   (Wed) Urges Gosse to pay a visit to Max Gate for a few days.
31   Takes the visiting Gosse to Bridport.

September
16   (Thurs) Invites John Alexander, keen to paint TH's portrait, to
     visit Max Gate.

October
Spend the first week of the month with Lady Portsmouth in Devon.
7   (Thurs) Death of William Barnes.
11   Funeral of Barnes. TH's walk there forms the basis for the poem
     'The Last Signal'.
16   Obituary notice of Barnes by TH appears in the *Athenaeum*.
19   Consoles Gosse after reading an attack by John Churton Collins
     on his *From Shakespeare to Pope*; 'I have suffered terribly at times
     from reviews – pecuniarily, & still more mentally, & the crown
     of my bitterness has been my sense of unfairness in such imper-
     sonal means of attack, wh. conveys to an unthinking public the
     idea of an immense weight of opinion behind, to which you can
     only oppose your own little solitary personality: when the truth
     is that there is only another little solitary personality against
     yours all the time' (*Letters*, I, 154).
31   Advises Miles Barnes to publish correspondence suggesting
     that there should be a memorial, funded by public subscription,
     to his father.

November
11   (Thurs) Thanks Coventry Patmore for his generous mention of
     TH in an article on Barnes.

December
Visit to the Society of British Artists causes TH to reflect on the
principles and practice of Impressionism (*Life*, p. 184). Eighth and
last Impressionist exhibition held.
13   (Mon) Agrees to help Barnes's daughter and prospective bio-
     grapher, Lucy Baxter, by supplying reminiscences of her father.

1887

Starts 'In a Wood' (finished 1896). Notes for *Jude the Obscure* begun
this year.

January
'January 1887 was uneventful at Max Gate . . . ' (*Life*, p. 185). A note
made this month, however, shows TH as far from complacent in his
reflections on artistic method: 'The "simply natural" is interesting no
longer. The much decried, mad, late-Turner rendering is now necessary to create my interest' (*Life*, p. 185).

February
4   (Fri) '8.20 P. M. Finished *The Woodlanders*. Thought I should feel
    glad, but I do not particularly, – though relieved' (*Life*, p. 185).
    The *Life* remarks that TH often felt that in some respects *The
    Woodlanders* was his best novel.
6   Visits his father, hearing from him about whippings in
    Dorchester in the 1830s.
8   *The Woodlanders* sent off.
9   Asks Frederick Macmillan to suggest terms for the book pub-
    lication of *The Woodlanders*, adding that he may wish to shorten
    some passages.
15 Accepts Macmillan's (wary) terms.

March
2   (Wed) Attends a conference arranged by the Incorporated So-
    cie-ty of Authors.
12 Agrees to turn his mind to a story ('Alicia's Diary') for Tillotson
    and Son on his return from abroad.
14 Attains a long-held ambition by leaving for a visit to Italy,
    visiting Turin, Genoa, Pisa, Florence, Rome (TH being more
    interested by its pagan than its Christian aspects), Venice and
    Milan. The 'Poems of Pilgrimage' in *Poems of the Past and the*

Present result from this trip, most of them after a considerable
interval, it appears. For TH's extensive account of their travels
see *Life*, pp. 187–96; for ELH's, her 'Diary 3'.

15 *The Woodlanders* published by Macmillan.
31 Visit the graves of Shelley and Keats, TH gathering violets from
the latter. Reports to Gosse 'I am so overpowered by the presence of *decay* in Ancient Rome that I feel it like a nightmare in
my sleep' (*Letters*, I, 163).

April
Attends the Royal Academy dinner.

May
16 (Mon) Meets James Russell Lowell.

June
21 (Tues) See the procession to celebrate Queen Victoria's Golden
Jubilee.
25 'At a concert at Prince's Hall I saw Souls outside Bodies' (*Life*,
p. 201).
26 Meets Browning at Anne Procter's. Browning complains that
too few writers have been invited to the Jubilee Service in
Westminster Abbey. The *Life* adds, 'The remainder of the
London season in the brilliant Jubilee-year was passed by the
Hardys gaily enough' (p. 201).
30 Lunch with the Stanley family. Later, talks to Arnold, Du Maurier
and others at the Royal Academy soirée.

July
Settle in a house in Campden Hill Road, near Holland Park.
12 (Tues) Thanks Lord Lytton for a letter of generous praise of *The
Woodlanders*.

August
Return to Max Gate. The *Fortnightly Review* publishes TH's choices of
the finest passages of poetry and prose as part of a series on the
subject.

September
The *Life* for this and the following month reveals much attention to
Dorset superstition.

October

1　(Sat) Offers 'The Withered Arm' to *Blackwood's Magazine.*

15　First instalment of 'Alicia's Diary' appears in the *Manchester Weekly Times.*

28　Thanks William Blackwood for his acceptance of 'The Withered Arm'.

November

Shapes another outline scheme for *The Dynasts,* ideas for the haunting of Napoleon perhaps showing the influence of recent absorption in local superstition.

December

11　(Sun) Thanks Blackwood for proofs of 'The Withered Arm' and reports that he is considering a natural death for the farmer.

31　'A silent New Year's Eve – no bell, or band, or voice.

　　'The year has been a fairly friendly one to me. It showed me the south of France – Italy, above all Rome – and it brought me back unharmed and much illuminated. It has given me some new acquaintances, too, and enabled me to hold my own in fiction, whatever that may be worth, by the completion of *The Woodlanders'* (*Life,* p. 203). A list of books read during the year follows this comment.

1888

January

'The Withered Arm' appears in *Blackwood's Magazine,* and the first instalment of 'The Waiting Supper' in *Murray's.*

14　(Sat) Reflects on the possibility of a sensational novel where the subject of the sensation is psychical evolution.

18　Congratulates Arthur Blomfield on being elected an associate of the Royal Academy.

24　'I find that my politics really are neither Tory nor Radical. I may be called an Intrinsicalist. I am against privileges derived from accident of any kind, and am therefore equally opposed to aristocratic privilege and democratic privilege. . . . Opportunity should be equal for all, but those who will not avail themselves of it should be cared for merely – not be a burden to, nor the rulers over, those who do avail themselves thereof' (*Life,* p. 204).

February

Late in the month begins correspondence with Dr A. B. Grosart on theological matters, failing to see any evidence for the idea of omnipotent goodness, and directing Grosart towards the *Life of Darwin* by G. T. Bettany, and works by Spencer and other agnostics. Also corresponds with the Bishop of Salisbury, John Wordsworth, over the effects of the migration of the peasantry.

29 (Wed) Asks Macmillan to consider publishing a collection of his short stories (*Wessex Tales*), adding that in the opinion of some well-known critics the stories are 'as good as anything I have ever written (however good that may be)' (*Letters*, I, 174).

March

'The Profitable Reading of Fiction' appears in the *Forum*.

1 (Thurs) Reflecting on four former village beauties, two of whom the *Life* identifies as influential on 'Lizbie Brown', and Arabella in *Jude*.

9 Reading in the British Museum, and conscious of the souls of the readers gliding about in a kind of dream. Accepts the terms offered by Frederick Macmillan for *Wessex Tales*.

April

15 (Sun) Death of Matthew Arnold.

16 Notes with approval the praise given by *The Times* to Arnold's enthusiasm for the nobler elements in humanity.

26 Reflecting on the success of Byron's *Childe Harold*.

28 Notes down an idea for a short story, a germ for *Jude*: 'A short story of a young man – "who could not go to Oxford" – His struggles and ultimate failure. Suicide. . . . There is something . . . the world ought to be shown, and I am the one to show it to them' (*Life*, pp. 207–8).

May

4 (Fri) *Wessex Tales* published.

7 Sends Browning as a birthday tribute an inscribed copy of *Wessex Tales*.

13 Lunches with Lady Catherine Gaskell, meeting Lord Houghton there.

28 Leave for a holiday in Paris. TH able here to see many memorials of the Revolution and of Napoleon, subjects which seem to have absorbed him particularly this year.

June

10 (Sat) Attend the Grand Prix de Paris at Longchamp.
13 See exhibition of Hugo's manuscripts and drawings.
14 Visits the Archives Nationales.

July

3 (Tues) Calls on Lady Portsmouth, 'one of the few, very few, women of her own rank for whom I would make a sacrifice' (*Life*, p. 210).
5 Asks Lord Carnarvon whether he would propose him as a member of the Athenaeum (TH eventually achieves election in 1891).
8 Attends a service at St Mary Abbots, Kensington, speculating at length on the congregation's absorption in wordly rather than sacred thoughts.
9 Sees Ada Rehan in *The Taming of the Shrew*. Reading Henry James's *Reverberator*, reflecting, 'The great novels of the future will certainly not concern themselves with the minutiae of manners' (*Life*, p. 211).
14 Dine with Walter Pater.
17 Complains to R. H. Hutton that the *Spectator* has failed to notice *Wessex Tales*.
24 Explains to Harry Quilter the substance of two short stories – 'The Melancholy Hussar' (which is in an advanced state) and 'A Tragedy of Two Ambitions' (which is at present only in note form) and offers him whichever he prefers for the *Universal Review*.

August

5 (Sun) Notes that 'To find beauty in ugliness is the province of the poet' (*Life*, p. 213).
15 Birth of T.E. Lawrence.
19 Sends off *A Tragedy of Two Ambitions* to Quilter.
28 Sends condolences to Gosse following the death of his father.

September

7 (Fri) Tells H. M. Alden that he hopes to finish 'The First Countess of Wessex' in about ten days.
30 Walks in the Frome Valley and near Evershot, mentally marking out the territory of *Tess of the d'Urbervilles*, seeing much evidence of 'The decline and fall of the Hardys', and reflecting 'So we go down, down, down' (*Life*, pp. 214–15).

October
7   (Sun) Regrets the prevailing insincerity of much modern liter-
    ature, especially in matters religious and moral. 'When dogma
    has to be balanced on its feet by such hair-splitting as the late
    Mr. M. Arnold's it must be in a very bad way' (*Life*, p. 215).
13 Encourages Robert Pearce Edgcumbe to stand as a candidate at
    the county-council and General elections. (County councils were
    established this year by the Local Government Act.)

December
'A Tragedy of Two Ambitions' appears in the *Universal Review*.
6   (Thurs) Specifies the qualities desirable in the illustrator of 'The
    First Countess of Wessex' (Alfred Parsons eventually selected).
17 Letter on the location of the Waterloo Ball appears in *The Times*.
24 Thanks Eliza Lynn Linton for her letter of praise of 'A Tragedy
    of Two Ambitions'.
31 Thanks W. P. Frith for the handsome compliment to TH in the
    final pages of *My Autobiogaphy*.

1889

Considerable poetic activity this year, including some planning of 'A
Drama of Kings', later to become *The Dynasts*.

January
8   (Tues) Notices the plight of horses drawing buses in London.
9   Greatly impressed by the late Turners at the Royal Academy,
    commenting, 'each is a landscape *plus* a man's soul' (*Life*, p. 216).
10 Elected to the council of the Dorset County Museum.
20 Specifies to Ward and Downey acceptable terms for a five-year
    lease on *Desperate Remedies*.
28 Entertain the landscape painter Alfred Parsons, consulting with
    him about the illustrations for 'The First Countess of Wessex'.

February
Tess well under way.
19 (Tues) Records idea for a story, partially incorporated in *The Well-
    Beloved* – a face which goes through three generations or more.

March

15   (Fri) Notes, 'Each new style of novel must be the old with added ideas, not an ignoring and avoidance of the old' (*Life*, p. 218).

April

Arrive in London at the end of this month, staying first at the West Central Hotel and later in two furnished floors of 20 Monmouth Road, Bayswater, until the end of July. Some work on *Tess* done during this period.

5   (Fri) Notes 'London. Four million forlorn hopes!' (*Life*, p. 218).

7   'A woeful fact – that the human race is too extremely developed for its corporeal conditions, the nerves being evolved to an activity abnormal in such an environment' (*Life*, p. 218).

14   Thanks J. A. Symonds for his letter praising *The Return of the Native*, confessing, 'I often begin a story with the intention of making it brighter & gayer than usual; but the question of conscience soon comes in; & it does not seem right, even in novels, to wilfully belie one's own views' (*Letters*, I, 190).

May

5   (Sun) Attend Bow Church, Cheapside.

12   Attend St James's, Westmoreland Street, hearing H. R. Haweis preach on Cain and Abel.

20   Calls on Alma-Tadema, meeting Hippolyte Taine.

29   Speculates on a girl seen on a bus, 'one of those faces of marvellous beauty which are seen casually in the streets but never among one's friends' (*Life*, p. 220), one of a number of such comments made at this time.

June

1   (Sat) Reports to Mary Sheridan his interest in an exhibition of Monet's paintings: 'In looking at them you could almost feel the heat of the sun depicted in the painting, & the dazzle of noonday' (*Letters*, I, 191).

7   Rosamund Tomson sends TH a copy of her book *The Bird-Bride*, the beginning of a brief affectionate relationship, which probably marked a significant stage in the deterioration of TH's marriage: 'From now onwards he was looking quite deliberately outside his marriage for emotional satisfaction, and potentially for sexual satisfaction' (Millgate, p. 298).

July

2   (Tues) At a dinner at the Gosses', sits next to Agatha Thornycroft, considered by him the most beautiful woman in England, and perhaps a physical model for Tess.

9   Notes, 'Love lives on propinquity, but dies of contact' (*Life*, p. 220).

14 Centenary of the fall of the Bastille. Hears a lecture by Frederic Harrison on the French Revolution.

19 Authorises dramatisation of *The Woodlanders*, recommending that Grace's future unhappiness with Fitzpiers should be made explicit.

23 Recalls the perfection of Agatha Thornycroft's mouth.

August

Settles down in Dorchester to the writing of *Tess*.

September

9   (Mon) Approximately half the manuscript of *Tess* sent to Tilllotson's.

21 Concludes that a 'spectral tone' must be adopted for *The Dynasts* (*Life*, p. 221).

25 Tillotson's return the manuscript of *Tess*, having found it unsuitable.

October

Sends part of the *Tess* manuscript to *Murray's Magazine*.

22 (Tues) 'The Melancholy Hussar' sent off to Tillotson's.

November

13 (Wed) Tells Arthur Locker that he is in a position to offer a full-length serial to his magazine, the *Graphic*.

15 Edward Arnold declines *Tess* on behalf of *Murray's Magazine*.

18 Agrees to Locker's suggested starting-date of July 1891, and suggests a fee of £800.

25 Mowbray Morris declines *Tess* for *Macmillan's Magazine*, commenting on 'rather too much succulence' (Millgate, p. 301).

29 Alters agreement with Locker for submission of manuscript.

December

'The First Countess of Wessex' appears in *Harper's New Monthly Magazine*.' 'At Middle-Field Gate in February' written around this time.

1 (Sun) On a visit to Bockhampton, hears from his father about old Stinsford burial customs.
12 Death of Browning.
16 Alerts the Secretary of the Society for the Protection of Ancient Buildings to the contemplated demolition of Stratton Church, near Dorchester.

1890

'The Lady Penelope' appears in *Longman's Magazine*. 'In a Eweleaze near Weatherbury' written.

January
'Candour in English Fiction' appears in the *New Review*.
4 (Sat) 'The Melancholy Hussar' begins serialisation in the *Bristol Times and Mirror*.
5 Looking at old copies of *Punch*.
24 Congratulates T. M. Dron on giving what he thinks is the first lecture on TH's writings to take place in Dorset.
29 'I have been looking for God 50 years, and I think that if he had existed I should have discovered him. As an external personality, of course – the only true meaning of the word' (*Life*, p. 224).

February
2 (Sun) Thanks Coventry Patmore for sending his *Principle in Art*.
14 Signs an agreement to provide Tillotson's with a new, lighter, serial to replace *Tess* (i.e. *The Well-Beloved*).

March
Scheme of *Jude* jotted down, from notes made from 1887 onwards.
5 (Wed) Starts 'Thoughts of Phena', the *Life* reporting that the woman intended (Tryphena Sparks) 'was dying at the time, and I quite in ignorance of it' (p. 224).
7 Sends Harper Brothers a description of *A Group of Noble Dames*.
15 Attend a crush at the Jeunes', TH noting that the beauty of the women would be far different if they were put into rough wrappers in a turnip field.
31 Offers detailed criticism of a dramatisation of *The Woodlanders* by C. W. Jarvis and J. T. Grein.

April
Osgood, McIlvaine, a subsidiary of Harper Brothers, establish themselves in London.

May
9   (Fri) *A Group of Noble Dames,* completed during the early months
    of this year, sent off to the *Graphic.*
15 Sees Irving in *The Bells.*

June
2   TH's fiftieth birthday.
25 William Algernon Locker, in the absence of his father, writes to
    say that *A Group of Noble Dames* in its present form is unsuitable
    for the *Graphic.*

July
23 (Wed) 'Lines', an epilogue hurriedly written the night before,
    for a special performance of *The Taming of the Shrew,* performed
    by Ada Rehan at the Lyceum Theatre. Part of the poem printed
    in the *Pall Mall Gazette* the same day. TH subsequently annoyed
    by criticism of his verse in the *Globe.*
30 Agreement reached with Arthur Locker on the publication of
    the bowdlerised *A Group of Noble Dames.*
31 Complete text of 'Lines' appears in the *Dorset County Chronicle.*

August
Returns from the London season to work on *Tess.* Visited at Max Gate
by Alfred Parsons. In the latter part of the month visits Paris with his
brother Henry. Reflections on the nature of art are a feature of TH's
notes around this time, the most famous being the definition that
'Art is a disproportioning . . . of realities, to show more clearly the
features that matter in those realities. . . . Hence "realism" is not Art'
(*Life,* p. 229).
11 (Mon) Death of Cardinal Newman.

September
17 (Wed) Sells 'To Please his Wife' to McClure's Syndicate.
25 Death of the Hardys' dog Moss.

October
8   (Wed) Manuscript of the first half of *Tess* sent off. For TH's
    reading after the completion of *Tess* (mostly satire) see *Life,* p. 230.

November

8 (Sat) Tells James Osgood that he would like to testify to Harper Brothers' fair dealing, following an attack on their conduct by Kipling.

29 Sends the Society for the Protection of Ancient Buildings further details of the Stratton rebuilding.

December

A Group of Noble Dames (i.e. six of the ten stories subsequently published under that name) appears in the *Graphic*.

2 (Tues) Begs the Hon. Jane Ashley to think again about the proposed restoration plans for Stratton Church.

4 'I am more than ever convinced that persons are successively various persons, according as each special strand in their characters is brought uppermost by circumstances' (*Life*, p. 230).

5 Delighted at reports of the likely success of an American Copyright Bill: 'nobody knows what difference it may make to us English authors' (*Letters*, I, 222).

11 Returns to Dorset from London, where he has been staying for a short time with Mary Jeune.

23 Execution of Mary Wheeler, whose case has caught TH's attention, and whose lack of sexual feelings may have influenced the characterisation of Sue.

25 'While thinking of resuming "the viewless wings of poesy" before dawn this morning, new horizons seemed to open, and worrying pettinesses to disappear' (*Life*, p. 230).

31 '*New Year's Eve*. Looked out of doors just before twelve, and was confronted by the toneless white of the snow spread in front, against which stood the row of pines breathing out: "'Tis no better with us than with the rest of creation, you see!" I could not hear the church bells' (*Life*, p. 231).

1891

During the early months of this year, corrects *Tess* proofs, finishes 'The Son's Veto' and 'On the Western Circuit', and prepares the first book edition of *A Group of Noble Dames*. Also makes several visits to London, some with, and some without, ELH, eventually finding a satisfactory flat at 12 Mandeville Place. Around this year, ELH begins to keep private and critical diaries about her husband's behaviour. J. T.

Grein founds the Independent Theatre Society, to introduce plays by Ibsen and other continental dramatists to the London stage.

February
10   (Tues) Speculates on the virtues of Newman and Carlyle, concluding that neither was 'truly a *thinker*' (*Life*, p. 233).

March
'For Conscience' Sake' appears in the *Fortnightly Review*; 'Wessex Folk', later retitled 'A Few Crusted Characters', begins serialisation in *Harper's New Monthly Magazine*. Moves the position of what he terms 'The Druid Stone' on the lawn at Max Gate.
26   (Thurs) 'The Doctor's Legend' (never collected by TH) appears in the *Independent*.

April
Elected a member of the Athenaeum. 'The Science of Fiction' appears in the *New Review*. Around this time, hears C. H. Spurgeon preach, and is much impressed by a visit to Whitelands Training College.
10   (Fri) Sees *Carmen up to Date*, the current burlesque at the Gaiety Theatre.
20   Taken by Gosse to see the opening performance in English translation of Ibsen's *Hedda Gabler*.
21   Assures Robert Pearce Edgcumbe that he will vote for him, but says that he cannot commit himself on the Irish question.
28   Converses with Kipling at the Savile Club.

May
'The Midnight Baptism', consisting largely of material excised from *Tess*, appears in the *Fortnightly Review*. Much impressed by a lengthy visit to a large lunatic asylum.
8   (Fri) Commiserates with Robert Pearce Edgcumbe on his lack of success in the election.
30   *A Group of Noble Dames*, now a collection of ten stories, appears in one volume, commencing almost a decade of association between TH and Osgood, McIlvaine.

June
Visits Stockwell Training College.
5   (Fri) Arrives to spend the weekend at the house of his new

friend Edward Clodd at Aldeburgh, who influences him into modern anthropological reading.

27   'To Please His Wife' published in *Black and White*.
30   Tells John Lane that he must decide whether the time is right for a bibliography of TH's work: 'Much of my work hitherto has been of a tentative kind, & it is but latterly that I have felt any sureness of method' (*Letters*, I, 239).

July
4   (Sat) *Tess* begins serialisation in the *Graphic*.
10   Replies, in letter to the *Pall Mall Gazette*, to that journal's review of *A Group of Noble Dames*.
15   Thanks Lord Lytton for his fulsome praise of *A Group of Noble Dames*, promising to tell him how much truth there is in some of the tales.
19   'At Mary Jeune's lunch to-day sat between a pair of beauties' (*Life*, p. 237).

August
Correcting *Tess* for its volume form, a process which largely consists of restoring passages excised from the serial edition.

September
Visit Scotland to stay with Sir George Douglas.
20   (Sun) Return to Max Gate, reached by way of leisurely stops at the cathedrals of Durham, York and Peterborough.

October
20   (Tues) 'Howells and those of his school forget that a story *must* be striking enough to be worth telling. Therein lies the problem – to reconcile the average with that uncommonness which alone makes it natural that a tale or experience would dwell in the memory and induce repetition' (*Life*, p. 239).
21   Offers W. E. Henley 'Saturday Night in Arcady' for the *National Observer*.
29   Thanks Thomas MacQuoid for his criticism of the character of Tess Durbeyfield, 'though I have not been able to put on paper all that she is, or was, to me' (*Letters*, I, 245).

November
8   (Sun) Thanks Douglas for their holiday. Sends Osgood, McIlvaine

a new title page for *Tess*, including the controversial subtitle
and epigraph.

14   'Saturday Night in Arcady', salvaged from the enforced ex-
      cisions in *Tess*, appears in the *National Observer*.

December

Tess appears in book form. The *Life* remarks that the book 'notwithstanding its exceptional popularity, was the beginning of the end of
his career as a novelist' (p. 240). 'On the Western Circuit' appears in
the *English Illustrated*.

1   (Tues) 'The Son's Veto' appears in the *Illustrated London News*.

17   Tells Tillotson's that he is suspending all other writing until *The
      Well-Beloved* is finished, which will probably be at the end of
      March.

26   The *Speaker* praises *Tess*, the first of the early reviews, which are
      mostly complimentary.

31   Thanks H. W. Massingham for his sympathetic review of *Tess* in
      the *Daily Chronicle*, remarking, 'Ever since I began to write –
      certainly ever since I wrote "Two on a Tower" in 1881 – I have
      felt that the doll of English fiction must be demolished, if Eng-
      land is to have a school of fiction at all: & I think great honour
      is due to the D: Chronicle for frankly recognizing that the devel-
      opment of a more virile type of novel is not incompatible with
      sound morality . . . ' (*Letters*, I, 250).

1892

Publication of *Tess* brings TH a new financial stability, of which
there are many signs, especially domestic, this year. The *Life* adds, '*Tess
of the d'Urbervilles* was also the cause of Hardy's meeting a good
many people of every rank during that spring, summer, and onwards, and of opportunity for meeting a good many more if he had
chosen to avail himself of it' (p. 245).

January

1   (Fri) Thanks Frederic Harrison for sending a Positivist calendar.

17   Outraged by the unfairness of a review of *Tess* in the *Saturday*.

18   Attempts to discover the identity of the *Saturday* reviewer from
      Gosse. Asks Tillotson's for more time to complete *The Well-
      Beloved*.

20 Pleased to report that the offending review appears only to
    have increased the novel's sales.

February
Third impression of *Tess* advertised.
4   (Thurs) Dismayed by the review of *Tess* by Andrew Lang in the
    New Review, telling Clodd, 'If Andrew, with his knowledge &
    opportunities, had a heart instead of a hollow place where his
    heart ought to be, he would by this time have been among the
    immortals of letters instead of in the sorry position of gnawing
    his quill over my poor production' (*Letters*, I, 257).
9   Thanks William Watson for the sensitivity of his review of *Tess*.
14 In a letter to Osgood, McIlvaine, reserves his right to withhold
    The Well-Beloved from publication in book form, 'the story being
    short & slight & written entirely with a view to serial publica-
    tion' (*Letters*, VII, 119).
26 Thanks Mary Harrison (the authoress 'Lucas Malet') for her
    praise of *Tess*.

April
13 (Wed) Tells Sir George Douglas, 'The few days that I spent in
    town were pleasant enough. I met among many other people
    "Lucas Malet", Frederic Harrison, Ellen Terry, Lord Randolph,
    Miss Norris (ballet dancer), Arthur Balfour, &c. &c.' (*Letters*, VII,
    121).
15 Hurt by a review of *Tess* in the *Quarterly*, whose critical tone is
    representative of a growing change in critical opinion at this
    time. 'Well, if this sort of thing continues no more novel-writing
    for me. A man must be a fool to deliberately stand up to be shot
    at' (*Life*, p. 246).

May
17 (Tues) Tells Roden Noel, 'Reading over the story after it was
    finished, the conviction was thrust upon me . . . that the heroine
    was essentially pure – purer than many a so-called unsullied
    virgin: therefore I called her so. . . . But the parochial British
    understanding knocks itself against this word like a humblebee
    against a wall, not seeing that "paradoxical morality" may have
    a very great deal to say for itself, especially in a work of fiction'
    (*Letters*, I, 267).

23   Attends the funeral in London of his publisher James Ripley Osgood, staying on in London thereafter.

June
3   (Fri) Leaves London for his father's sickbed.
8   Declines to propose Robert Pearce Edgcumbe as Liberal candidate for South Dorset, explaining to Joseph Eldridge, 'I am & have always been compelled to forego all participation in active politics' (*Letters*, I, 272).

July
1   (Fri) 'The art of observation . . . consists in this: the seeing of great things in little things, the whole in the part . . . ' (*Life*, p. 248).
19   Advises John Hales of the meaning of the dialect phrase 'goodnow'.
20   Death of TH's father, which 'seems to have removed an essential element of good-humoured kindliness that had served to temper latent hostilities and keep the Bockhampton and Max Gate households linked' (Millgate, p. 326).
27   Contributes to the Shelley memorial fund.
29   Suggests a date on which he might sit for his portrait to William Strang.
31   Present at the memorial service for his father in Stinsford Church. Four verses of Psalm 90 sung, these being claimed by TH as the traditional Stinsford graveside hymn, and specially printed for the occasion.

August
Visited at Max Gate by Sir Arthur Blomfield.
11   (Thurs) Gladstone forms his fourth ministry, following Salisbury's resignation.
14   Hears his mother reminisce about his father in earlier years.
26   Answers queries on phrases and allusions in *Tess* to assist with the Russian translation.
31   Contribution to the symposium 'Why I Don't Write Plays' appears in the *Pall Mall Gazette*.

September
Buys 51 High West Street Dorchester as an investment. Discusses transference of rights on his novels to Osgood, McIlvaine.
7   (Wed) Visit Swanage with the Owen sisters.

12 Cultivates the interest of George Alexander in dramatizing *The Well-Beloved*.
15 Sees a fire at Stinsford House, 'a bruising of tender memories for me' (*Life*, p. 250).
30 *Tess* issued in one-volume form, with an addition (dated July 1892) to the Preface.

October
Visits Fawley, Berkshire: 'Though I am alive with the living I can only see the dead here, and am scarcely conscious of the happy children at play' (*Life*, p. 251).
1 (Sat) First instalment of *The Well-Beloved* appears in the *Illustrated London News*.
6 Death of Tennyson.
11 Thanks Blomfield for sending a portrait of himself; 'I always reckon it as among the most fortunate circumstances of my life that destiny gave me an introduction to you in our younger days, which has led to so much pleasantness' (*Letters*, I, 286).
12 Attends Tennyson's funeral in Westminster Abbey.

November
'Our Exploits at West Poley' begins serialisation in the *Household*.

December
17 (Sat) Final instalment of *The Well-Beloved* appears in the *Illustrated London News*.

1893

'The Division' written. Leslie Stephen's *An Agnostic's Apology* published.

January
3 (Tues) Congratulates J. Henry Harper on his safe arrival in New York.
13 Posts 'The Fiddler of the Reels', completed during the end of the previous year, to Scribner's in New York.
14 Assures Edward Marston that there was nothing personal in his recent remarks on publishers' royalty payments.

15 Declines invitation to contribute an article on 'The Canons of Criticism' to the *New Review*.
17 Thanks Madeleine Stanley for sending a photograph of her mother, Lady Jeune.
29 Acknowledges Lord Houghton's gift of a copy of his *Stray Verses*.

February
12 (Sun) Complies with Stuart Reid's request to send a photo of himself.
23 Reflects in Notebook, 'A story must be exceptional enough to justify its telling. We tale-tellers are all Ancient Mariners . . . ' (*Life*, p. 252).
25 Again writes to Reid, this time thanking him for sending a copy of Lord Stanmore's *Life of Lord Aberdeen*.

March
?11 (Sat) Encourages Robert Pearce Edgcumbe to restore some of Dorchester's historic street names.
?16 Communicates with Emma about domestic arrangements at Max Gate.
28 Sends Clement Shorter, editor of the *Illustrated London News*, the manuscript of 'Master John Horseleigh, Knight', published in the Summer number.

April
4 (Tues) Warmly praises William Frederick Collier's *Tales and Sayings of William Robert Hicks, of Bodmin*.
13 Attends the Trocadero Music Hall.
14 Offers W. M. Colles a story ('An Imaginative Woman').
19 J. M. Barrie suggests that TH should make a play out of 'The Three Strangers' (dramatised as *The Three Wayfarers*).
21 Shows interest in Barrie's suggestion, and invites him to call at 70 Hamilton Terrace, St John's Wood, the Hardys' residence for three months. (This is the first time that they have rented a whole house for the London season.) As the *Life* records, 'In London this spring they again met many people, the popularity of Hardy as an author now making him welcome anywhere' (*Life*, p. 253).
27 Records a low opinion of A. J. Balfour's speech at the Royal Literary Fund dinner the previous evening: 'he dwelt with much

emphasis on the decline of the literary art, and on his opinion that there were no writers of high rank living in these days' (*Life*, p. 254).

28 Observes pictures of landscapes from his novels in a private view at the Royal Academy.

29 Sends Clement Kinloch-Cooke, on request, a photo of himself.

May

'The Fiddler of the Reels' appears in *Scribner's*.

3 (Wed) Declines to read anything aloud at a meeting of the Authors' Club.

7 In a letter to William Archer, discusses the baptism scene in *Tess* and a similar scene in the short story 'Befriad' by the Swedish writer Elin Ameen, defending the *Tess* scene as based on real life.

9 Writes a letter to the *Westminster Gazette* about this similarity.

10 Attends a conversazione of the Royal Society, in the company of many of the intelligentsia, scientific and otherwise, of the day, 'without (I flatter myself) betraying excessive ignorance in respect of the points in the show' (*Life*, p. 254).

15 Sends the amended dramatised version of *The Three Wayfarers* to the actor-manager Charles Charrington.

18 Leave London for Dublin, via Llandudno, Holyhead and Kingstown.

19 Arrive at the Viceregal Lodge in Dublin, where they are guests of Lord Houghton. Received by Florence Henniker, a 'charming, *intuitive* woman apparently' (*Life*, p. 254), for whom TH very quickly entertains an affection. The typescript of the *Life* originally added, 'The chief significance of Hardy's visit to Dublin was his meeting there with Mrs Arthur Henniker (Florence Henniker) who became afterwards one of his closest and most valued friends, remaining so until her death many years after. Some of his best short poems were inspired by her . . .' (*Personal Notebooks*, p. 240).

23 Visits the scene of the Phoenix Park murders.

24 Impressed by the Queen's birthday review.

25 After a visit to the Guinness brewery, set off on tour of the Killarney lakes.

29 Return to England in the company of Florence Henniker.

31 Responds favourably to W. T. Stead's suggestion of organised visits to historic religious and non-religious shrines.

June

Attends performance of several plays by Ibsen in the course of this month, including *Hedda Gabler*, *Rosmersholm* and *The Master Builder*. Also visits Oxford during the Commemoration, perhaps with a view to researching the background for *Jude*.

3   (Sat) Attends first night of *The Three Wayfarers* with Lady Jeune and other friends. Tells Florence Henniker, 'much desire to go somewhere with you' (*Letters*, II, 10).

?6   Thanks Clement Shorter for birthday greetings.

?7   Offers Florence Henniker lessons in architectural appreciation: 'Oral instruction in actual buildings is, of course, a much more rapid and effectual method than from books, and you must not think it will be any trouble to me' (*Letters*, II, 11).

8   Confirms his intention of withdrawing *The Woodlanders* and *Wessex Tales* from Macmillan's list, to allow their inclusion in Osgood, McIlvaine's forthcoming collected edition.

9   Declines to help Harry Quilter, who has failed to secure election to the Slade Professorship of Fine Art at Cambridge.

10   Enlists the help of W. M. Colles in his dispute with Macmillan. Offers Florence Henniker friendly criticism of her novel *Sir George*.

12   'Master John Horseleigh, Knight' appears in the *Illustrated London News*. Continued correspondence with Macmillan over copyright.

16   Congratulates Charles Charrington on his performance as the hangman in *The Three Wayfarers*.

17   Sends 2 guineas towards a memorial stone for James Osgood.

20   Offers Florence Henniker an architecturally instructive tour of Westminster.

28   Congratulates Augustin Daly on his acting in *The Taming of the Shrew*, which TH attended the previous evening.

29   Lunches with Gosse and Pater at the National Club.

July

16   (Sun) Criticises Florence Henniker for her belief in 'ritualistic ecclesiasticism' (*Letters*, II, 23), one of a number of indications that she is not responding satisfactorily to his advances.

August

Involved from this month until the following May in designs for the restoration of West Knighton Church. The experience possibly plays a part in the genesis of *Jude*, which TH later claimed to have begun writing in detail this month. At some stage in the month the Hardys visit the Milnes-Gaskells at Wenlock Abbey, Shropshire.

 8 (Tues) Visits Winchester alone with Florence Henniker, perhaps clasping her hand beside the Cathedral high altar.

September
 8 (Fri) Second Irish Home Rule Bill rejected by the Lords.
14 Sends Colles the manuscripts of 'An Imaginative Woman', a story which has links with his recent affair.

Towards the end of the month, visit the Jeunes at Arlington Manor, Berkshire.

October
22 (Sun) Tells Florence Henniker that *Life's Little Ironies*, collected together this month, is ready to be sent to the publisher, and that he hopes to begin work in earnest on *Jude* in the coming winter.

November
Poem 'The Young Glass-Stainer', partly arising out of Hardy's work at West Knighton, written this month. Also writes 'He Wonders about Himself'.

December
Reading galley proofs of *Life's Little Ironies*.
 1 (Fri) Tells Florence Henniker he thinks they have been satisfactorily remunerated for their joint production 'The Spectre of the Real'.
18 Writes affectionately to Florence Henniker, 'If you have only *one* good quality, a good *heart*, you are good enough for me' (*Letters*, II, 44). Sends her story 'Bad and Worthless' off to Shorter. 'A Thunderstorm in Town', a poem associated with Florence Henniker, carries this year's date.
23 Thanks Lena Milman for sending a portrait of herself, and announces himself at work on the *Jude* manuscript.
25 Spend Christmas at Max Gate.

1894

Writes 'The Slow Nature'.

January

9 (Tues) Confirms with Clarence McIlvaine that the royalty for
   Life's Little Ironies will be 15 per cent.
15 Hopes for continued association with Florence Henniker,
   through writing and through campaigns for animal rights, adding, 'I have been thinking that the sort of friend one wants most
   is a friend with whom mutual confessions can be made of
   weaknesses without fear of reproach or contempt.' Reports that
   he is 'creeping on a little' with *Jude* (*Letters*, II, 47).
20 Tells Sir Douglas Straight, editor of *Pall Mall Magazine*, that he
   must always consider himself at liberty to cut unsuitable passages in TH's work.

February

One day this month spent with Henry Hardy supervising the erection of their father's tombstone in Stinsford churchyard.
1 (Thurs) Regrets that he is too busy to commit himself to writing
   a short story for Shorter.
4 Meets a religious enthusiast, the germ for the poem 'On
   Stinsford Hill at Midnight'.
18 Thanks Robert Pearce Edgcumbe for his influence in securing
   TH's appointment as a JP for Dorset.
19 Regrets that pressure to have a uniform edition of the novels
   means that he must remove *Desperate Remedies* from William
   Heinemann's list.
22 Publication of *Life's Little Ironies*. Shortly afterwards, visits Osgood, McIlvaine to negotiate a higher royalty payment for *Jude*.

March

3 (Sat) Resignation of Gladstone as Liberal leader, having split the
   party over Home Rule.
4 Tells ELH of his recent social engagements and postpones return to Dorchester in order to attend another of these, a party
   given by Lady Jeune.

April

Take accommodation for the season at 16 Pelham Crescent, South
Kensington.

1 (Sun) Answers an anthropological query from Clodd, assever-
ating that 'every superstition, custom, &c., described in my
novels may be depended on as true records of the same' (*Letters*,
II, 54).

7 Warns Harpers Brothers that the *Jude* manuscript is threatening
to become controversial, and offers either to cancel the agreement or to allow them to alter the manuscript.

30 Visits George Meredith at Box Hill, Surrey.

May
'The Pink Frock' suggested by some words of Marcia, Lady
Yarborough, in a meeting this month.

4 (Fri) Asks Lady Jeune to write a letter defending *Life's Little
Ironies* from the charge of impropriety.

9 Tells William Archer that he regards their friendship as un-
affected by Archer's criticisms of the sensuality of *Life's Little
Ironies*.

11 Begins a five-day visit to Clodd at Aldeburgh, Suffolk, where he
meets Edward Whymper.

21 Signs an agreement whereby Macmillan relinquish their dis-
puted entitlement to the publication of *The Woodlanders* and
Wessex Tales in return for the inclusion of all TH's fiction in their
Colonial Library series (not for sale in the United Kingdom or
the United States).

22 Thanks Grant Allen for sending a copy of his *The Lower Slopes*,
with a generous inscription.

June
Returns for a few days to Dorchester, to make arrangements for
extensions to Max Gate. ELH, in a display of the independence
which she is beginning to espouse, prefers to travel to Hastings for a
brief holiday. Contribution to the symposium 'The Tree of Knowledge' appears in the *New Review*.

29 (Fri) Regrets that he cannot undertake to write a series of stories
for Ernest Rhys.

July
Sends John Lane a copy of the original manuscript of 'The Fire at
Tranter Sweatley's' for use in Lane's book *The Art of Thomas Hardy*.
Hurts his back while moving out of their London accommodation,

symptomatic of the physical aging by which he is beginning to be inconvenienced.

30   (Mon) Death of Pater.

August

Further correspondence with Lane this month to improve the accuracy of Lane's book, which appears later this year.

18   (Sat) 'The Hon. Mrs. Henniker', a brief sketch by TH, appears in the *Illustrated London News*.

September

18   (Tues) In a letter to Frederick Macmillan, clarifies the number of alterations he intends to make in the Wessex Novels edition (published by Osgood, McIlvaine), so that Macmillan can incorporate the changes in the Colonial Library.

October

16   (Tues) Meets Henry Harper in London.

November

ELH writes to Mary Haweis, probably in this month, expressing dissatisfaction with her marital relationship with TH. Particular interest now shown by ELH in women's rights, as instanced in her pointed aside, 'He understands only the women he *invents* – the others not at all' (Millgate, p. 356).

17   (Sat) 'The Spectre of the Real', TH's collaboration with Florence Henniker, appears in *To-day*.

25   Advises H. Macbeth-Raeburn, who is to provide frontispieces for the Wessex Novels edition, on transport to and accommodation in Dorchester.

December

Jude (as *The Simpletons* and then *Hearts Insurgent*) begins serialisation in *Harper's New Monthly Magazine*. The poem 'At Mayfair Lodgings' is suggested by an experience this month.

16   (Sun) Suggests to Macbeth-Raeburn that he should visit Cornwall before drawing the *Pair of Blue Eyes* frontispiece, rather than relying on photographs.

1895

January

1 (Tues) Congratulates Robert Pearce Edgcumbe on his knighthood.

10 Hastens to assure George Herriot, at the London office of the Duchy of Cornwall, he is not responsible for a newspaper report suggesting that they had disagreed over the grant of the land for Max Gate.

17 Denial by TH of any difficulty in purchasing the site of Max Gate from the Duchy of Cornwall published in the *Dorset County Chronicle*.

February

16 (Sat) Congratulates Grant Allen on his *The Woman Who Did*.

24 Tells Clarence McIlvaine that he would like to alter the title *Hearts Insurgent* when the serial (i.e. *Jude*) appears in book form.

March

Manuscript of *Jude* finished.

1 (Fri) Offers Clement Shorter a short story by Florence Henniker, 'A Page from a Vicar's History', for the *Illustrated English Magazine*.

3 Regrets that he cannot accept an invitation to visit Sir George Douglas on account of the work involved in preparing copy for the Wessex Novels edition.

April

1 (Mon) Inquires unsuccessfully of Eliza Lynn Linton whether they might be accommodated as her tenants for the season.

4 *Tess* appears, the first of the Wessex Novels edition, one novel per month being published until 1896. Each novel proof-read, and supplied with a new preface, by TH.

24 Advises Grant Allen on the sort of terms to expect from Tauchnitz.

May

8 (Wed) Informs ELH that he has taken a flat at 90 Ashley Gardens, and asks her to make the necessary arrangements at Max Gate.

10   Advises ELH to travel up to London on the same train as the
     Max Gate servants, but not in the same class.
15   Invites Shorter to call at Ashley Gardens.
25   Oscar Wilde found guilty on homosexual charges.

June
 3   (Mon) Asks Winifred Thomson to suggest when would be con-
     venient for him to begin sittings for her portrait.
25   Lord Salisbury forms a Unionist ministry.
29   Attends the ceremony at which the foundation stone of West-
     minster Cathedral is laid. Death of T. H. Huxley.

July
 1   (Mon) Congratulates Lord Houghton on being made an earl. In
     a letter to Winifred Thomson, complains about the drudgery of
     proof-reading the Wessex Novels edition.
10   Tells Beatrice (Mrs Patrick) Campbell that she must play the
     title role if *Tess* is staged. TH later claimed to have had many
     requests from leading actresses of the day to appear in the title
     role in any dramatisation of the novel, and seems to have 'caused
     himself considerable embarrassment by allowing a number of
     more or less imperious women to believe that he had each of
     them definitively in mind for the part' (Millgate, p. 363).
24   Reading Max Nordau's *Conventional Lies of our Civilization*.
29   Acknowledges the gift of a pamphlet by Havelock Ellis, prob-
     ably his *Sexual Inversion in Women*.

August
12   (Mon) Revising *Jude* for book publication, reporting himself to
     Florence Henniker 'more interested in this Sue story than in any
     I have written' (*Letters*, II, 84). Copy, with a preface, sent to the
     publishers later this month. The *Life*, however, records, 'On ac-
     count of the labour of altering *Jude the Obscure* to suit the
     magazine, and then having to alter it back, I have lost energy for
     revising and improving the original as I meant to do' (p. 269).
     The alterations probably contributed some bitterness to TH's
     'long-standing and still-accumulating dissatisfaction with the
     novel-writer's trade' (Millgate, p. 349).

September
Corrects, with particular interest and attentiveness, the proofs of
Jude.

4 (Wed) Enjoys local festivities at Rushmore, Wiltshire, the home of General Augustus Pitt-Rivers and his wife Alice, where he stays for a week. For the last time in his life TH dances in the open air on grass, particularly enjoying the company of his newly met partner, the Pitt-Riverses' daughter, Agnes Grove. The couple meet and correspond with some frequency in the coming years, and Agnes soon takes Florence Henniker's place as a kind of literary pupil.

6 Invites Gissing, his uneasy friendship and correspondence with whom have lapsed, to make a weekend visit to Max Gate.

11 Tells Florence Henniker he intends to get a copy of Mill's *On the Subjection of Women*.

14 Gissing and McIlvaine spend the weekend at Max Gate, Gissing taking away a poor opinion of ELH's behaviour.

15 Agrees terms with Frederick Macmillan for the Colonial Library edition of *Jude*.

19 Invites William Archer to pay a weekend visit to Max Gate.

October

28 (Mon) Agrees to appear on a list of prospective contributors to the *Savoy* magazine.

November

1 (Fri) Publication of *Jude the Obscure*.

3 Advises Agnes Grove to revise a draft article on female suffrage.

5 Swinburne sends his comments on *Jude*.

10 An unusually energetic and impassioned day of correspondence, indicative of a level of feeling about *Jude* detectable in many letters of this time. Millgate comments that, while TH 'had deliberately used the success of *Tess* . . . as a springboard from which to launch the final comprehensive challenge of *Jude*, he remained quite unprepared for the violence of the critical response' (p. 374). Agrees with Clodd that modern views of marriage are 'a survival from the custom of capture & purchase, propped up by a theological superstition' (*Letters*, II, 92), and comments on the treatment of the marriage issue in *Jude*. In an unusually forthcoming letter, congratulates Gosse on the discrimination evident in his review of the novel, remarking, 'You have hardly an idea how poor & feeble the book seems to me, as

executed, besides the idea of it that I had formed in prospect'
(*Letters*, II, 93). Congratulates the illustrator William Hatherell
on his illustration of Jude at the milepost: 'I do not ever before
remember having an artist who grasped a situation so thoroughly' (*Letters*, II, 94). Unconvincingly tries to persuade Florence Henniker that he is indifferent to public reception of the
novel, and sends her a list identifying the Oxford worthies.

14   Acknowledges in a letter to William Archer that this has been
the first book in which 'I feared that the Job-cum-Ezekiel moral-
ist loomed too largely behind the would-be artist' (*Letters*, II, 96).

15   Sends the pig-killing scene from *Jude* to the editor of *The Animals' Friend*, suggesting its publication.

17   Points out in a letter to Lady Jeune that *Jude* nowhere gives his
own views on marriage, and voices his former fear that the
novel would seem too 'High-Churchy' (*Letters*, II, 98).

20   A similar argument seen in a letter to Sir George Douglas: 'I feel
that a bad marriage is one of the direst things on earth, & one of
the cruellest things, but beyond that my opinions on the subject
are vague enough' (*Letters*, II, 98). Sends Gosse a frank letter on
the novel, describing the book as 'all contrasts' (*Letters*, II, 99).

December
Identifies his favourite hymns in response to query from W. T. Stead
(see *Life*, p. 275).

17   (Tues) Assures Shorter that he will soon turn his mind to the
short story promised him.

22   Tells Chavelita Clairmonte, 'I have been intending for years to
draw Sue, & it is extraordinary that a type of woman, compar-
atively common & getting commoner, should have escaped
fiction so long' (*Letters*, II, 102).

24   Tells Harper Brothers that they may withdraw *Jude* in America
if it is giving offence to the American public.

1896

Finishes 'In a Wood' (begun 1887). The 'In Tenebris' collection of
poems date from this and the preceding year. Writes 'The Dead Man
Walking'.

January
   2 (Thurs) Thanks William Archer for a sympathetic review of
      Jude as 'the book of the year' in the *Daily Chronicle*, also report-
      ing the completion of the *Tess* play.
   4 Thanks Gosse for his review of Jude in *Cosmopolis*, expressing his
      firm belief that the novel 'makes for morality' (*Letters*, II, 105).
   5 Complains to Sir George Douglas about the reviews of *Jude*.
  26 Fixes dates for final sittings for portrait by Winifred Thomson.
  28 Sends a letter of condolence to George Macmillan following the
      death of his father, Alexander.

February
ELH suffers the first of a series of attacks of poor health, probably
caused by shingles.
   2 (Sun) Begins a brief trip to London.
   3 Attends the funeral of Lord Leighton.
   9 Asks Harper Brothers to act as agents for the play *Tess* in
      America.
  15 *Jude* by now in its twentieth thousand.

March
Moves into 16 Pelham Crescent, South Kensington, for the season.
  15 (Sun) Asks Henry Arthur Jones for advice over royalties for
      plays.

April
  14 (Tues) Advises Agnes Grove on what she might include in an
      article on 'What Children Should Be Told'. Invites Richard Le
      Gallienne to visit.
  19 Returns to Agnes Grove a draft of her article, with forthright
      suggestions for improvement.
  24 Tells Agnes Grove that he has sent her article to the *Free Review*,
      remarking, 'The trouble has been nothing. You are such a good
      little pupil that it is a pleasure to offer you suggestions' (*Letters*,
      II, 117).

May
Takes a brief holiday in Brighton this month to aid recovery from a
rheumatic attack.
  12 (Tues) Invites Agnes Grove to call at Pelham Crescent.
  16 Informs the Glasgow University Liberal Club that he regrets

that he cannot accept their nomination as a candidate for the Lord Rectorship. Congratulates Dorothy Stanley on her engagement to Henry Allhusen, whilst regretting that it is likely to limit his own opportunities of taking her to the theatre.

17   Informs Arthur Symons that he does not feel able to enter into a definite agreement for a short story.

31   Tells Harper Brothers that he hopes that *Tess* will be staged in America first, and therefore hopes for news from them.

June
1   (Mon) Reproves Florence Henniker for suggesting that he is an advocate of free love, and reports that he has been inundated with requests for fiction following the publication of *Jude*.

29   Invites Richard Le Gallienne to call again, hoping that he will be able to meet the actress Beatrice Campbell.

July
'Our Children. What Children Should Be Told' by Agnes Grove, with fulsome assistance from TH characteristic of their relationship at this time, appears in the *Free Review*.

3   (Fri) Signs an agreement with Harrison Grey Fiske for an American production of *Tess*, Lorimer Stoddard subsequently undertaking the necessary revisions to TH's dramatisation.

4   In a letter published in the *Critic*, denies any plagiarism in the drilling-scene of *The Trumpet-Major*.

8   Tells Shorter that he is anxious to complete 'A Committee-Man of "The Terror"' for him, and sends best wishes for his marriage the next day to Dora Sigerson.

16   Declines to give an interview to Jeannette Gilder about *Jude*: 'Those readers who, like yourself, could not see that "Jude" . . . makes for morality more than any other book I have written, are not likely to be made to do so by a newspaper article, even from your attractive pen' (*Letters*, II, 126).

27   Commiserates with C. Kegan Paul on the accident which has necessitated his retirement.

August
7   (Fri) Tells Beatrice Campbell that he has dismissed for the time being all thoughts of staging *Tess* in England.

25   Visit Stratford as part of an eight-week English and then continental holiday.

September

24 (Thurs) Sends Florence Henniker from Liège an account of European travels so far.

28 Provides Bertram Windle with a lengthy list of Wessex place identifications for incorporation in a Dorset and Wiltshire guidebook, and promises further assistance.

October

2 (Fri) Visit Waterloo.

3 Death of William Morris.

4 Lord Rosebery resigns the Liberal leadership.

12 Reports return to England in a letter to Florence Henniker: 'The eight weeks of nearly continual movement has been upon the whole an agreeable & instructive time' (*Letters*, II, 134).

17 Notes that controversial opinions give less offence when expressed in verse rather than prose: 'If Galileo had said in verse that the world moved, the Inquisition might have let him alone' (*Life*, p. 285).

25 Acknowledges lukewarmly W. M. Colles's request for a serial, and proposal for the placing of short stories.

30 Sends Clodd details of a folkloric custom for incorporation in his research.

November

22 (Sun) 'A Committee-Man of "The Terror"' appears in the *Illustrated London News*.

29 Suggests to Florence Henniker that she should go to see Ibsen's *Little Eyolf*.

December

Finishes 'Wessex Heights'.

6 (Sun) Congratulates Florence Henniker on her recently published short story 'A Brand of Discord'.

14 'The Duke's Reappearance' appears in the *Saturday Review*.

30 Sends Florence Henniker New Year greetings.

1897

'Valenciennes' finished. 'The Dead Quire' written.

January
 1 (Fri) Congratulates Agnes Grove on her achievements in the
    year past.
15 Subscribes a guinea towards a portrait of Herbert Spencer.
17 Congratulates Clodd on the appearance of his *Pioneers of
    Evolution from Thales to Huxley*, praising the book's scope and
    criticising the insidious effect of 'dogmatic ecclesiasticism'
    (*Letters*, ii, 143).
24 Complains to Florence Henniker about treatment of authors by
    the Dorset nobility: 'Dorset landowners only tolerate an author;
    they do not associate with him' (*Letters*, ii, 144). Also remarks
    that of all dead men Shelley is the one he would most like to
    meet.

February
14 (Sun) Assists A. R. Hope Moncrieff with identification of 'Wessex'
    locations for the introduction to a new edition of *Black's Guide to
    Dorset*.
28 Agrees with William Rothenstein a date for a portrait sitting.

March
 2 (Tues) First performance of *Tess* in New York. A reading of the
    play also given at the St James's Theatre, London, for copyright
    reasons – 'a farce which will cost me more than twenty pounds',
    as TH reports to ELH (*Letters*, ii, 149). Later attends dinner for
    the US Ambassador at the Mansion House.
 4 Apologises to Florence Henniker for leaving London earlier
    than he had expected, adding, 'Driving up Regent St in the rain
    one day, & looking at the tyranny of the strong over the weak I
    met an electric omnibus, & it seemed a joyful presage of the
    future' (*Letters*, ii, 150).
 7 Replies non-committally to Beatrice Campbell's plea for *Tess* to
    be staged in London. Asks Shorter to arrange for a reference in
    a newspaper to the New York production of *Tess*.
16 *The Well-Beloved* published in book form, with alterations from
    the serial text. TH again disappointed by the severity of the
    novel's reception, 'and so ended his prose contributions to lit-
    erature (beyond two or three short sketches to fulfil engage-
    ments), his experiences of the few preceding years having killed
    all his interest in this form of imaginative work, which had ever
    been secondary to his interest in verse' (*Life*, p. 286). The *Life*

(p. 291) elaborates further on the reasons underlying TH's renunciation of prose fiction. Thanks Rebekah Owen for her report of the New York performance and asks if the accent of the
leading lady was sufficiently English to pass as such on the
London stage.

21 Thanks Gosse for so perceptive a review of *The Well-Beloved*.
Congratulates Lady Grove on the improvements in her style
evident in her new article, 'Of Women in Assemblies.'

24 Review of *The Well-Beloved* appears in the *World*, declaring that
'Of all forms of sex-mania in fiction we have no hesitation in
pronouncing the most unpleasant to be the Wessex-mania of
Mr. Thomas Hardy.'

25 Complains to Sir George Douglas about the *World* review.

27 Declines Lewis Hind's invitation to write a reply to the *World*
review for the *Academy*, whilst again criticising it with force.

29 Reports himself to Lady Jeune 'much surprised & distressed by
a ferocious attack in The World on my poor little book' (*Letters*,
II, 156), one of several such letters at this time.

31 Tells Florence Henniker, 'You mistake in supposing I admire
Zola. It is just what I don't do. I think him no artist, & too
material' (*Letters*, II, 157).

April
1 (Thurs) Agrees to the inclusion of *The Well-Beloved* in Macmillan's
Colonial Library. Thanks Swinburne for his letter about the
novel, also expressing his lengthy and intense admiration for
Swinburne's writing.

3 Osgood, McIlvaine advertise a second edition of *The Well-
Beloved*.

May
14 (Fri) Dines at the Gosses'; Henry James and Edward Marsh
amongst the guests. Unable to rent an apartment in London, the
Hardys make Dinmont House, Basingstoke, their base for the
season, travelling up for selected functions.

June
12 (Sat) Thanks Winifred Thomson for presenting him with the
portrait she has recently painted.

15 Leave for a Swiss holiday, 'thus entirely escaping the racket of
the coming Diamond Jubilee, and the discomfort it would bring

upon people like them who had no residence of their own in
London' (*Life*, p. 292).

20   The Diamond Jubilee of Queen Victoria.

26   Thanks Richard Watson Gilder for sending an account of Minnie
Fiske's portrayal of Tess. Clarifies the meaning of the phrase 'to
chaw high', in response to a request from Joseph Wright.

27   Sits out till midnight in the garden of the Hôtel Gibbon,
Lausanne, imagining Gibbon completing *Decline and Fall* in the
same spot 110 years earlier. The poem 'Lausanne' results from
this experience.

28   Reports to Clodd that the view of the Matterhorn has reminded
him of Edward Whymper's description at Aldeburgh of the first
successful attempt at reaching the summit. The view inspires
the sonnet 'To the Matterhorn', finished some time subsequently.

July

3   (Sat) Reports travel news to Florence Henniker, telling her 'I
have not given a single thought to novels of my own or other
peoples since I finished the corrections of the W. B.' (*Letters*, II,
169).

7   Return to Max Gate. Clarifies for Madeleine Rolland the situation he believed himself to be in when offering her the translation rights of *Tess*.

8   *The Times* publishes a letter from TH giving information on the
disappearance in Switzerland of James Robert Cooper.

9   Tells the editor of the *St James's Budget* that the draft of 'The Grave
by the Handpost' is finished, and that the revised version can be
with him by the 26th.

August

7   (Sat) Recounts to Kate Hardy details of a romantic visit to
Salisbury, part of a nine-day tour of Somerset and Wiltshire
made whilst alterations were being made at Max Gate, and
suggests that she might join him in Salisbury on a subsequent
day.

10   Visit to Salisbury provides the germ for 'A Cathedral Façade at
Midnight', written this year.

September

Spends several days bicycling with Kipling, who is considering purchasing a house in the locality.

21 (Tues) Suggests terms to Madeleine Rolland for her translation of *Jude*.
28 Sends Thackeray Turner, Secretary of the Society for the Protection of Ancient Buildings, a detailed report on the state of East Lulworth Church tower.

October
12 (Tues) Reports to Thackeray Turner on the state of the White Horse Inn, Maiden Newton.
31 Reports to Winifred Thomson his satisfaction with a new Rover Cob bicycle. The *Life* reports, 'Bicycling was now in full spirit with the Hardys – and, indeed, with everybody – and many were the places they visited by that means' (*Life*, pp. 296–7). Professor Millgate expands: TH's 'discovery of the bicycle, his abandonment of fiction, and his return to poetry seemed to be combining in a single movement of liberation and renewal' (Millgate, p. 389).

November
10 (Wed) Agrees to become President of the Wessex Society of Manchester.
27 Regrets having to decline an invitation to speak at a dinner of the Royal Institute of British Architects.
30 'The Grave by the Handpost' appears in the *St James's Budget*.

December
19 (Sun) Thanks Sir George Douglas for sending his *Poems of a Country Gentleman*, and gives his opinion on Tennyson, whose biography by Hallam Tennyson he was reading at the time: 'a great artist, but a mere Philistine of a thinker' (*Letters*, II, 183).

1898

'The Peasant's Confession' written.

January
4 (Tues) Suggests to Gosse how he ought to proceed in preparing a seventieth-birthday tribute for Meredith, the subject of several communications this month.

18   Death of the Greek lexicographer Henry George Liddell. TH
      writes the poem 'Liddell and Scott' some time this year.

February
22   (Tues) Thanks Elspeth Thomson for sending a valentine.

March
 3   (Thurs) Tells Sir George Douglas he is greatly disappointed by
      the poetry of Stephen Phillips.

April
 9   (Fri) Sends Lady Grove the first of two detailed letters of criti-
      cism of an unidentified short story which she has recently com-
      pleted.

May
?5   (Thurs) Move into their accommodation for the season,
      9 Wynnstay Gardens, Kensington. TH does some reading for
      The Dynasts at the British Museum.
19   Death of Gladstone.
22   Declines to write an article on Gladstone for the *Daily Chronicle*.
26   Sends Kate Hardy an account of his visit to Gladstone's lying-
      in-state.

June
24   (Fri) Declines to write an introduction to a Fielding edition,
      complaining about Fielding's condescension towards the lower
      classes.

July
Bicycling holiday taken in the later part of this month, visiting Bristol, Gloucester, Cheltenham and several other towns.

August
12   (Fri) Writes to Florence Henniker to suggest that her husband
      might stay at Max Gate during army manoeuvres in the neigh-
      bourhood.

September
 8   (Thurs) Sends Gosse suggested alterations to his introduction to

the Constable edition of Fielding, elaborating his theory that
Fielding dealt unsatisfactorily with the lower classes.

22   Reveals to Florence Henniker that he has been at work on the
     illustrations for *Wessex Poems* and on the poems themselves:
     'Some of them have been lying about for many many years –
     with no thought on my part of publishing them' (*Letters*, II, 202).

October
10   (Mon) Involved with the proofs of *Wessex Poems*.
31   Sympathises with Clodd on the death of his mother.

November
Begins 'Lines to a Movement in Mozart's E-Flat Symphony'.
1   (Tues) Acknowledges the gift from the publisher, Grant Richards,
     of A. E. Housman's *A Shropshire Lad*.
10   Returns contract for the American edition of *Wessex Poems* to
     Harper Brothers.
13   Reports to Florence Henniker, 'Beyond some pleasant bicycle
     rides . . . I have no activities just now' (*Letters*, II, 205).
19   Writes 'June Leaves and Autumn'.
24   Explains to William Archer that the likelihood of critical mis-
     understanding and outrage makes him disinclined to attempt
     another novel.

December
Wessex Poems published. Critical reaction generally puzzled; con-
nubial reaction hostile.
21   (Wed) Thanks Archer for his review of *Wessex Poems*.
27   Explains to Gosse, 'Well: the poems were lying about, & I did
     not quite know what to do with them' (*Letters*, II, 208).

1899

'An August Midnight' and 'On Martock Moor' written.

January
1   (Sun) Sends Florence Henniker New Year greetings and tells
     her the titles of Swinburne's favourites in *Wessex Poems*.
2   Tells Ian Forbes-Robertson that it will not be possible for Beatrice
     Campbell to appear as Tess on the London stage.

20 Letter, 'A Plea for the Horses', printed in *War against War*.
30 In a letter to Florence Henniker, expresses disgust at reviews of
    Wessex Poems and reports 'the cheerful sense of coming long
    days has begun, & of the outdoor possibilities of summer, & I
    already think of excursions to Cathedrals & Abbeys, with a fine
    disregard of railway timetables' (*Letters*, ɪɪ, 210).

February
'On a Fine Morning', 'His Immortality' and 'To Sincerity' written.
 2 (Thurs) 'I Have Lived with Shades' written.
 9 Thanks Lionel Johnson for his sympathetic review of *Wessex
    Poems*, whilst continuing his criticism of other reviewers.
14 Tells Gosse he now much regrets not having revised *Wessex
    Poems* more extensively.
15 Having read Florence Henniker's 'Three Corporals', suggests
    that she might write a series of military stories. Also hopes that
    she will accompany him to the Rembrandt exhibition at the
    Royal Academy.
26 Thanks Theodore Watts-Dunton for his appreciation of *Wessex
    Poems*.

March
 6 (Mon) Offers Gosse his opinion on Browning: 'The longer I live
    the more does B.'s character seem *the* literary puzzle of the 19th
    century. How could smug Christian optimism worthy of a dis-
    senting grocer find a place inside a man who was so vast a seer
    & feeler when on neutral ground?' (*Letters*, ɪɪ, 216).
13 Thanks Pearl Craigie for sending a copy of her play *A Repent-
    ance*.

April
Again take a flat in Wynnstay Gardens, this time at no. 20.
 2 (Sun) Confirms that the right to issue *Tess* in French rests with
    Madeleine Rolland and Hachette.

May
19 (Fri) Begins a weekend visit to Clodd at Aldeburgh.

June
 7 (Wed) Takes Clodd to see Pinero's *The Gay Lord Quex*.

11 Asks Kate Hardy to supervise one or two domestic alterations at Max Gate.
18 Meets A. E. Housman, probably for the first time.
20 Visits Swinburne in Putney, and, perhaps as a result of a conversation there, revisits St Mildred's, Bread Street, where Shelley and Mary Godwin married.

July
2 (Sun) Declines to become a member of the Rationalist Press Association, arguing that imaginative writers need to preserve detachment.
12 Declines to comment on the Dreyfus affair.
25 Finishes reading Tolstoy's *What is Art?*
31 Suggests terms to Harper Brothers for an edition of *Life's Little Ironies*.

August
11 (Fri) Congratulates Lady Grove on her article on female suffrage, and suggests that she should concentrate on essays rather than fiction.
13 Reports to Florence Henniker on a recent bicycling holiday in Hampshire and Wiltshire.
24 The *Daily Chronicle* publishes 'Shall Stonehenge Go?', an interview with TH largely written by the interviewee himself.

September
17 (Sun) Asks Florence Henniker whether her husband is likely to have to serve in the war with the Boers, which now looks inevitable: 'It seems a justification of the extremest pessimism that at the end of the 19th Centy we settle an argument by the Sword, just as they wd have done in the 19th centy B. C.' (*Letters*, II, 229).
20 Invites Lady Grove to visit Woodbury Hill Fair with him.

October
'Embarcation', 'Departure' and 'The Colonel's Soliloquy' written.
1 (Sun) Tells Gosse that he is unable – and indeed disinclined – to write an introduction to a translation of a novel by Zola.
11 Tells Florence Henniker, 'I constantly deplore the fact that "civilized" nations have not learnt some more excellent & apostolic

way of settling disputes than the old & barbarous one, after all these centuries; but when I feel that it must be, few persons are more martial than I, or like better to write of war in prose & rhyme' (*Letters*, II, 232). Expresses disappointment with Swinburne's patriotic poem 'The Transvaal. October 9, 1899'.

12 Boer War begins.
19 Wishes Major Arthur Henniker good fortune in the war.
20 Cycles to Southampton to see troopships depart.
21 Sends his nephew Gordon Gifford to report on Major Henniker's departure from Southampton.
22 Writes 'Murmurs in the Gloom'.
25 'The Departure', later retitled 'Embarcation', appears in the *Daily Chronicle*.
27 Commiserates with the widow of Grant Allen on her loss.

November
5 (Sun) Invites Gissing to call when he is in the Dorchester area.
9 Asks Florence Henniker to send a recent photograph of her husband.
11 'The Going of the Battery', based on the departure from Dorset of a troop of local artillery, published in the *Graphic*.
13 Asks Charles Lacey if he might reprint 'The Going of the Battery' in the *Dorset County Chronicle*.
25 'The Dead Drummer', later retitled 'Drummer Hodge', published in *Literature*.

December
'At the War Office, London', 'The Souls of the Slain', 'A Wife in London' and 'Birds at Winter Nightfall' written.
1 (Fri) Agrees to send Shorter 'A Changed Man'.
4 Harper Brothers go into temporary receivership.
15 Britain's 'Black Week' in the Boer War ends with the repulse of Buller's force at Colenso.
17 Responds favourably to an inquiry from Macmillan as to whether the firm might become his publisher.
19 In a letter to Florence Henniker, records his alarm at the war news: 'This Imperial idea is, I fear, leading us into strange waters' (*Letters*, II, 241).
23 'A Christmas Ghost-Story' appears in the *Westminster Gazette*.
25 Writes to the *Daily Chronicle* in response to its claim that the

soldier's phantom in 'A Christmas Ghost-Story' is unheroic (letter printed 28 Dec).

29 Tells Macmillan that he would like if possible to see his published as well as future books on their list.

1900

Freud publishes *Die Traumdeutung* (*The Interpretation of Dreams*). TH arranges the suppression of biography: the *Life* reports, 'Hardy's memoranda on his thoughts and movements – particularly the latter – which never reached the regularity of a diary – had of late grown more and more fitful, and now (1900) that novels were past and done with, nearly ceased altogether, such notes on scenes and functions having been dictated by what he had thought practical necessity; so that it becomes difficult to ascertain what mainly occupied his mind, or what his social doings were. His personal ambition in a worldly sense, which had always been weak, dwindled to nothing, and for some years after 1895 or 1896 he requested that no record of his life should be made' (p. 305).

January
20 (Sat) Death of Ruskin.
24 Asks Charles Blomfield if he would give Gordon Gifford unpaid work-experience in his architectural practice.
26 Reading, and admiring, Otway's *Venice Preserved*.
27 'At the War Office after a Bloody Battle', later retitled 'At the War Office, London', published in the *Sphere*.

February
6   (Tues) Visits Dorchester Barracks, seeing the Imperial Yeomanry before their departure for South Africa.
25 Explains to Florence Henniker his inconsistency in being fascinated but also disgusted by the war.
27 Labour Party founded.

March
2   (Fri) Sends 'The Souls of the Slain' to the *Cornhill*, where it appears the next month.
10 Asks Harper Brothers to arrange publication of 'The Souls of the Slain' in America.

11 Sends Reginald Smith a revised version of the poem.
21 Wittily declines an invitation from the *Daily Mail* to act as its Irish correspondent during the Queen's visit.
24 Sends off the Winifred Thomson portrait for exhibition in London.

April
Move for the season to London, staying at the West Central Hotel rather than taking a flat. 'The Souls of the Slain' appears in the *Cornhill*.
20 (Fri) Sends Thomas Perkins information on the topography of *The Return of the Native*.
21 First instalment of 'A Changed Man' appears in the *Sphere*.

May
 3 (Thurs) Invites Sir George Douglas to meet him at the Royal Academy Exhibition.
14 Reports to ELH that Gordon Gifford is performing satisfactorily in Blomfield's office.

June
 1 (Fri) Thanks Clodd for sending his *The Story of the Alphabet*. Reading Arthur Symons' *Images of Good and Evil*, and, with less enthusiasm, his *The Symbolist Movement in Literature*.
 2 TH's sixtieth birthday.
11 Agrees to sit for a portrait by William Rothenstein.
26 Tells the American writer Charlotte Pendleton that he would have no objection to her writing a libretto of *Tess* to be set to music by Elliott Schenck. (The opera is never written.)

July
13 (Fri) Invites Clodd, also now sixty, to stay for a weekend in August.
14 'To Sincerity' appears in the *Review of the Week*.
17 Declines to elaborate in print his idea that the British crown should descend from woman to woman.

August
Entertain various literary friends at Max Gate in the course of this month. Much cycling in the immediate neighbourhood, and out into the counties beyond, in this and the coming two months.

28 (Tues) Thanks William Rothenstein for sending a copy of his recent book on Goya.

September
28 (Fri) Sends Arthur Symons autobiographical information to be used in the entry on TH in the *Encyclopaedia Britannica*.

October
14 (Fri) Declines to write a paper on Cerne Abbey for the Dorset Natural History and Archaeological Field Club.
21 Sends small corrections for the Barnes entry in the *Dictionary of National Biography*.
22 Tells Florence Henniker that he is considering gathering together a further collection of poems, but is deterred by their likely critical reception. Also deplores the current state of criticism of the novel: 'I am of opinion that the present condition of the English novel is due to the paralysing effect of English criticism upon those who would have developed it' (*Letters*, II, 269–70).

November
Defends the doctrinal accuracy of the clergyman's refusal to bury Tess's baby.
6 (Tues) Sends a letter of local and feline news to ELH.
14 Advises Henry Davray on rights for translation of the novels into French, and encourages him to consider translating *Two on a Tower*.
28 Sends 'Song of the Soldiers' Wives' to the *Morning Post*, which publishes it two days later.
30 Death of Wilde.

December
'Enter a Dragoon' appears in *Harper's Monthly Magazine*.
10 (Mon) Sends 'The Lost Pyx' to Shorter for the *Sphere*.
11 Advises ELH on the correct procedure to adopt following the death of her sister Helen, whom she has been nursing at her home in Hampshire.
22 'The Lost Pyx' appears in the *Sphere*.
24 Tells Florence Henniker that he is disappointed with Arthur Quiller-Couch's *Oxford Book of English Verse*.
29 'The Darkling Thrush' appears in the *Graphic*.

1901

'Bereft', 'Autumn in the Park' and 'The Dear' written.

January
18 (Fri) Thanks Nathaniel Sparks for sending a drawing of St Mary Redcliffe, Bristol, as a New Year gift.
22 Death of Queen Victoria. Accession of Edward VII.
27 'V. R. 1819–1901' written. Death of Verdi, TH noting 'a similar modulation from one style into another by a great artist' (*Life*, p. 300).
29 'V. R. 1819–1901' appears in *The Times*. Millgate comments, 'Hardy felt somehow reinvigorated by the initiation of a new century and a new reign' (Millgate, p. 412).

February
9 (Sat) Congratulates Madeleine Rolland on her translation of *Tess*.
10 Approves the text of an interview to be published in William Archer's *Real Conversations* (also published in the *Pall Mall Magazine* for April).

March
17 (Sun) Clarifies his future publishing-plans for Bertram Windle.

April
3 (Wed) Suggests to Sir George Douglas, busy rereading TH's work, that 'Her Death and After' and 'The Dance at the Phoenix' are 'two as good stories as I have ever told' (*Letters*, II, 283).
9 Agrees to meet Gosse in London during May.
26 Sees Sir Henry Irving as *Coriolanus*.

May
'The Superseded' appears in *The May Book*.
1 (Wed) Attempts to arrange London accommodation for ELH. A few weeks this month and the next spent in London, at 27 Oxford Terrace, but in general residence in London limited this year, with no house or flat taken for long.

June
2 (Sun) Gives Florence Henniker an account of a recent visit to Clodd at Aldeburgh.

12 Attends the funeral of Sir Walter Besant.

25 Sends Sarah Bernhardt a copy of the French translation of *Tess*, suggesting that she might like to produce the play *Tess* in French, with herself in the title role.

27 Suggests to *Humanity* that there should be a meeting to celebrate the fall of the Royal Buckhounds (letter appears in the August issue).

29 Entertain members of the Whitefriars Club on a visit to Max Gate, erecting a marquee for their better accommodation. Jemima Hardy, despite the interdiction of her daughters, waves a handkerchief at the passing carriages as they approach Max Gate.

July

25 (Thurs) Tells Florence Henniker that he is gathering together *Poems of the Past and the Present* for publication.

29 Thanks Frederic Harrison for his praise of *Far from the Madding Crowd*, describing it as 'the work of a youngish hand' but conceding that it has qualities he might not now be able to reproduce (*Letters*, ii, 294).

31 'Wives in the Sere' appears in the *Tatler*.

August

15 (Thurs) Clarifies terms with Harper Brothers for a cheap uniform edition of the Wessex novels and poems. Promises them *Poems of the Past and the Present* in a few days.

17 The Royal Titles Act, as an expression of imperialist sentiment, adds the words 'and of the British Dominions beyond the Seas' to Edward VII's style.

September

9   (Mon) Declines an invitation to contribute the volume on George Eliot to the Modern English Writers series.

October

13 (Sun) Sends the vicar of Fordington suggested minor alterations to the wording of an appeal pamphlet.

November

Publication of *Poems of the Past and the Present*.

7   (Thurs) Congratulates Bertram Windle on the appearance of his *The Wessex of Thomas Hardy*.

23 'In the Old Theatre, Fiesole', in an early version, appears in the *Academy*.
25 'The Dead Quire' appears in the *Graphic*.

December
'The Homecoming' written.
 2 (Mon) Sends Theodore Watts-Dunton a copy of *Poems of the Past and the Present*.
17 Writes 'A Daughter Returns'.
31 Records the following reflection: 'After reading various philosophic systems, and being struck with their contradictions and futilities, I have come to this: *Let every man make a philosophy for himself out of his own experience*' (*Life*, p. 310).

1902

'The Man He Killed', 'Yell'ham Wood's Story' and most of the sequence 'At Casterbridge Fair' written.

January
 1 (Wed) Notes, 'A Pessimist's apology. Pessimism (or rather what is called such) is, in brief, playing the sure game. You cannot lose at it; you may gain. It is the only view of life in which you can never be disappointed' (*Life*, p. 311).
 7 Sends good wishes for the future of the Wessex Society of Manchester to its secretary, A. R. Andrews, and a signed copy of one of his volumes of short stories to Dorothy Allhusen.
17 Declines to write an introduction to Thackeray's work for the projected Bedford Edition.
25 Attends the wedding of Lord Stavordale to Lady Helen Stewart at St Peter's, Eaton Square and sends ELH news of the event. Afterwards accompanies Madeleine Stanley to see *Blue-Bell in Fairyland* at the Vaudeville Theatre.

February
12 (Wed) Thanks Dorothy Allhusen for sending her portrait, comments on the Stavordale wedding, and gives advice on what to see in Milan and Genoa.
21 Apologises to Clement Shorter for not making better progress with a new short story apparently promised to him.

26 Tribute by TH to Victor Hugo (see *Life*, p. 311) appears in *Il piccolo della sera*.
27 Congratulates Clodd on his *Thomas Henry Huxley*, and gives his own views on religion.
28 Writes to Clarence McIlvaine, as a prelude to letting his contract with Harper Brothers lapse.

March
4 (Tues) Thanks Reginald Smith for accepting 'At Casterbridge Fair' for the *Cornhill*.
4 Consults the Incorporated Society of Authors over his proposed break with Harper Brothers.
10 Agrees to communicate his views on agricultural conditions in Dorset to Rider Haggard, for publication in the latter's *Rural England*. Proposes what he sees as generous handover terms to McIlvaine.
18 Approaches Frederick Macmillan about his firm's offer to become TH's British publisher.
22 Proposes terms to Macmillan.
26 Death of Cecil Rhodes.
29 Thanks Arthur Tomson for letting him see his stories, on which he offers some advice.
31 Returns a draft agreement to Macmillan, suggesting also an annotated edition of the novels.

April
At work on 'A Trampwoman's Tragedy'. 'At Casterbridge Fair', later retitled 'At Casterbridge Fair: I. The Ballad-Singer', appears in the *Cornhill*.
1 (Tues) Warmly thanks A. C. Benson for sending a private printing of his *Ode to Japan*.
2 Executes Memorandum of Agreement with Macmillan.
6 Declines E. W. Kerr's suggestion that he should write an introduction to a new guide to Dorchester, but offers to meet members of the town council to discuss the reinstitution of old street names.
9 Asks the Dorset Undersheriff, E. A. Ffooks, to put him down as a Grand Juror at the Dorset Assizes. The *Life* explains, 'He was not infrequently . . . on Grand Juries at the Assizes, where he would meet with capital offences' (p. 317). In fact, the Grand Jury only commented on whether the available evidence war-

ranted a full trial, thus giving TH involvement with the legal process, but a cushioning distance from ultimate responsibility.

24   Offers to write down his proposals for Dorchester street names.
28   Sends off remarks on tourist facilities in Dorchester, renaming ancient sites, and so on, to the Town Clerk.

May

17   (Sat) Sends good wishes, and complaints about a flu, to Clodd. Letter 'M. Maeterlinck's Apology for Nature' appears in *Academy and Literature*.
19   Thanks Arthur Symons for writing about the Maeterlinck letter, and reports little creative activity: 'A growing sense that there is nobody to address, no public that knows, takes away my zest for production' (*Letters*, III, 21).
20   'One We Knew' written.
22   Invites Sir George Douglas to stay at Max Gate, and mildy praises Douglas's recently published *Diversions of a Country Gentleman*.
25   Writes in part 'Thoughts at Midnight'.
29   Letter on Edmund Kean's connections with Dorchester appears under a pseudonym in the *Dorset County Chronicle*.
31   Agreement ending the Boer War signed in South Africa.

June

'The Dear' appears in the *Monthly Review*. Spends some time this month researching further details of Kean's connections with Dorchester, and again writing to the *Dorset County Chronicle*.

2   (Mon) Flag flown at Max Gate to celebrate news of the conclusion of the Boer War.
6   Declines Clement Shorter's invitation to write a poem on the end of the Boer War, and reports that he cannot supply him with the intended short story.
17   Agrees to sign Arthur Symons' petition protesting against the banning of Maeterlinck's play *Monna Vanna*.
30   Praises William Watson's *Ode on the Day of the Coronation* in a letter to the author: 'my regret at coming to the last page was that there was no more of the poem' (*Letters*, III, 26).

July

Turns his attention to finishing *The Dynasts*, part I.

9   (Wed) Authorises Macmillan to begin printing their new edi-
    tion of his works, and asks to make minor changes to specified
    parts of *Far from the Madding Crowd*, *Tess* and *Jude*.
10 The last of TH's letters about Kean appears in the *Dorset County
    Chronicle*.
12 On the retirement of Lord Salisbury, A. J. Balfour becomes
    Prime Minister.
14 Again declines to write an introduction to a new guide book to
    Dorchester.
24 Agrees to Edgar Lane becoming tenant of his house at 51 High
    West Street, Dorchester.

August

'Time's Laughingstocks, a Summer Romance', later retitled 'The
Revisitation', appears in the *Fortnightly Review*.
9   (Sat) Coronation of Edward VII.
18 Invites Arthur Symons to visit.

September

25 (Thurs) Writes to Florence Henniker, having noticed that her
    husband is sailing home at the end of his Boer War service.
27 Asks the bookseller Walter T. Spencer to look out for a copy of
    the Vulgate.
29 Death of Zola.

October

1   (Wed) Declines invitation from Clive Holland to attend dinner
    of the Institute of Journalists, at the same time lamenting the
    death of Zola: 'a real moralist, reformer, & truth-seeker, though
    perhaps not an artist – indeed, certainly not' (*Letters*, III, 34).
2   Thanks Oswald Crawfurd for sending his *Two Masques*.
8   Advises the rector of All Saints, Dorchester, on where ground
    plans of the church might be found.
10 Permits Clement Shorter to publish 'The Man He Killed' in the
    Sphere.
11 Increasingly conscious of the appeal to readers of a topograph-
    ical Wessex, asks Frederick Macmillan to add the half-title
    'Wessex Novels' to the new edition of *Tess*. During this decade
    guide books to and topographical studies of the region prolif-
    erate; and, while generally keeping his distance, TH frequently

seeks at least covert means of encouraging them, as a means of increasing his own sales.

November

8   (Sat) 'The Man He Killed' appears in *Harper's Weekly*.

11 Thanks Benjamin De Casseres for sending a copy of his article 'Thomas Hardy's Women' from the previous month's *Bookman*, and praises the article for its sympathetic nature.

22 Thanks Nathaniel Sparks for sending him a cello.

23 Sends the *Dorset County Chronicle* his 'Recollections of "Leader Scott"', which appear in the paper four days later.

24 'The Rash Bride' appears in the *Graphic*.

28 Thanks Edmund Gosse for attacking Sir Edward Clarke's contention that contemporary authors are inferior to those of the 1850s.

December

2   (Tues) In a letter to Sir George Douglas, reports enthusiastically on a recent visit to Bath and asks for Douglas's opinion on Leslie Stephen's article 'Browning's Casuistry'.

18 Replies to a query from Joseph Wright about the word 'trangleys'.

24 Sends postcards illustrated by himself to Alfred Pretor (with an inscription largely in Latin) and to his sisters, Mary and Katharine (with an inscription largely in English).

1903

Occupied with arrangements for the erection of a brass in Stinsford Church commemorating his family's musical connections with the building. 'The Market Girl (Country Song)', later retitled 'At Casterbridge Fair: IV. The Market-Girl', appears in the *Venture*.

January

2   (Fri) Expresses his admiration for Frederick Harrison's review of the events of the past year.

4   Thanks Florence Henniker for a gift of *A Shropshire Lad*, and arranges to call on her when visiting London for Madeleine Stanley's wedding.

28 Speculates on 'awkward tricks of fact in imitating fiction' in letter to Sir George Douglas (*Letters*, III, 48).

February

1 (Sun) Resigns from the Restoration Committee of St George's Church, Fordington, partly in disappointment at recent alterations of the tower.

9 Congratulates Arthur Quiller-Couch on his article in the *Daily News* on war poetry.

25 Declines an invitation to visit Lady Grove, and tells her that 'no person of serious thought in these times could be said to stand aloof from Positivist teaching & ideals' (*Letters*, III, 53).

26 Answers a query from Thomas Perkins about the font in Fordington Church.

March

17 (Tues) Tells Florence Henniker that he and ELH have been reading *The Wings of the Dove*, '& find we have wholly conflicting opinions thereon. At the same time James is almost the only living novelist I can read . . . ' (*Letters*, III, 56).

23 Advises Macmillan on translations of his novels, also claiming that *Tess* 'possibly suggested Tolstoi's Resurrection' (*Letters*, III, 57).

29 Congratulates Florence Henniker on her volume of short stories *Contrasts*.

April

4 (Sat) Thanks Arthur Symons for sending his *Lyrics*.

26 Sends Reginald Smith 'A Trampwoman's Tragedy' for the *Cornhill* (declined as unsuitable).

28 Suggests to Edward Clodd that he should write an article defending the achievement of Crabbe.

May

24 (Sun) Sends ELH elaborate instructions on how to find an illustration for 'Leipzig' in *Wessex Poems*, now required for reprinting.

June

20 (Sat) Sends ELH news of his activities in London.

24 Attends the first night of Hermann Sudermann's *The Joy of Living*.

July
1 (Wed) Attends the wedding of Anthony Hope Hawkins.
9 Answers another lexicographical query from James Murray.
21 Offers G. W. Thomson a photograph of himself.

August
21 (Fri) Approves the title page of 'The Sergeant's Song', a setting of words from *The Trumpet-Major* by Gustav Holst.

September
2 (Wed) Sends Laurence Housman 'The Market Girl (Country Song)' for publication in the *Venture*.
13 Writes at some length to Florence Henniker.
14 Returns corrected proof of 'The Trampwoman's Tragedy' for publication in the *North American Review*.
28 Sends Macmillan *The Dynasts*, part I.

October
1 (Thurs) Agrees with Macmillan a price of 4s. 6d. for *The Dynasts*, part I.
4 Returns to William Archer, with some alterations, the interview subsequently printed in *Real Conversations*. Approves specimen pages of *The Dynasts*, part I.
15 Suggests alterations in royalty terms for *The Dynasts*.
16 Agrees to attend the forthcoming Dorset Assizes.
19 Writes at length to Arthur Moule, with observations on things Chinese, and barbed references to Western and Christian interference with them.
21 Returns the *Dynasts* agreement to Macmillan, with slight amendments. Offers Shorter 'One We Knew' for the *Tatler*.
31 Writes in a friendly manner to Sir George Douglas, protesting 'I am a Victor-Hugo-ite still. . . . his misérables are not so real as Dickens's, but they show, to my mind, one great superiority, that of universality . . . ' (*Letters*, III, 81).

November
13 (Fri) Sends ELH, visiting Dover and France with her niece Lilian, news of (non-) developments at Max Gate, one of several such letters sent during this trip.
15 Thanks Gosse for his praise of 'A Trampwoman's Tragedy', which has appeared this month in the *North American Review*.

20 Returns proof of *The Dynasts*, part I.
21 Visited by the Miss Shirleys.
23 'The Homecoming' appears in the *Graphic*.
25 Attends evensong at St Paul's Cathedral, subsequently being shown round the organ loft by the organist, Sir George Martin.
29 Reports to ELH (whom he encourages to return – evidence of his worry that her trip is lasting too long) meetings with Henry James, Kipling and other distinguished personalities.

December
1 (Tues) Selects cloth for cover of *The Dynasts*, part I.
2 'One We Knew' appears in the *Tatler*.
8 Death of Herbert Spencer.
9 Thanks Oswald Crawfurd for sending his *The Sin of Prince Eladane*.
10 Sends E. Pasco information on two folkloric queries, confirming that 'folk-lore in my books is traditionary, & not invented' (*Letters*, III, 94).
22 Sends Clodd a copy of *Poems of the Past and the Present*.
23 Sends Florence Henniker Christmas greetings.
25 Authorises the French translation of *The Mayor of Casterbridge* by Madeleine Rolland.

1904

'The Christening' and 'After the Last Breath' written.

January
'A Sunday Morning Tragedy' and 'Shut Out That Moon' written.
6 (Wed) Helps Thomas Perkins with a query about restoration at Puddletown Church.
13 *The Dynasts*, part I, finally published, after delays caused chiefly by difficulties in finding an American publisher.
16 Thanks Frederic Harrison for his acknowledgement of a gift of *The Dynasts*, part I, criticising a reviewer in *The Times* for being upset by the 'Positive view of the universe in the book' (*Letters*, III, 98).
17 In a letter to Gosse, again complains of *odium theologicum* in reviews of *The Dynasts*. Reviews are lukewarm, perhaps largely because of the novelty of the genre. TH consistently suspects

theological bias, forgetting even his own recognition that the writing is of mixed quality.
21   Congratulates Henry Balfour Gardiner on his setting of 'The Stranger's Song'.
27   Grants permission for translation into German of *A Group of Noble Dames*.
31   Congratulates Gosse on his *Jeremy Taylor*, 'a personage who is now far more interesting to me than ever he was before' (*Letters*, III, 102).

February
3   (Wed) Unsuccessfully recommends James Sparks for a post at the Plymouth School of Art.
5   Authorises George Bryan and Co. to start a series of postcards to be known as the Wessex Novels series. TH's letter about the recent review of *The Dynasts* by A. B. Walkley appears in *The Times Literary Supplement*, a reflection of his depth of resentment of the reviews in general.
10   Declines Henry Newbolt's invitation to the Omar Khayyám Club dinner: 'I have got out of the way of going to dinners, & this winter has given me a troublesome neuralgia in the face, which may not entirely go off till the spring' (*Letters*, III, 104).
11   Thanks William Archer for sending a copy of *Real Conversations*, and for his review of *The Dynasts*.
16   Agrees to serve, though only incognito, on a committee for a memorial to W. E. Henley.
19   A second letter from TH about the *Dynasts* review appears in *The Times Literary Supplement*. The *Life* reports that TH was disappointed by the inability of reviewers to perceive that the work was 'advanced not as a reasoned system of philosophy, nor as a new philosophy, but as a poem, with the discrepancies that are to be expected in an imaginative work' (p. 319).
20   Sends back to Rebekah Owen her copy of *The Dynasts*, signed.
22   Death of Leslie Stephen.
23   Regrets having to decline an invitation to visit Lady Grove.

March
1   (Tues) Advises Hermann Lea, who is planning to photograph local buildings described in *The Mayor of Casterbridge*, on locations.
2   Gives the Revd S. Whittell Key his low opinion of blood sports:

'In the present state of affairs there would appear to be no reason why the children, say, of overcrowded families should not be used for sporting purposes' (*Letters*, III, 110).

5   States to Charles Hannan his terms for dramatisation of *Two on a Tower*, which Hannan subsequently declines.

8   Recommends to Hermann Lea a photo by Thomas Perkins of 'Blooms-End'.

13 Thanks Henry Newbolt for his review of *The Dynasts*, part I.

14 In a letter to Florence Henniker, comments on reviews of *The Dynasts*.

20 Sends Arthur Moule, following the death of his brother Henry, a lengthy letter of condolence dwelling on shared memories.

22 Thanks Clodd for his praise of *The Dynasts*, part I, giving his definitions of the Will and the Pities.

28 Offers Sir James Knowles 'The Revisitation' for the *Nineteenth Century and After*. Offer declined.

April

3   (Sun) Death of Jemima Hardy, 'the single most important influence in his life' (*Millgate*, p. 435). The *Life* comments 'She had been a woman with an extraordinary store of local memories, reaching back to the days when the ancient ballads were everywhere heard at country feasts, in weaving shops, and at spinning-wheels; and her good taste in literature was expressed by the books she selected for her children in circumstances in which opportunities for selection were not numerous' (p. 321).

8   Thanks Shorter for his sympathy, sends a photo of his mother's portrait for the *Sphere*, and corrects minor inaccuracies in some obituaries: for instance, 'my mother's "tiny cottage" is an eight-roomed homestead with an acre & half of land attached' (*Letters*, III, 119).

10 Funeral of Jemima Hardy at Stinsford. ELH not present, for reasons that are not known, though grief is not suspected. Sends portrait of Jemima to the *Graphic*, suggesting it might be printed.

12 Thanks Clodd for his condolences: 'The gap you speak of is wide, & not to be filled. I suppose if one had a family of children one would be less sensible of it' (*Letters*, III, 119).

18 Acknowledges letters of sympathy from Florence Henniker and Louise MacCarthy.

21 Tells Hermann Lea why one of his stories was refused by maga-

zines: 'The "Young Person", in fact, blocks the way of all progress in English fiction – or rather she is made to do so by her parents' (*Letters*, III, 122).

May

'During May he was in London reading at the British Museum on various days – probably historic details that bore upon *The Dynasts* – and went to Sunday concerts at the Queen's Hall, and to afternoon services at St. Paul's whenever he happened to be near the Cathedral, a custom of his covering many years before and after' (*Life*, p. 322).

3 (Tues) Tells Mary Hardy that Hubert von Herkomer so admires their mother's profile that he declares he would have painted her without fee. Sends a letter to E. Pasco answering minor queries on the novels.

8 Visits the Gosses, meeting Max Beerbohm and Yeats.

June

9 (Thurs) Reports to Reymond Abbott his activities in the London season: 'I have been twice to St Paul's, but have done very little of a solid kind' (*Letters*, III, 126).

16 Agrees to publication of Cyril Scott's song 'Trafalgar', a setting of a lyric from *The Dynasts*.

19 Attends party at the Gosses', Henry James also being present.

22 Clodd, following a dinner with the Hardys, records in his diary that ELH's reproofs of her husband were responded to with patient forbearance. In general, Jemima Hardy's death seems to have caused a temporary improvement in TH's marital relationship, though the lack of argument was partly the result of the independence-offering spaciousness of Max Gate.

26 Attends first performance of Yeats's play *Where there is Nothing* at the Royal Court Theatre, accidentally exchanging umbrellas with another guest in Lady Gregory's box.

27 Invites the novelist Isobel Violet Hunt to visit.

28 Writes to *The Times* in praise of Tolstoy's 'masterly general indictment of war as a modern principle, with all its senseless and illogical crimes' (*Life*, p. 322).

July

1 (Fri) Acknowledges receipt of Arthur Tomson's romance *Many Waters*.

11 Tells Sir George Douglas, 'The effort of getting away from Town is what keeps me in it mainly' (*Letters*, III, 130).

11 Asks Alfred Pope to advise him on the consequences of defects in the Dorchester sewage system.

19 As a guest of Gosse, takes tea at the House of Lords with Lord Salisbury, A. J. Balfour and others.

22 Returns to Dorchester from London.

August
'Again in the country in August, Hardy resumed his cycling tours, meeting by accident Mr. William Watson, Mr. Francis Coutts (Lord Latymer), and Mr. John Lane at Glastonbury, and spending a romantic day or two there among the ruins' (*Life*, p. 322).

September
5 (Mon) Tells Gerald Maxwell that he cannot supply him with a story for the *Court Journal*: 'five years past I have not written a line of fiction or thought of the subject – my interests having lain in another direction' (*Letters*, III, 132–3).

8 Explains to Arthur Symons how Browning came to be included amongst the 'ghostly presences' in *Jude*, adding that he has often thought how much he would like to produce an anthology of English verse.

12 Thanks Laurence Housman for sending his novel *Sabrina Warham*.

25 Acknowledges a letter from Florence Henniker, including reflections on the Battle of Jena.

30 Declines to make any contribution to the Sherborne Pageant, but agrees to join the General Committee for the Sherborne celebration.

October
Writes 'An Autumn Rain-Scene'. 'Life's Opportunity', later retitled 'The Unborn', appears in *Wayfarer's Love*.

2 (Sun) Writes 'Last Words to a Dumb Friend'.

4 Asks Hamo Thornycroft where he can buy a chisel suitable for cutting the name of their recently deceased cat Snowdove on a tablet to be erected in the Max Gate pets' cemetery.

6 Shows a guiding interest in Hermann Lea's plans for *A Handbook to the Wessex Country of Thomas Hardy's Novels and Poems*, continued in correspondence later in the month.

23   Suggests to Arthur Symons that someone should write a critical
      appreciation of 'Laurence Hope', the *nom de plume* of Violet
      Nicolson, who recently poisoned herself after the death of her
      husband.
26   Declines an invitation from Hammond Hall, editor of the *Daily
      Graphic*, to speak about the marriage question, maintaining that
      he cannot say more than is already contained in *Jude*.
29   Obituary of Violet Nicolson by TH appears in the *Athenaeum*.
      Apart from this, and various letters to newspapers, 'he appears
      to have printed very little during this year 1904' (*Life*, p. 322).

November
 1   (Tues) Agrees with Archer's suggestion that there should be a
      National Theatre.
 8   Writes an open testimonial for W. M. Colles.
 9   Asks Hermann Lea to refrain from including in his *Handbook*, as
      part of his coverage of *Under the Greenwood Tree*, photographs of
      spots in Higher Bockhampton.
12   Agrees to look over Hermann Lea's manuscript.
13   Invites Clodd to stay the weekend with him.
16   In a letter to Walter Tyndale, identifies models for various fic-
      tional locations in his work.
21   Indulges in slight critical confrontation in a letter to Edward
      Garnett.
29   Declines Reginald Smith's invitation to the *Cornhill* dinner.

December
 9   (Fri) Congratulates Richard Garnett on his play *William Shakes-
      peare, Pedagogue and Poacher*.
21   Thanks Rider Haggard for a Christmas present of pheasants,
      whilst mildly pointing out that at Max Gate there is no gun by
      which an animal might feel threatened.
22   Sends Christmas greetings and news to Florence Henniker.

1905

'Orphaned, a Point of View', later retitled 'Unrealized', appears in
The Queen's (Christmas) Carol. Einstein states his first theory of relativity. Motor buses introduced in London, and the Underground
network expanded.

January
'The Farm-Woman's Winter' appears in the *Pall Mall Magazine*.
3   (Tues) Provisionally accepts an invitation to a dinner to be given by Gosse at the National Club on the 23rd.
4   In response to a request by Reginald Smith, sends him a poem, 'The Noble Lady's Story', for the *Cornhill Magazine*.
8   Declines a request from Douglas Sladen to write about copyright for a newspaper, feeling that his previous pronouncements on the question have all been to no avail.
11 Willingly grants Henry Newbolt permission to include 'The Night of Trafalgar' (from *The Dynasts*) in Newbolt's collection *The Year of Trafalgar*.

February
18 (Sat) 'The Noble Lady's Story', later retitled 'The Noble Lady's Tale', appears in *Harper's Weekly*.
23 Thanks the Revd Herbert Pentin, vicar of Milton Abbey, for sending a greatly appreciated collection of local doggerel rhymes, also remarking on local history.
24 In a letter to Henry Symonds denies comments attributed to him (TH) about faith in the Middle Ages and strongly criticises all those who inhabit a religious fool's paradise: 'I should say that, upon the whole, whatever may be true, is best known, & not disguised' (*Letters*, III, 157).
25 Attempts to persuade Edgar Lane not to give up the tenancy of 51 High West Street, Dorchester. Agrees to become Vice-President of the Society of Dorset Men in London.
26 Sends Florence Henniker a chatty refusal of an invitation.

March
5   (Sun) Thanks J. M. Bulloch for his congratulations on the award of an LLD from Aberdeen University.
24 Thanks Mary Augusta (Mrs Humphry) Ward for sending him a copy of her *The Marriage of William Ashe*, and adds many compliments on the book.
25 Sends Agnes Goldman 'Geographical Knowledge', for publication in the *Outlook*.
29 Sends Lea comments on recently taken photos of himself, and on suggested new photographs for 'Wessex' postcards.

April

1 'Geographical Knowledge' appears in the *Outlook*.

6 Leaves Euston for Aberdeen by overnight sleeper. Subsequent degree-day pleasantries are much enjoyed by TH, who appears to find in the occasion some compensation for his earlier lack of formal education. The *Life* concludes its detailed report of the proceedings with the comment that the whole episode 'was of a most pleasant and unexpected kind, and it remained with him like a romantic dream' (p. 324).

11 Sends a letter of condolence to Lady St Helier, formerly Lady Jeune, on the death of her husband: 'the pain of the shock was as great as anything I have ever undergone. . . . But you must remember that people have borne such things before & will have to bear them so long as human nature lasts' (*Letters*, III, 167).

12 Recommends the services of Desmond MacCarthy to J. L. Garvin.

May

This spring the Hardys return to a more than usually strenuous round of social engagements in London, having rented 1 Hyde Park Mansions for the season. The succession of dinners, concerts and plays is interspersed with social calls, such as visits to Swinburne and Meredith.

24 (Wed) Sends back to Lea the proofs of the latter's *Handbook*.

28 Declines to write a poem celebrating the hundredth anniversary of the Battle of Trafalgar for the *Cornhill*.

June

1 (Thurs) Redrafts phrases about the geographical boundaries of 'Wessex', and the relationship between fictional and actual locations in the novels, for Lea's *Handbook*.

July

1 (Sat) Reports in a letter to Sir George Douglas on a long chat with Swinburne, who told him of a paragraph in a Scottish newspaper: 'Swinburne planted, & Hardy watered, & Satan giveth the increase' (*Letters*, III, 175).

9 Declines to contribute anything to a new edition of Shakespeare on the grounds of having too much work to do helping with biographies of H. J. Moule and Leslie Stephen.

11 Suggests to Clive Holland Dorset sights which might entertain members of the Institute of Journalists on their visit to the area.

16   Asks William Heinemann to return the introduction written by TH to Laurence Hope's *Indian Love*, and to explain why it has not been published.

27   Acknowledges the kindness of J. A. Spender in drawing his attention to Vernon Lee's article 'Of Hardy and Meredith' in the recent issue of the *Westminster Gazette*.

August

7   (Mon) Suggests to the Mayor of Dorchester that prolonged litigation over the nuisance caused by the new sewage works represents a waste of ratepayers' money.

10   Gives permission to the young journalist Florence Dugdale, later to become the second Mrs Hardy, to visit him at Max Gate. It is uncertain whether this visit occurred, and it remains unknown how the two first came into contact.

12   In a letter to R. R. Talbot, tartly resents the Council's opposition to his views on the sewage case.

September

1   (Fri) Receive members of the Institute of Journalists at Max Gate.

12   Writes to Florence Henniker, reassuring her before an operation, praising her play *The Courage of Silence*, and hoping to arrange to see her.

14   Thanks Walter Tyndale for the gift of a Wessex watercolour.

15   Sets off for Aldeburgh in the company of Shorter and Clodd for celebrations to mark the 150th anniversary of the birth of George Crabbe, a writer whom TH admires 'as an apostle of realism who practised it in English literature three-quarters of a century before the French realistic school had been heard of' (*Life*, p. 327).

20   Suggests to Frederick Macmillan that *The Dynasts* should be advertised for a couple of months, to take advantage of centennial interest in Trafalgar.

23   Sends Frank Heath a brief foreword for a guide to Dorchester, despite earlier reservations.

28   Manuscript of *The Dynasts*, part II, finished.

October

Dorchester (Dorset), and its Surroundings, by F. R. and Sidney Heath, with a foreword by TH, published.

11 (Wed) Sends manuscript of *The Dynasts*, part II, to Macmillan, where it is received with little enthusiasm following the lack of commercial success of part I.

20 Acknowledging the gift of Arthur Symons' *Spiritual Adventures*, dedicated to TH, discourses on techniques of novel-writing and acclaims one of the stories in the volume, 'Seaward Lackland', as 'an almost perfect bit of narrative art' (*Letters*, III, 183).

21 Congratulates Florence Henniker on her recovery, and tells her how Dorchester is celebrating the centenary of Trafalgar.

26 Workers in St Petersburg form the first Soviet; mutiny on the battleship *Potemkin*.

November

Proofs of *The Dynasts*, part II, read in the early part of this month. Note reprinted in the *Life* records 'First week in November. The order in which the leaves fall this year is: Chestnuts; Sycamores; Limes; Hornbeams; Elm; Birch; Beech' (*Life*, p. 327).

5 (Sun) As a result of a request for clarification from Clive Holland, speculates on his possible relationship to Captain Hardy.

7 Tells Gosse that he is 'oppressed just now by a practical gloom', chiefly caused by the burden of proof-reading *The Dynasts*, part II, and anxieties as to its reception, but none the less asserts, 'Why people make the mistake of supposing pessimists, or what are called such, incurably melancholy, I do not know' (*Letters*, III, 187).

December

21 (Thurs) Sends Christmas greetings to Florence Henniker.

25 Henry Campbell-Bannerman forms a Liberal ministry following the resignation of A. J. Balfour.

26 Sends Habberton Lulham limited compliments on his *Devices and Desires*.

30 Congratulates Harrison on his verse drama *Nicephorus*.

1906

'New Year's Eve' written. TH's recollection of Leslie Stephen published in F. W. Maitland's *Life and Letters of Leslie Stephen*.

January

H. J. Moule's *Dorchester Antiquities* published, with a preface by TH.

2   (Tues) Thanks Florence Dugdale for her visit: 'I do not think you stayed at all too long, & hope you will come again some other time' (*Letters*, III, 193). The flowers she sent are reported fresh and in water on the table. ·

12   Liberal landslide in the General Election enables Campbell-Bannerman to embark on sweeping social reforms.

23   Asks Gosse to do what he can to help secure the election of Harrison's son Austin to the Savile Club.

24   Asks Clement Shorter if he might be able to obtain a photo of 8 Adelphi Terrace, and explains his emotional attachment to the house.

27   'The Ejected Member's Wife', later retitled 'The Rejected Member's Wife', appears in the *Spectator*.

February

4   (Sun) Asks Holland, who in his forthcoming *Wessex* mentions that TH witnessed the hanging of Martha Browne, to tone down the passage in question.

9   *The Dynasts*, part II, published. TH sends a copy to Newbolt, fearing that the book's art will be 'made the scape-goat of its philosophy' (*Letters*, III, 195).

11   Asks Florence Henniker to send news of her whereabouts, so that he can forward to her a copy of *The Dynasts*, part II.

12   Sends Clodd the second volume of *The Dynasts*, having received from him his *Animism: The Seed of Religion*.

20   Thanks Reginald Bosworth Smith for his compliments on *The Dynasts*, and identifies a word in the Greek version of the Magnificat as the source of the title.

28   Thanks Gosse for his praise of *The Dynasts*, confessing that its fault 'lies in the hurried execution of the blank & other verse in some places' (*Letters*, III, 198).

March

2   (Fri) Tells Arthur Symons, 'Your theory that verse should be confined to emotional expression is one that I used to hold, & was very uncomfortable under' (*Letters*, III, 199).

4   Suggests to Hermann Lea some names for his new house.

5   Sends a small donation to the Keats–Shelley memorial fund.

21   Thanks G. M. Trevelyan for his review of *The Dynasts*, which treated 'an imperfect work so handsomely' (*Letters*, III, 200).

April
Letter to Israel Zangwill on the subject of the Jewish Territorial Organisation appears in the *Fortnightly*.
  8   (Sun) Thanks Galsworthy for sending a copy of his *The Man of Property*, the first volume of *The Forsyte Saga*.
10   Frédéric d'Erlanger's opera *Tess* receives its premiere at the Teatro San Carlo, Naples.
16?   Leave to spend the season in London, returning to their accommodation of the previous year at 1 Hyde Park Mansions. 'It was this year that Hardy met Dr. Grieg, the composer, and his wife, and when, discussing Wagner music, he said to Grieg that wind and rain through trees, iron railings, and keyholes fairly suggested Wagner music; to which the rival composer responded severely that he himself would sooner have the wind and rain' (*Life*, pp. 329–30).
22   Tells Clodd that he is 'not in trim for public functions' (*Letters*, III, 202). Accordingly, entertainments during the season are generally artistic rather than social, with several theatre trips, and visits to concerts of music by Wagner and, especially, Tchaikovsky. A note in the *Life* explains TH's preference for late Wagner, as for late Turner, in terms which perhaps reflect TH's views on his own development: 'When a man not contented with the grounds of his success goes on and on, and tries to achieve the impossible, then he gets profoundly interesting to me' (p. 329).
23   Refuses the Revd Frederick Langbridge dramatisation rights for *Tess*.
26   Meets Clodd at the Savile Club.
28   Regrets in a letter to d'Erlanger that Vesuvius should have erupted on the first night of his opera, remarking that 'for an opera to have won any sort of approval in such circumstances, it must have been an unusually strong one' (*Letters*, III, 204).

May
'The Spring Call' appears in the *Cornhill*.
11   (Fri) Agrees with George Macmillan that Alfred Hyatt, a friend of Florence Dugdale, should be allowed to compile extracts

from TH's works, published later in the year as *The Pocket Thomas Hardy*.

16 Inquires whether Florence Henniker may be able to meet him in London.

21 Writes to General Arthur Henniker on hearing from him that Florence Henniker has undergone another operation. Letter from TH recounting his recollections of J. S. Mill on the hustings in 1865 appears in *The Times*.

23 Takes an uncharacteristic initiative in writing an unsolicited letter of praise to John McTaggart, approving the clearness of his *Some Dogmas of Religion*, and remarking that McTaggart's conclusions have much in common with the philosophical framework of *The Dynasts*. Death of Ibsen.

28 Takes Clodd to tea at Holman Hunt's.

31 Thanks Shorter for photos of Adelphi Terrace.

June

5 (Tues) Goes with Henry Arthur Jones to see H. B. Irving in *Othello*. Regrets that he cannot join the Dorset Field Club on its visit to Wool.

6 Invites Arthur Symons to dinner at the Savile.

9 Asks Dorothy Allhusen to meet the French painter Jacques Blanche, who is painting a portrait of TH. The next day the same invitation is extended to Shorter.

12 Asks Florence Henniker for news of her health.

19 Draws the attention of the Secretary of the Royal Society for the Prevention of Cruelty to Animals to the treatment of animals in a current show at the Alhambra Theatre.

20 TH's paper 'Memories of Church Restoration' read in his absence at the General Meeting of the Society for the Protection of Ancient Buildings. 'At the end of the lecture great satisfaction was expressed by speakers that Hardy had laid special emphasis on the value of the human associations of ancient buildings . . . since they were generally slighted in paying regard to artistic and architectural points only' (*Life*, p. 331). Agrees to add his signature to a letter to *The Times* appealing for funds for the purchase of the house in Rome in which Keats died.

29 Asks Florence Henniker for further news of her health, and praises her story 'His Best Novel'.

July
Declines an invitation to visit America to attend the opening of the
new building of the Pittsburgh Institute.

3   (Tues) Offers Reginald Smith his paper on church restoration
    for the *Cornhill*, where it appears the following month. Attends
    a party given by Gosse at the House of Lords.

4   Declines an invitation to review Treves's *Highways and Byways
    in Dorset* for the *Dorset County Chronicle*.

11 Lunches with Sir George Douglas at the Conservative Club.

16 Returns to Max Gate.

19 Agrees on the binding for Macmillan's Pocket Edition of his
    work.

20 Alters title page of *The Mayor* so that the title reads *The Life and
    Death of the Mayor of Casterbridge: A Story of a Man of Character.*

25 Identifies the illustrator of *Far from the Madding Crowd* as Helen
    Allingham in a letter to Gosse, speaking of her in terms 'quite
    romantical' (*Letters*, III, 218). Also reports some progress on *The
    Dynasts*, part III.

27 Thanks Shorter for sending him Paul Gruyer's *Napoléon, roi de
    l'île d'Elbe*.

30 Sends the publisher Theodore Watt the poem 'Aberdeen'.

August
15 (Wed) Grants Arthur Quiller-Couch permission to include ex-
    tracts from his work in an anthology, agreeing that some new
    art form must replace the novel as it grows inadequate as a form
    of expression.

17 Sets out with Henry Hardy on a tour of English cathedrals,
    including Lincoln, Ely and Canterbury.

28 Sends Harold Hodge 'A Church Romance'.

30 Agrees to help Henry Nevinson with his article on TH's fiction.

September
'Aberdeen' appears in the quater centenary number of the Aberdeen
University magazine *Mater*. Gives Florence Dugdale two photos of
himself, a reflection of the deepening of their relationship which has
taken place over the summer.

8   (Sat) 'A Church Romance' appears in the *Saturday Review*.

12 Writes to Florence Henniker, mentioning *inter alia* that he has
    abandoned reading Galsworthy's *A Man of Property*.

13 Suggests to Madeleine Rolland that she should translate into French 'An Imaginative Woman'.

15 Thanks Arthur Symons for his praise of 'A Church Romance'.

21 Congratulates Frederick Macmillan on the appearance of the Pocket Edition, and indicates no preference as to whether the *Wessex Poems* volume should include his original drawings.

30 Fulsomely congratulates Henry Nevinson on the draft of his article, while suggesting that he (TH) might more accurately be referred to as an author or writer rather than as a novelist.

October

3 (Wed) Thanks Arthur Symons for sending a copy of his article 'A Note on the Genius of Thomas Hardy', which has recently appeared in the *Saturday Review*.

17 Thanks Harrison for sending his *Memories and Thoughts*, and lengthily compares Harrison's views with his own, suggesting that both are 'meliorists' but that, amongst other things, TH's belief that nature is 'unmoral' prevents him being as hopeful as Harrison (*Letters*, III, 231).

21 Offers Arthur Symons detailed criticism of his recently published *The Fool of the World and Other Poems*.

23 Gives Adam Gowans permission to include 'Hap' and any two or three other poems in his anthology *The Ways of God*, particularly recommending "ΑΓΝΩΣΤΩι ΘΕΩι" ('To the Unknown God').

31 Reports to Gosse that he is 'at present distractedly trying to give something like a clear picture of that maelstrom of confusion the Battle of Leipzig' (*Letters*, III, 233).

November

4 (Sun) Tells Henry Newbolt that he does not intend to take part in the dispute over the Net Book Agreement. Answers a question from James Rose on the ancestry of the Hardys.

10 Henry Nevinson's article 'Thomas Hardy; The Son of the Earth' appears in the *Reader*.

11 Suggests a possible fee to Gosse for 'Autumn in My Lord's Park'. Advises the Society for the Protection of Ancient Buildings on the proposed restorations at Fordington Church.

17 'Autumn in My Lord's Park', later retitled 'Autumn in the Park', appears in *Books: A Literary Supplement to the 'Daily Mail'*.

22 Expresses himself happy to serve as a vice-president of the

English Association, in response to an invitation from Sidney
Lee.

24 Congratulates F. W. Maitland on his recently published *The Life
and Letters of Leslie Stephen*, to which TH has contributed. Remarks that he feels Stephen's diverse writings do have a unity
about them: 'A man with such a special manner of looking at
everything makes one subject of all the subjects he takes in
hand' (*Letters*, III, 238).

30 Tells Millicent Fawcett that he has long been in favour of female
suffrage, though for reasons which he fears she may find
unorthodox.

December

6 (Thurs) Sends back to the father of Pearl Craigie ('John Oliver
Hobbes') all the letters he received from her, for use in a projected biography.

8 Asks Reymond Abbott if he would find out the composer of the
military march *The Downfall of Paris*.

15 Declines to write an introduction to Harry Harding's *Dorset: A
Reading-book for Schools*. TH's letter of congratulation on the
seventieth birthday of Henry Mills Alden appears in *Harper's
Weekly*.

19 Suggest to Arthur Symons that he should put together an anthology of English lyrical poetry, regretting that the alteration
of the *Golden Treasury* means that there is no longer any satisfactory such publication. Death of F. W. Maitland.

27 Christmas greetings sent to Gosse, Clodd and Florence Henniker.

1907

January

2 (Wed) Thanks Clodd for his letter about 'New Year's Eve' (just
published in the *Fortnightly Review*) and remarks, 'it is paralyzing
to think what if, of all that is so incomprehensible to us (the
Universe) there exists no comprehension anywhere' (*Letters*, III,
244). TH's preoccupation with religious and philosophical matters in the early part of this year is indicated by extensive notes
in the *Life* for this month.

19 Offers to make a selection of Barnes's poems for the Clarendon
Press.

23 Suggests to Frederick Macmillan that the Oxford University Press should not be allowed to include one of the Wessex novels in their World's Classics series.

February
2 (Sat) Recommends old Dorset songs to Harry Pouncy for use in recitals.
8 ELH takes part in a Suffragette procession in London.

March
16 (Sat) Declines an invitation to attend Holman Hunt's eightieth-birthday dinner.
21 Tells Florence Dugdale that she must not risk damaging her health by checking details of *The Dynasts* for him in the British Museum Library, and gives her advice on getting good terms for her own work.
22 Points out to J. M. Bulloch that certain admired scenes in recent drama reproduce details which were not admired when included in TH's fiction many years earlier, asking, 'How is it that dramatists are always praised for imitating what novelists are condemned for inventing?' (*Letters*, III, 250).
29 First complete draft of *The Dynasts*, part III, completed.

April
'Wagtail and Baby' appears in the *Albany Review*.
3 (Wed) Asks Shorter if he would include a picture of the recently deceased Revd Thomas Perkins in the *Sphere*.
12 Accepts an invitation to the *Cornhill* dinner.
21 Reports to Gosse on activities so far in the London season (again spent at 1 Hyde Park Mansions): 'I have been nowhere yet, feeling dreadfully tired & disinclined to do anything' (*Letters*, III, 252). None the less, in the course of this season TH meets Shaw, Maxim Gorky, H. G. Wells, Joseph Conrad and J. M. Barrie, and begins to strike up a particularly close friendship with Barrie.
27 Praises Arthur Symons' *An Introduction to the Study of Browning*, and agrees to see his play *Cleopatra in Judaea*.
29 Thanks Florence Dugdale for her continued research for *The Dynasts*, and suggests that they meet at the South Kensington Museum. The coming months see an intensification of TH's efforts on Florence Dugdale's behalf, and an increasing frustration with the restraints imposed by his own marriage.

May

10 (Fri) Thanks Hermann Lea for photographing two portraits of him.

June

2 (Sun) Sends Edward Wright a lengthy letter on the philosophy of *The Dynasts*, claiming it as 'a generalized form of what the thinking world had gradually come to adopt' (*Letters*, III, 255).

10 Lunches with Gosse at the House of Lords.

22 Attends a Garden Party at Windsor Castle.

July

1 (Mon) Tells H. W. Massingham that he feels that the exciting developments in the novel have been stunted by critical disapproval, and that poetry may be expected to be a particularly interesting genre in the future. Declines an interview with Bram Stoker, whilst admitting, 'if I were to be interviewed there is nobody whom I should prefer to yourself for performing the operation' (*Letters*, III, 259).

6 Gives James Rose advice on his early literary biography.

8 Writes Maurice Macmillan a fulsome letter of introduction for Florence Dugdale, hoping that the firm may give her some work on educational books.

9 Writes a similar letter of introduction to Archibald Marshall, editor of the *Daily Mail* books supplement.

13 Writes an open testimonial recommending Nathaniel Sparks as an art master.

17 Return from London to Max Gate, where work begins on revising *The Dynasts*, part III.

29 Commends the proofs of Hermann Lea's 'Some Dorset Superstititons', published in Thomas Perkins and Herbert Pentin's *Memorials of Old Dorset*.

August

3 (Sat) Sends Dorothy Allhusen advice on avoiding rheumatism, and Clement Shorter an amusing indictment of the inconsistencies of his reviewers.

8 Tells Lady Grove he will be honoured by her dedication to him of *The Social Fetich*, a light-hearted survey of contemporary manners, which he offers to help proof-read. Reveals to Flor-

ence Henniker that he is cutting portions of *The Dynasts*, part III, so that the last part will not be too long.
11 Advises Lady Grove on the wording of her dedication.
15 Visited by Madeleine Rolland.

September
21 (Sat) Regrets that he cannot stand as a godparent to Henry John Moule, great-grandson of the Revd Henry Moule: 'I feel that I must maintain my objection in practice as well as in theory' (*Letters*, III, 273).
25 Manuscript of *The Dynasts*, part III, reaches its final form.
26 Thanks Reginald Smith for reading Florence Dugdale's story 'The Apotheosis of the Minx' and accepting it for the *Cornhill*.
27 Tells Frederick Macmillan that the last part of *The Dynasts* should soon be finished, and suggests that in due course 'Saturday Night in Arcady' should be incorporated in a new edition of *Tess*, after due publicity.
29 Congratulates Florence Henniker on her novel *Our Fatal Shadows*: 'It is quite Trollopian, indeed, in its limitation within certain strict lines of naturalness' (*Letters*, III, 275).
30 Tells Desmond MacCarthy, 'I am, as you know, trying hard to get The Dynasts ended & printed: it has dragged its slow length along through too many years already. This uses up all my energy of which I have no superabundance' (*Letters*, III, 276).

October
10 (Thurs) Sends the manuscript of *The Dynasts*, part III, to Frederick Macmillan, claiming the completed work to be 'the longest English drama in existence' (*Letters*, III, 277).
15 Congratulates Edward Garnett on his play *The Breaking Point*, and protests about the degree of censorship still pertaining in magazines. Gives the example of his own 'A Sunday Morning Tragedy', rejected twelve days earlier by W. L. Courtney, editor of the *Fortnightly Review*.
19 Thanks Margaret Woods for sending her *Poems Old and New*.
21 Tells Harry Pouncy that he enjoyed his presentation 'Hours in Hardyland', and suggests slight improvements which might be made.
29 TH's signature appears amongst seventy others in a letter to *The Times* protesting against the current censorship of plays.
30 Writes 'The Inscription'.

November

'In November he complied with a request from the Dorsetshire Regiment in India, which had asked him for a marching tune with the required local affinity for the use of the fifes and drums, and sent out an old tune of his grandfather's called "The Dorchester Hornpipe"' (*Life*, p. 336).

3   (Sun) Sends Gosse his rather random impressions on reading *Father and Son*.

15   Elected President of the Society of Dorset Men in London, continuing in office until 1909, and providing forewords for the Society's yearbooks.

23   Advises William Arnold on poems by Dorset writers suitable for setting to music.

26   Alerts the Society for the Protection of Ancient Buildings to an unsatisfactory restoration project being proposed at St Mary's, South Perrott.

December

3   (Tues) Congratulates Lady Grove on the appearance of *The Social Fetich*, whilst also warning her, 'I am not going to agree to your always frittering yourself away on those whimsical subjects' (*Letters*, III, 284).

6   Writes to Rebekah Owen about the curious uncertainty over the exact venue of the Brussels Ball.

26   Answers a query from A. M. Broadley about 'Overcombe' in the *The Trumpet-Major*, returning him a query about titles of hymn tunes.

31   Tells Clodd, 'In two or three days I shall have done with the proofs of Dynasts III. It is well that the business should be over, for I have been living in Wellington's campaigns so much lately that, like George IV, I am almost positive that I took part in the battle of Waterloo, & have written of it from memory' (*Letters*, III, 287). A lassitude resulting from a sense of anti-climax follows the completion of this task. Sends New Year greetings to Florence Henniker.

1908

'God's Funeral' begun (completed 1910).

January

7 (Tues) Helps A. M. Broadley to identify places in the Weymouth neighbourhood where George III held military reviews.

22 Asks his second cousin Charles Meech Hardy to discuss building improvements at 51 High West Street, Dorchester.

23 Helps Madeleine Rolland with queries over her translation of 'A Committee-Man of "The Terror"'.

29 Tells Walter Raleigh that he is now able to undertake the Barnes selection, and explains his proposed editorial method.

February

6 (Thurs) Agrees to present the Dorset County Museum with a complete set of his writings.

9 Declines to write an appreciation of Meredith for the *Daily News*, on the grounds that he cannot manage a sufficiently detached viewpoint.

11 *The Dynasts*, part III, published. 'Its long-term importance lay in his own increased confidence in his capacity to write effectively in a wide range of forms, and in the public perception of him henceforth as not merely a greater writer but *the* great writer of his day' (Millgate, p. 452).

12 A sentence of tribute by TH on Meredith's eightieth birthday appears in the *Daily News*.

16 Thanks Noyes for his generous review of *The Dynasts*, part III, indicative of the generally acclamatory nature of reviews of this volume.

18 Tells R. W. Chapman that he hopes to include some previously unpublished poems in the Barnes selection, also undertaking to provide marginal glosses.

20 Agrees to consider Charles Cartwright's suggestion for a dramatisation of *The Mayor of Casterbridge*. Thanks Clodd for his commendation of the presentation of the Waterloo fauna on the eve of the battle: 'in the many treatments of Waterloo in literature, those particular personages who were present have never been alluded to before' (*Letters*, III, 298).

27 Tells George Macmillan that the dramatisation by the Dorchester Debating and Dramatic Society of *The Trumpet-Major* should not be published.

March

Thanks Violet Hunt for sending her novel *White Rose of Weary Leaf*:

'You are a bit slip-shod in your English in the early pages, by the way, but get more facile & masterly as you get on' (*Letters*, III, 301).

2   (Mon) Sends the Barnes selection off.

3   Regrets that he cannot go to London to see Dorothy Allhusen, and comments on her possible reaction to John Singer Sargent's portrait of her.

8   Tells C. T. Hagberg Wright that he would like to be at least nominally associated with the recognition of Tolstoy's eightieth birthday.

11 Thanks Harrison for his generous appreciation of *The Dynasts*, and inquires after his *National and Social Problems*, commenting, 'My quarrel with Socialists is that they don't make it clear what Socialism is. I have a suspicion that I am of their way of thinking, but I don't know for the above reason' (*Letters*, III, 304–5). Acknowledges Arthur Symons' praise of *The Dynasts*: 'Well, there it is: some pages done carefully, some galloped over, & now staring me accusingly in the face' (*Letters*, III, 305).

12 Tells A. M. Broadley, 'Now that The Dynasts is finished I am quite in a whirl of small drudgeries that have been postponed' (*Letters*, III, 306).

17 Asks A. G. Gardiner to alter some phrases in his recently published article 'Thomas Hardy: A Character Study' if it should ever be reprinted.

19 Clarifies his objections to Gardiner's article, defining what some might call pessimism as 'only a reasoned view of effects & probable causes, deduced from facts unflinchingly observed' (*Letters*, III, 308).

25 Sends Shorter the manuscripts of his novels for binding, allowing him to keep that of *The Return of the Native* as a gift.

April

7   (Tues) Accepts an invitation to become an honorary member of the Dorset Field Club.

8   Asquith becomes Prime Minister following the resignation through ill health of Campbell-Bannerman.

10 Sends back proof of early pages of the Barnes selection.

25 Informs William Watkins that his presidential address will be ready for the dinner of the Society of Dorset Men in London, where it will be read out in TH's absence.

26 Asks Sir Frederick Macmillan to add to publicity material for

The Dynasts a statement to the effect that the play carries the reader along like an exciting novel.

May
10 (Sun) Declines a second time to join a committee for the erection of a Shakespeare memorial theatre at Stratford, arguing that the fact that Shakespeare wrote for a theatrical audience rather than for a reading public 'was an accident of his social circumstances that he himself despised' (*Letters*, III, 313).
21 Sends Florence Henniker news of his social encounters in London. This season he stays at the West Central Hotel and uses the Athenaeum as his main base. His explanation to Florence Henniker that ELH feels too ill to housekeep is something of a half-truth since he seems to have influenced her to remain in Dorchester even after she recovered, perhaps in order to facilitate his own meetings with Florence Dugdale. The *Life* passes hastily over the decision: 'It appears that the Hardys did not take any house or flat in London this year, contenting themselves with short visits and hotel quarters, so that there is not much to mention' (p. 342).

June
4 (Thurs) Thanks Shorter for arranging the binding of the novel manuscripts, and reports that for the first time for many seasons, he and ELH have taken no London flat or house.
19 Corresponds with R. W. Chapman over a further textual problem in the Barnes selection.

July
1 (Wed) Tells R. W. Chapman that he would like to write a preface to the Barnes selection.
2 Finalises domestic arrangements and social engagements with ELH.
3 First sitting for the portrait by Herkomer.
10 Attends the Milton celebrations in Cambridge: '*Comus* was played at the theatre, in which performance young Rupert Brooke appeared as the attendant Spirit, but Hardy did not speak to him, to his after regret' (*Life*, p. 342).
23? Returns to Dorchester.
24 Thanks Gosse for sending *The Poems of John Donne*, introduced by Frank L. Babbott, as a birthday gift.

31 Attempts to get a story by Florence Dugdale published in the *Strand Magazine*.

August

8 (Sat) Explains to Lady Grove why she has not seem him in London.

17 Recommends a story, probably by Florence Dugdale, to Shorter.

18 'The Poet takes note of nothing that he cannot feel emotively.
'If all hearts were open and all desires known – as they would be if people showed their souls – how many gapings, sighings, clenched fists, knotted brows, broad grins, and red eyes should we see in the market-place!' (*Life*, pp. 342–3).

22 Compliments J. McT. E. McTaggart on his *The Relation of Time and Eternity*, offering observations of his own.

25 Declines an invitation from Lady Grove, on the grounds that he is too busy proof-reading the Barnes selection, 'which is a lot of trouble, though I like doing it' (*Letters*, III, 330).

September

9 (Wed) Offers 'A Sunday Morning Tragedy' to Ford Madox Hueffer for the first number of the *English Review*.

12 Invites Harold Child to see the first performance by the Dorchester Debating and Dramatic Society of *The Trumpet-Major*.

15 Reports to ELH, who is visiting Calais, on building-arrangements and feline developments at Max Gate, the first of a number of such letters from this period.

26 Communicates with R. W. Chapman over developing copyright problems with the Barnes edition.

27 Advises the Society for the Protection of Ancient Buildings on possible restoration of St Catharine's Chapel, Abbotsbury.

29 Attempts to sort out unexpectedly troublesome copyright issues over the Barnes selection, a problem which necessitates considerable correspondence in the coming weeks.

October

9 (Fri) TH's article 'Maumbury Ring' appears in *The Times*.

12 Suggests to Lady Grove that, if she wishes Lord Morley to write about her book *The Human Woman*, she should send it direct.

16 Gives the vicar of Stinsford, Cyril Wix, his comments on an

architect's report on the church, outlining details of the previous restorations.

19 Reports to ELH 'it is very dull staying here alone' (*Letters*, III, 347).
20 Declines to take the chair at the next dinner of the Royal Literary Fund.

November

1 (Sun) Warmly thanks Valery Larbaud for an appreciative essay on *The Dynasts*.
4 Commiserates with Rhoda Symons on the illness of her husband Arthur, who has suffered a nervous breakdown and been certified insane.
5 Asks Asquith if the proposal of a knighthood might be held over for a year, and expresses admiration for the Prime Minister's 'talents & courage in acting up to principles that I share' (*Letters*, III, 353). The offer is not, however, renewed.
13 Congratulates Lady Grove on her *The Human Woman*. Agrees to let Vaughan Williams set a soldiers' song from *The Dynasts*.
18 First performance, in Dorchester, of *The Trumpet-Major*, the first of the so-called Hardy Plays performed by the Dorchester Debating and Dramatic Society (called from 1916 the Hardy Players). TH, who gives the productions minor assistance, and follows their progress with interest, is prevented from attending this inaugural production by illness.
24 *Select Poems of William Barnes* published by the Clarendon Press.
29 Corresponds with Balfour Gardiner and Vaughan Williams over musical settings of his work.

December

'A Sunday Morning Tragedy' appears in the *English Review*. 'In Praise of Calais', by ELH, appears in the *Dorset County Chronicle*. Its slighting reference to Calais Cathedral is indicative of the hardening at this time of her religious prejudices into psychological obsessions.
9 (Wed) Attends a banquet at the Mansion House to honour the tercentenary of Milton's birth.
10 Answers queries from Harry Pouncy about local history.
21 Death of the cat Comfy, aged twenty. Writes 'The Child and the Sage'.
22 Declines an invitation to have his name given as a possible future contributor to a Suffragette newspaper.

29   Agrees to help Harry Pouncy in obtaining an agent.
31   Tells H. W. Nevinson, 'I have been doing virtually nothing lately, having had a cold off & on' (*Letters*, III, 363).

1909

'A Plaint to Man' written in this and the following year.

January
'The House of Hospitalities' appears in the *New Quarterly*.
 7   (Thurs) Grants Henry Balfour Gardiner permission to produce 'The Three Strangers' as an opera.
 9   Complains to William Archer that situations which would appear stale in novels or poems are praised when presented in plays.
13   Comments on Lady Grove's preface to T. W. Berry's *Professions for Girls*. Asks Frederick Macmillan to consider a single-volume *Dynasts*, as well as reprints of the poems.
15   TH's letter on the Poe centenary (written 4 Jan) appears in *The Times*.
16   Thanks Newbolt for an enthusiastic review of *The Dynasts*, and gives amusing reflections on *In Memoriam*: 'why Tennyson, who knew so much, should not have seen the awful anticlimax of finishing off such a poem with a highly respectable middle class wedding, is a mystery, when it ought to have ended with something like an earthquake' (*Letters*, IV. 5).
18   Agrees to the publication of *The Dynasts* and his two volumes of poems as a single volume and not as part of a collected edition, though dropping a hint that one day he would like to see a de luxe complete edition.
31   Sends Ford Madox Hueffer 'The Two Rosalinds' and 'Reminiscences of a Dancing Man', allowing him to choose which he wishes to print in the *English Review*.

February
 3   (Wed) Thanks Reginald Smith for agreeing to print 'Let Me Enjoy' in the *Cornhill*.
12   Gives advice to W. T. Horton on possible illustrations for 'Wessex' scenes.

14 Informs Frederick Macmillan that corrections to *Wessex Poems* and *Poems of the Past and the Present* are complete.

March
10 (Wed) Despatches final copy of the one-volume *Poems* to Macmillan.
11 Sympathises with Clodd on the loss of his cousin, and reports, 'The raw east wind has reduced my mind no less than my body to a vertical greyness, out of which not a single thought will sprout' (*Letters*, IV, 12).
20 'The Two Rosalinds' appears in *Collier's*.
24 Unsuccessfully recommends a story by Florence Dugdale to *Chambers's Journal*.
27 'Reminiscences of a Dancing Man' appears in *Collier's*.

April
'Let Me Enjoy' appears in the *Cornhill*.
10 (Sat) Death of Swinburne.
15 Prevented by rheumatism from attending Swinburne's funeral.
19 Reports himself incensed at the lack of appreciation shown in obituaries of Swinburne. Agrees to join the Stinsford Church restoration committee.
20 Agrees with Maurice Macmillan that a new volume of poems should appear, the proposed one-volume complete poems being held over to a later date.
25 Sends the Stinsford Church restoration committee detailed proposals on what work should be carried out, such work being in accordance with 'the only legitimate principle for guidance', namely 'to limit all renewals to *repairs for preservation*, and never to indulge in alterations' (*Letters*, IV, 18).

May
1 (Sat) Undertakes to be with Clodd for Whitsun: 'The only scruple I have about it lies in my domestic circumstances which, between ourselves, make it embarrassing for me to return hospitalities received, so that I hesitate nowadays to accept many' (*Letters*, IV, 21).
5 Expresses qualified approval of A. H. Evans' dramatisation of *Far from the Madding Crowd*.
18 Death of Meredith, which leaves Hardy in a position of clear

pre-eminence amongst living English authors. TH sees the announcement on a newspaper poster in Dover Street. 'He went
on to the Athenaeum and wrote some memorial lines on his
friend, which were published a day or two later in *The Times*' (*Life*,
p. 345).

22   Attends the memorial service for George Meredith in Westminster Abbey. 'G. M.' appears in *The Times*.

24   Writes to Florence Henniker about the achievements of Meredith,
terming him a greater writer than Wordsworth but a smaller
thinker.

28   Apologises to Clodd for being unable to join him at Aldeburgh
because of flu.

29   Suggests to George Macmillan that the new volume of poems
be called *Time's Laughingstocks, and Other Verses*.

June
9   (Wed) Declines the presidency of the Incorporated Society of
Authors, vacant after the death of Meredith.

11   Advises Maurice Hewlett that he is unsuitable as President
because of the controversial nature of his writings: 'for on one
point I am determined – to exhibit what I feel ought to be
exhibited about life to show that what we call immorality, ir-
religion, &c, are often true morality, true religion, &c, quite
freely to the end' (*Letters*, IV, 28). 'However, the matter ended by
the acceptance of the Presidency by Hardy on further represen-
tations by the Council' (*Life*, p. 346).

July
2   (Fri) Begins a four-day visit to Clodd at Aldeburgh, taking him
into his confidence over his marital difficulties, and mentioning
his friendliness with Florence Dugdale. This revelation marks a
new intimacy in TH's relationship with Clodd.

13   Attends a rehearsal of the opera *Tess* at Covent Garden. Asks
Clodd to take Florence Dugdale to a performance, promising to
visit the couple in their seats.

14   Smooths over a personal misunderstanding with Gosse. With
ELH, attends the first night of *Tess*: 'Though Italianized to such
an extent that Hardy scarcely recognized it as his novel, it was
a great success in a crowded house, Queen Alexandra being
among the distinguished audience. Destinn's voice suited the

title-character admirably; her appearance less so' (*Life*, p. 347).

19   Thanks John Drinkwater for sending a copy of his *Lyrical and Other Poems*.

22   Thanking Clodd for his kindly opinion of Florence Dugdale and describing himself as 'very anxious about her health & welfare', he acknowledges Clodd's invitation to bring her to Aldeburgh and asks for a possible date (*Letters*, IV, 35).

24   Thanks Lady Gregory for sending her *Seven Short Plays* and a good opinion of *The Dynasts*, and hopes soon to see further verse by Yeats.

25   Asks Gosse to tell F. A. Hedgcock that there is no direct influence of Schopenhauer on his work.

28   Regrets that Florence Dugdale is too ill to travel to Clodd's, and asks for a further invitation.

August

5   (Thurs) Declines to sign a Suffragette petition.

13   Travels to Aldeburgh with Florence Dugdale. Letter on 'The Censorship of Plays' appears in *The Times*.

16   Stuck in a boat with Clodd and Florence Dugdale on a mudbank on the river Alde, an incident which is reported in the local press.

22   Asks Shorter not to publicise the stranding in the national press, presumably because this would alert ELH to his companion. Holidays with Florence Dugdale in the party are, however, taken later this year, so others must have been aware of the relationship. The consequent frustrations give rise to low spirits, and a number of fine poems such as 'On the Departure Platform' later in the year.

30   Thanks Clodd warmly for the holiday.

September

Time's Laughingstocks sent off to Macmillan.

18   (Sat) Asks Frederick Macmillan to consider whether 'Panthera' should be included in the forthcoming volume.

October

6   (Wed) Absolutely refuses to attend a dinner of the Whitefriars Club advertised, as a result of a misunderstanding with Shorter, as being held in TH's honour.

10   Reports to Reymond Abbott on his recent cathedral visits, made with Florence Dugdale and Henry Hardy, praising a chant heard in Edinburgh and the choir at York, and regretting the city at Durham. Congratulates Gustav Holst on his settings of TH's poems.
12   Thanks Maurice Lanoire for his appreciative article on *The Dynasts*.
20   Agrees to sign a petition against dramatic censorship, though requesting that his name should appear well down the list of petitioners.

November

4   (Thurs) In a letter to Alfred de Lafontaine, regrets alterations in and around Dorchester, but declares himself devoid of local influence.
17   Attends the first performance, by the Dorchester Debating and Dramatic Society, of A. H. Evans' dramatisation of *Far from the Madding Crowd*. 'Hardy had nothing to do with the adaptation, but thought it a neater achievement than the London version of 1882 by Mr. Comyns Carr' (*Life*, pp. 347–8).
25   Thanks A. M. Broadley for the gift of his *Doctor Johnson and Mrs Thrale*, though stating that he is 'not strictly a Johnsonian' (*Letters*, IV, 60).
28   Tells Florence Henniker that *Time's Laughingstocks* will soon be appearing and that she will be sent a copy.
30   The House of Lords rejects the Asquith government's Finance Bill.

December

2   (Thurs) Thanks Henry Jones, Professor of Moral Philosophy at the University of Glasgow, for a letter about *Tess*, declaring that the book 'was not written to prove anything, either about Heaven or Earth' (*Letters*, IV, 62). Asquith obtains a dissolution of Parliament as a result of the Finance Bill crisis.
3   *Time's Laughingstocks* published. Inscribed copies sent to Clodd and Gosse. Supports Gosse in his attempts to prevent shoddy censorship by librarians.
12   Thanks Gosse for his acknowledgement of the gift of *Time's Laughingstocks*, and disputes whether the collection should rightly be found sad.

13 Writes to the *Daily News* complaining about a review of *Time's Laughingstocks* (letter published 15 Dec).

18 Pleased to hear that *Time's Laughingstocks*, favourably received by the critics, will need to be reprinted, and sends a list of errata.

24 Sends Christmas greetings to Florence Henniker.

29 Swaps opinions of *Time's Laughingstocks* with Lady Grove.

31 Afflicted by flu. 'At twelve o'clock he crouched by the fire and heard in the silence of the night the ringing of the muffled peal down the chimney of his bedroom from the neighbouring church of St. George' (*Life*, p. 348).

1910

'God's Funeral' completed. 'Before and after Summer' and the group of poems 'Satires of Circumstance' written.

January
'An Impromptu to the Editor', later retitled 'The Jubilee of a Magazine', appears in the *Cornhill*, and 'The Satin Shoes' appears in *Harper's Monthly Magazine*. 'Some Old-Fashioned Psalm-Tunes Associated with the County of Dorset' appears in the *Yearbook* of the Society of Dorset Men in London.

3 (Mon) Sends Gustav Holst a copy of *Time's Laughingstocks*.

14 Proposes to Shorter that he should publish an article on journalists who print inaccurate interviews.

15 The General Election, fought on the issues of Lloyd George's budget, the power of the Lords, and Irish Home Rule, results in the return of the Liberals with a reduced majority.

February
Writes 'The Year's Awakening'.

7 (Mon) Suggests to the Society for the Preservation of Ancient Buildings that they should oppose the restoration of Puddletown Church.

13 Invited by Gosse to become one of the thirty founder members of the English Academy of Letters.

24 Agrees to meet John Acland, curator of the Dorset County Museum, and other interested locals, to discuss the renaming of Dorchester streets.

March

4   (Fri) Agrees to appear as an honorary vice-president of the Royal Institute of British Architects in publicity for the Institute's forthcoming Town Planning Conference.

23 Visits the grave of Swinburne with Florence Dugdale, a stimulus to the completion of 'A Singer Asleep'. 'It is remembered by a friend who accompanied him on this expedition how that windy March day had a poetry of its own, how primroses clustered in the hedges, and noisy rooks wheeled in the air over the little churchyard. Hardy gathered a spray of ivy and laid it on the grave of that brother-poet of whom he never spoke save in words of admiration and affection' (*Life*, p. 349).

26 Spends the Easter weekend, accompanied by Florence Dugdale, with Clodd.

April

'A Singer Asleep' published in the *English Review*.

1   (Fri) Thanks Edward Whymper, whom he has just met again at Aldeburgh, for sending portraits of himself and his family.

3   Sends the *Daily Mail* a note (published on 5 Apr) requesting it to explain that the subject of 'A Singer Asleep' is Swinburne.

8   Asks ELH to choose among various possibilities of accommodation for the season.

13 Thanks Lady Grove for sending her *On Fads*, approving of some of it but adding, 'your ideas come tumbling out in such a torrent that they make your sentences turgid & involved' (*Letters*, IV, 82).

18 Advises Lady Grove on whether to carry on writing professionally: 'A very good test rule is, would you rather lose money & opportunities by writing than gain them by not writing? If you can honestly say yes, I think you are called by nature to do it. I remember testing myself by that query when I stood at the parting of the ways' (*Letters*, IV, 83–4).

24 Declines an invitation to write a serialised autobiography for *Harper's Monthly Magazine*.

27 Further consultation with ELH on London accommodation.

28 Finance Bill finally passed.

May

Letter on the rights of animals appears in the *Humanitarian*.

2   (Mon) Brings protracted deliberations to an end by putting in

an offer for 4 Blomfield Court, Maida Vale. 'At the flat – the last
one they were to take, as it happened – they received their usual
friends as in previous years, and there were more performances
of the *Tess* opera . . . ' (*Life*, p. 350).

6   Death of King Edward VII. Accession of George V.
13 Advises Lady Grove on several possibilities for clearer phras-
    ing, reminding her, 'you are, you know, rather inclined to let
    your pen run away with you at times!' (*Letters*, IV, 89).
20 Funeral of Edward VII. TH subsequently writes 'A King's
    Soliloquy'.
22 Congratulates Austin Dobson on his poems on the death of
    Edward VII.

June
2   (Thurs) TH's seventieth birthday.
3   Thanks Clodd for his birthday greetings, the first of a series of
    such notes.
7   Accepts an invitation from Lady Gregory to see Synge's *Playboy
    of the Western World*, asking if he may bring 'a young cousin' (i.e.
    Florence Dugdale) with him if ELH should be unable to go
    (*Letters*, IV, 95).
12 Thanks the editor, G. W. Foote, for the praise of TH recently
    published in the *Freethinker*.
15 Visits Peterborough with Florence Dugdale.
17 Asks Clodd if he would allow Florence Dugdale to prepare
    a seventieth-birthday interview with him for the *Evening
    Standard*. Negotiates with Lillah McCarthy on three matinee
    performances of *Tess*.
19 Visit the Gosses.
23 Florence Dugdale, having enjoyed several introductions to ELH
    in the course of the season, reports to Clodd that she admires
    TH more as an author than as a man. Florence Dugdale now
    accepted by ELH almost as part of the household.
24 Owing to a prolonged and troublesome stomach complaint,
    regretfully rescinds acceptance of an invitation to dine with Sir
    Frederick and Lady Macmillan.

July
4   (Mon) Asks William Dean Howells to call, telling him, 'It is a
    great many years since we met – too many!' (*Letters*, IV, 102).

9 TH's appointment to the Order of Merit announced in the Birthday Honours List. Many letters of thanks for congratulations follow, their sentiment being summed up in a letter to Lady Grove: 'this incident of my existence has pleased a great many of my friends – all of them, in fact – & that is enough to make it worth having' (*Letters*, IV, 111).

18 Sends domestic news to ELH, including his refusal to sign an anti-Suffragette letter to *The Times* organised by Lord Curzon.

19 Invested with the Order of Merit. ELH not present, but requests Florence Dugdale to check that TH is properly dressed.

20 Leaves London.

22 Clarifies his views on female suffrage in letter to Moberly Bell: 'I hold that a woman has as much right to a vote as a man; but at the same time I doubt if she may not do mischief with her vote' (*Letters*, IV, 106).

23 Warmly thanks Henry Newbolt for dedicating his *Collected Poems, 1897–1907* to him.

24 Informs the librarian of the Royal Library, Windsor Castle, that arrangements are in hand for a portrait by William Strang, to be kept with those of other members of the Order of Merit at Windsor Castle. Agrees to see F. A. Hedgcock, on the understanding that nothing seen or heard at Max Gate is to be printed.

28 Tells Sir George Douglas, 'I have done absolutely nothing (except a poem to Swinburne) since my last poems came out' (*Letters*, IV, 111).

August

5 (Fri) Discusses with Clodd arrangements for another visit to Aldeburgh with Florence Dugdale.

7 Agrees to Lady Gregory's suggestion that he should sign a petition for a Civil List pension for Yeats.

9 Asks the Dorchester police superintendent to caution boys caught stealing Max Gate apples, a repeated nuisance.

11 Sends the Society for the Protection of Ancient Buildings further news on developments at Puddletown Church.

12 Successfully recommends Florence Dugdale's story 'Blue Jimmy the Horse-Stealer' to the *Cornhill*.

13 'After the Visit' appears in the *Spectator*.

September

2 (Fri) Begins a five-day visit to Clodd's with Florence Dugdale.

16 Invites William Strang to come to Max Gate for the portrait sittings.

20 Asks Macmillan when they think it will be advisable to bring out the poetry in one volume. Successfully recommends Florence Dugdale's poem 'Trafalgar! How Nelson's Death Inspired the Tailor' to the *Daily Chronicle*.

22 Discusses poem publication with Sir Frederick Macmillan, hinting that a new volume of verse is envisaged.

October

5 (Wed) Thanks Strang for sending a portrait of Florence Dugdale. Reports with horror to the Society for the Protection of Ancient Buildings developments in the restoration of Puddletown Church.

12 Agrees in principle with Sir Frederick Macmillan to an American twenty-volume de luxe edition of the complete works.

19 Recommends various strengthenings in the plot of *The Mellstock Quire*, an adaptation of *Under the Greenwood Tree* being rehearsed in Dorchester.

22 Invites Henry Newbolt to see *The Mellstock Quire* in Dorchester.

24 Approves A. H. Evans' alterations to *The Mellstock Quire*.

November

Writes 'The Roman Gravemounds'.

11 (Fri) Sends Clodd a ticket for a London performance of *The Mellstock Quire*, and reports 'Miss D. – my handyman, as I call her – appeared yesterday with her typewriter' (*Letters*, IV, 128). For her part, Florence, reflecting on the Hardy marriage, reports in a letter to Clodd, 'I am intensely sorry for her, sorry indeed for both' (Millgate, p. 470).

16 Receives the Freedom of the Borough of Dorchester. TH's great pleasure at this tardily awarded honour reflected in a formal speech of unusual length. The *Life* judges the speech as 'perhaps the most felicitous and personal' of TH's public speeches, and reprints the text (*Life*, pp. 351–3). First performance, in Dorchester, by the Dorchester Debating and Dramatic Society, of *The Mellstock Quire*.

17 Text of TH's speech appears in *The Times*.

23 Expresses pleasure at the appearance of the one-volume edition of *The Dynasts*.

December

'The Torn Letter' appears in the *English Review*.

5 (Mon) Thanks Clodd for his appreciation of *The Mellstock Quire*, and recalls the rejection of *The Poor Man and the Lady*, remarking, 'It was the most original thing (for its date) that I ever wrote' (*Letters*, IV, 130).

15 Advises John Lane not to proceed with the publication of a translation of Sudermann's *Das hohe Lied*.

19 Thanks Florence Henniker for her sympathy over the death of Kitsey, a white Max Gate cat, whose burial earlier in the month was the occasion of TH's poem 'The Roman Gravemounds'.

20 Thanks Angus Maclachlan for sending him his unpublished setting of 'Sing Ballad-Singer', acknowledging it as one of his favourite poems in *Time's Laughingstocks*.

25 Christmas Day marked by a heated dispute between ELH and TH as to whether Florence Dugdale should accompany TH on a visit to his sisters, ELH fearing that they will poison Florence's mind against her. Florence subsequently avoids visiting Max Gate when TH and ELH are both in residence.

26 Defends his view of the Sudermann novel in letter to George Moore: 'though obscenity is innocuous, sensuality is not quite the same' (*Letters*, IV, 133).

29 Takes ELH on board HMS *Dreadnought*, and then to a dance on board the United States flagship *Louisiana*, both ships being anchored in the Portland Roads.

31 Declines Shorter's request for a coronation ode.

1911

ELH's literary productions increase this year. At the beginning of the year she completes the manuscript of *Some Recollections*, and at the end her collection of verse *Alleys* is privately printed in Dorchester.

January

4 (Wed) Clarifies the terms under which F. O. Saxelby may compile his *A Thomas Hardy Dictionary*.

11   Sends Florence Dugdale as birthday presents a copy of Hermann Lea's *Handbook*, and a lamp to read it under.
19   Gives Grosvenor Bartelot his views on a possible memorial to Edward VII in Dorset.

February
22   (Wed) Asks Sir Frederick Macmillan to investigate further Louis Vincent's suggestion for a film of *Tess*.

March
2   (Thurs) Declines an invitation to the Coronation.
17   Agrees, in response to a request by Florence Henniker, to join the committee of the Council of Justice to Animals, but says he will not be sending her a copy of the twelve soon-to-be-published 'Satires of Circumstance', since 'We have drifted so far apart in our views of late years' (*Letters*, IV, 143). Thanks Gilbert Murray for sending his *Nefrekepta*.
26   In a letter to Grosvenor Bartelot, bluntly expresses his opposition to alterations to Fordington Church. Asks Adam L. Gowans to send further copies of his anthology *The Ways of God*. An autographed copy is given to Florence Dugdale the next month.
30   Joins the committee set up to honour the life of Théophile Gautier.
31   Suggests that the Dorchester Debating and Dramatic Society should make *The Three Wayfarers* and 'The Distracted Preacher' its next presentation.

April
Eleven of the 'Satires of Circumstance' group appear in the *Fortnightly Review*.
13   (Thurs) Arrives at Aldeburgh to spend the Easter weekend with Clodd. Florence Dugdale in attendance.
18   Begins a five-day cathedral tour with Henry Hardy, Florence Dugdale and her sister Constance. Lichfield and Hereford amongst the cities visited.
23   Tells A. H. Evans that he cannot at present grant permission for a dramatisation of *The Mayor of Casterbridge*.
26   Tells Clodd, 'I never had a more cheerful time at Aldeburgh. The air, material & spiritual, was wonderful; & really your hospitality is beyond thanks' (*Letters*, IV, 150).
29   Attends the annual dinner at the Royal Academy, meeting Sargent, Barrie, Kipling and others.

May

4   (Thurs) Thanks Shorter for sending a copy of George Herbert
     West's *Gothic Architecture in England and France.*

21   Visits the Gosses, meeting Yeats and Hugh Walpole.

June

2   (Fri) Spends his seventy-first birthday at Bockhampton with his
     family and Florence Dugdale. TH seems to have tried to arrange
     at this time for his brother Henry to marry Florence's sister
     Constance.

3   Thanks J. B. Bury for sending his *Romances of Chivalry on Greek
     Soil*, and discusses modern superstition, rustic and ecclesiasti-
     cal.

8   Advises George Putnam on routes to take when touring Wessex.

15   Counsels Austin Harrison not to be too outraged by a criticism
     of the moral tone of the *English Review* in the *Spectator.*

16   Begins, with Henry Hardy, Florence and Constance Dugdale,
     and their father Edward, an eight-day North Country tour, 'to
     escape the glories of the Coronation' (*Letters*, IV, 160). Visit
     Carlisle, the Lake District and Rugby, returning to Dorset via
     London.

22   Coronation of George V. TH subsequently writes 'The Corona-
     tion'.

24   Tells Macmillan that he proposes dividing the novels in the
     Wessex Edition into two groups.

26   Agrees to Galsworthy's request to consider signing a petition
     against the use of aircraft in war, believing it 'an insanity that
     people in the 20th Century should suppose force to be a moral
     argument' (*Letters*, IV, 161).

28   Tells Sir Frederick Macmillan that he would like to see proofs of
     the proposed American de luxe edition.

July

Takes Kate Hardy and Florence Dugdale on a brief trip to north
Somerset. Writes 'In the Days of Crinoline'.

13   (Thurs) Sends Frank Hedgcock his observations on his *Thomas
     Hardy, penseur et artiste*, with no mention of the subsequently
     contentious biographical chapter.

August

22   (Tues) Writes to Florence Henniker, 'It occurred to me the other

day that this year completes the eighteenth of our friendship. That is rather good as between man & woman, wh. is usually so brittle' (*Letters*, IV, 168).

September
Writes 'Beyond the Last Lamp'.

6   (Wed) Thanks Florence Dugdale for sending revised prefaces for the Wessex Edition, typed.

7   Tells Reymond Abbott that he has been reading *Clayhanger*, describing it as 'the contents of a reporter's note-book emptied on to the pages' (*Letters*, IV, 172).

9   Returns to F. O. Saxelby altered proofs of his *A Thomas Hardy Dictionary*, insisting that the book should not appear to be authorised by TH.

16   Death of Edward Whymper.

22   Thanks Handley Moule for sending a pamphlet on Buddhism, and suggests that Buddhism may have influenced Christianity.

26   Asks Lea to remind him of the models for certain Wessex locations in *A Group of Noble Dames*.

29   Visited at Max Gate by Sydney Cockerell, who urges TH to distribute his manuscripts to selected British and American libraries. Cockerell subsequently entrusted with making the appropriate arrangements.

October
'The Calf', subsequently attributed to TH, appears in Florence Dugdale's *The Book of Baby Beasts*.

3   (Tues) Agrees to Clodd's proposal to invite him and Florence Dugdale to revisit Aldeburgh. Thanks Florence Henniker for occasionally having Florence Dugdale to stay, and sets out his views on termination of marriages. Visits Florence Dugdale at Weymouth.

5   In a letter to Cockerell, sends his views on placement of manuscripts.

7   Discusses *Thomas Hardy's Wessex* with Hermann Lea.

14   Agrees to send Austin Harrison 'Among the Roman Gravemounds' for the *English Review*, reporting that at present it wants 'touching up at the end a little' (*Letters*, IV, 182).

18   ELH reports to Lilian Gifford that she has been widely dispersing extreme Protestant pamphlets, symptomatic of her increasing religious zeal.

24   Agrees to provide Alfred Pope with information about dewponds.
25   Thanks Cockerell for arranging the placement of the manuscripts successfully. Sends Macmillan a map of Wessex and promises to send copy for the first of the novels for the Wessex Edition, *Tess*, in a few days.
26   Agrees to give Clodd a manuscript. Proclamation of the Chinese Republic.
27   *Tess* dispatched to Macmillan, with an assurance that no subsequent novel will contain as much additional matter.

November
'The Sacrilege' appears in the *Fortnightly Review*.
 5   (Sun) Thanks Masefield for sending his *The Everlasting Mercy*, and compliments him on his previous poetry.
10   Agrees to send the manuscript of *The Mayor of Casterbridge* to the Dorset County Museum.
15   First performance by the Dorchester Debating and Dramatic Society of *The Distracted Preacher* (dramatised by A. H. Evans), on which TH has offered some advice in the preceding weeks, and TH's own dramatisation *The Three Wayfarers*. Note by TH printed in the programme.
21   Suffragette riots in Whitehall.

December
'Night in a Suburb', later retitled 'Beyond the Last Lamp', appears in *Harper's Monthly Magazine*. 'Among the Roman Gravemounds', later retitled 'The Roman Gravemounds', appears in the *English Review*. 'The Abbey Mason' written after a visit to Gloucester Cathedral.
 1   (Fri) Asks J. M. Barrie to recommend an agent to handle rights for performances of *The Three Wayfarers*. Thanks John Drinkwater for sending his play *Cophetua*.
20   'To Meet, or Otherwise' appears in the *Sphere*.
24? Sends Florence Dugdale seasonal greetings, adding the Scriptural quotation 'Ye have been called unto liberty' (*Letters*, IV, 195), perhaps a reference to some event on their recent West Country holiday, on which they were accompanied by TH's sister Kate.

1912

January

2   (Tues) Tells Dorothy Allhusen that he hopes to meet her more frequently in the coming year.

7   Plans for an American de luxe edition having fallen through, TH asks Sir Frederick Macmillan to propose more generous terms for the projected Wessex Edition.

10 Agrees to a royalty of 1s. 6d. per volume, and agrees the title for the series. The subsequent work of proof-reading all his earlier work seems to have occasioned TH considerable satisfaction.

15? Sees Max Reinhardt's production of *Oedipus Rex* at Covent Garden.

19 Tells Clarence McIlvaine that he would be prepared to let John Pierpont Morgan have the manuscript of 'The Romantic Adventures of a Milkmaid'.

February

Brief contribution by TH to a symposium on Dickens appears in the *Bookman*. 'The Forsaking of the Nest', later refashioned into 'The Third Kissing-Gate', appears in *Nash's Magazine*.

2   (Fri) Agrees to Morgan's offer of £100 for the manuscript of 'The Romantic Adventures of a Milkmaid' and some verse (eventually 'The Abbey Mason').

3   Advises Barrie of his feelings about the censorship of Eden Phillpotts's play *The Secret Woman*.

9   States the terms under which he will sign a letter of protest about the censorship to *The Times*.

15 Returns proofs of early pages of *Tess*.

25 Returns the final instalment of *Tess* proofs to Macmillan.

March

'God's Funeral' appears in the *Fortnightly Review*. TH's contribution to the symposium 'How Shall We Solve the Divorce Problem?' appears in *Nash's Magazine*.

3   (Sun) In a letter to Clodd, clarifies the date at which he wrote 'God's Funeral' and adds that at present he is not hopeful of getting away to spend time with Florence Dugdale.

9   Letter of tribute to William Dean Howells appears in *Harper's Weekly*.

11 Sends William Rothenstein his reminiscences of rural deprivation in the 1830s and 1840s.
25 Sends off the manuscripts of 'The Romantic Adventures of a
Milkmaid' and 'The Abbey Mason' to Morgan.
28 The Commons reject the Women's Franchise Bill.
31 Clarifies his preferred order of publication for the Wessex
Edition volumes.

April
ELH's prose volume *Spaces* completed, 'the product of a mind at
once obsessed, muddled, and naïve' (Millgate, p. 479).
2 (Tues) Agrees to classify *A Pair of Blue Eyes* as a 'Romance and
Fantasy' in the Wessex Edition.
15 Sinking of the *Titanic*.
19 Tells Cockerell that he would gladly accept an honorary degree
if Cambridge were to offer one.
21 Thanks Florence Henniker for sending her novel *Second Fiddle*,
on which he offers detailed criticism.
22 Reports progress on proof-reading to Florence Dugdale, remarking that Clym is 'the nicest of all my heroes' and that
The Woodlanders is '*as a story*' the novel he likes best of all
(*Letters*, IV, 212).
23 Accepts invitation to Clodd's, and writes to Florence Dugdale
to ask her too.
24 'The Convergence of the Twain' completed.
30 The first two volumes of the Wessex Edition, *Tess* and *Far from
the Madding Crowd*, appear. Two volumes of the twenty-volume
complete edition issued in each subsequent month. The edition
is of great textual importance, since for it TH revised all his
novels for the last time.

May
10 (Fri) Begins a four-day stay at Clodd's with Florence Dugdale.
14 'The Convergence of the Twain' published in the programme
for a Covent Garden matinee in aid of the *Titanic* disaster fund.
17 Thanks Percy Ames, Secretary of the Royal Society of Literature, for the award of the Society's gold medal.
22 Glad to hear of Florence Henniker's pleasure in 'A. H., 1855–
1912', the poem composed by TH in memory of her recently
deceased husband.

29 Encourages Sir Frederick Macmillan to secure terms with Harper Brothers for the American publication of the Wessex Edition.

June
2 (Sun) The gold medal of the Royal Society of Literature presented to TH at Max Gate by a deputation consisting of Henry Newbolt and W. B. Yeats. TH discusses architecture with Newbolt, while ELH informs Yeats of the merits of the cats seated beside her lunch plate. ELH excluded from the subsequent presentation, a reflection of TH's concern at her growing mental instability.
4 TH's speech of acceptance of the gold medal, 'A Plea for Pure English', appears in *The Times*.
11 Strike of transport workers, a reflection of this year's acute social unrest, begins.

July
2 (Tues) Through B. F. Stevens and Brown, American literary agents, authorises George Barr McCutcheon to print a limited edition of 'The Convergence of the Twain'.
16 ELH gives her last garden party at Max Gate: 'The afternoon was sunny and the guests numerous on this final one of many occasions of such a gathering on the lawn there, and nobody foresaw the shadow that was so soon to fall on the house . . . ' (*Life*, p. 359).

August
29 (Thurs) Gives Sir Arthur Quiller-Couch permission to include any poems he may wish in his *Oxford Book of Victorian Verse*.

September
5 (Thurs) Visited at Max Gate by Gosse and A. C. Benson.
9 Asks Sir Frederick Macmillan to make sure that the printers use the first edition of *The Dynasts*, in three separate parts, as copy for the Wessex Edition.

October
'A. H., 1855–1912', never collected by TH, appears in Florence Henniker's memorial volume *Arthur Henniker*. 'The Yellow-Hammer', subsequently attributed to TH, appears in Florence Dugdale's *The Book of Baby Birds*.

8   (Tues) Declines an invitation to visit Clodd, an indication of his determination swiftly to finish proof-reading the Wessex Edition, a job which has taken up a considerable amount of his time this year.

10   Commiserates with d'Erlanger on the poor returns on the opera *Tess*, expressing his enthusiasm for it and a wish that it should be heard further. Discusses with Sir Frederick Macmillan whether the original illustrations to *Wessex Poems* should be reproduced in the Wessex Edition.

19   Congratulates George Forrest on his *A History of the Indian Mutiny*.

29   Sends Gosse praise of his article on Swinburne in the *Dictionary of National Biography*.

November

10   (Sun) Discusses in a letter to James Douglas what action might or should be taken against Morley Roberts's *The Private Life of Henry Maitland*, a fictionalised account of the life of George Gissing.

19   First performance, in Dorchester, by the Dorchester Debating and Dramatic Society, of A. H. Evans' dramatisation of *The Trumpet-Major*.

21   Writes 'The Bird-Catcher's Boy'.

22   ELH goes out for the last time (recalled in 'A Leaving').

25   Rebekah and Catharine Owen, visiting Max Gate, notice ELH's weakness (the duration of which is a matter of some controversy) and record her refusal to see a doctor. 'The Last Performance', written this year, records one incident in ELH's decline.

27   The Max Gate maid, Dolly Gale, summons TH to ELH's room following an alarming deterioration in her condition. ELH dies minutes later.

30   Funeral of ELH at Stinsford. No London literati or Gifford relatives present. The card attached to TH's wreath is inscribed 'From her Lonely Husband, with the Old Affection'.

December

'The Abbey Mason' appears in *Harper's Monthly Magazine*.

12   (Thurs) Tells Ellen Gosse, 'I have been full of regrets that I did not at all foresee the possibility of her passing away thus, but

merely thought the few days of illness a temporary ailment which I need not be anxious about' (*Letters*, IV, 239).

13 Writes a letter of acknowledgement to Clodd, one of a large number of such letters at this time, commenting, in words which suggest that the 'Poems of 1912–13' were already taking shape in his mind, 'One forgets all the recent years & differences, & the mind goes back to the early times when each was much to the other – in her case & mine intensely much' (*Letters*, IV, 239).

28 Attempts to offer his resignation as a governor of the Dorchester Grammar School.

1913

'Many poems were written by Hardy at the end of the previous year and the early part of this – more than he had ever written before in the same space of time. . . . To adopt Walpole's words concerning Gray, Hardy was "in flower" in these days, and, like Gray's, his flower was sad-coloured' (*Life*, p. 361). Such poems are 'The Spell of the Rose', 'St Launce's Revisited' and the group 'Poems of 1912–13'.

January
4 (Sat) 'The Bird-Catcher's Boy' appears in the *Sphere*.
5 Thanks Henry Newbolt for sending his *Poems: New and Old*.
20 Tells Harper Brothers that he needs time to consider what a new volume of short stories might contain.
28 Suffragette demonstration following withdrawal of the Franchise Bill.
29 Reports to Florence Dugdale his feelings on going through ELH's diaries, highly critical of his conduct, and adds, 'If I once get you here again won't I clutch you tight: you shall stay till spring' (*Letters*, IV, 255).
30 Agrees to lend support to Robert Francillon's application for a grant from the Royal Literary Fund.

February
Writes 'On a Discovered Curl of Hair'.
1 (Sat) Tells Clodd that he feels he must now begin to shake off his grief, and invites him to visit.
22 Accepts with pleasure an honorary doctorate from the University of Cambridge.

March

6 (Thurs) 'On March 6 – almost to a day, forty-three years after his first journey to Cornwall – he started for St. Juliot . . . ' (*Life*, p. 361).

8 Writes 'It Never Looks like Summer'.

9 Reports to Florence Dugdale on his visit to Cornwall with Henry: 'The visit to this neighbourhood had been a very painful one to me, & I have said a dozen times I wish I had not come. What possessed me to do it!' (*Letters*, IV, 260).

28 Sends the vicar of St Juliot a photograph of the church before restoration, adding that he is designing a tablet for the north-aisle wall. Sends instructions for the lettering on ELH's grave.

April

Writes 'Old Excursions'.

8 (Tues) Authorises Harper Brothers to allow a film to be made from *Tess*. This appears later in the year.

13 Asks the vicar of Stinsford for permission to erect ELH's tomb.

14 Asks Clodd if he might conveniently be visited at Aldeburgh.

16 The gift to Florence Dugdale of a bunch of dried flowers marks a significant stage in their relationship – perhaps TH's first proposal. Certainly by the summer he had proposed and she had accepted.

22 Arrives at Southwold for brief East Anglian holiday, visiting Florence Henniker and Clodd, in the company of Florence Dugdale.

May

3 (Sat) Clarifies a variant reading in *Tess* for William Macmillan.

16 Congratulates William Stebbing on his *Five Centuries of English Verse*.

29 Declines Shorter's invitation to write something about George Borrow, reporting, 'I am writing nothing about anybody at present' (*Letters*, IV, 275), a statement which the 'Poems of 1912–13', in progress at this time, magnificently disprove.

June

Travels to Cambridge this month to receive aꞁ honorary LittD.

1 (Sun) Sends the vicar of St Juliot a fee for the erection of the tablet to ELH, adding, 'I should much like to see the memorial, but sad memories so crowded upon me when I last visited the

spot that I suppose I shall never venture to go again' (*Letters*, IV, 275).

2 Writes 'Exeunt Omnes'.

3 Congratulates J. M. Barrie on being made a baronet, and Gosse on his lecture 'The Future of English Poetry'.

4 Corresponds with Macmillan on the film rights for *Tess*.

15 Calls on the Gosses.

20 The Cockerells arrive to spend the weekend with TH and Florence Dugdale at Max Gate. She arrived in the spring, and was thenceforward a near-permanent resident.

July

6 (Sun) Advises the British and Foreign Blind Association on which of his works might best be put into braille.

11 Asks Hermann Lea to omit the picture of the birthplace from his forthcoming book. Clodd and the Shorters arrive to take up their invitation to stay for the weekend.

18 Tells Gosse that his gratitude for a recent gift of miscellaneous manuscripts has been excessive, and refers to the Poet Laureateship, which TH may have hoped to obtain at this time.

24 Congratulates George Dewar on his appointment as editor of the *Saturday Review*, also discussing *A Pair of Blue Eyes*.

24 Offers to help John Lane with research for a book on Alfred Stevens.

25 Sends Austin Harrison 'The Place on the Map' for the *English Review*.

28 Accepts with pride an honorary fellowship of Magdalene College, Cambridge. Agrees to collaborate with Sir Edward Elgar, suggesting (unfortunately in vain) *A Pair of Blue Eyes* as suitable for musical setting.

August

6 (Wed) Tells Maurice Macmillan, 'I find that enough poems to fill a volume are lying in my drawer ready for the press at some indefinite date' (*Letters*, IV, 293).

9 Declines invitation to meet 300 Canadian teachers at Weymouth: 'I have not gone out anywhere this year' (*Letters*, IV, 294).

11 Sends correction of 'The Place on the Map' to Austin Harrison.

19 Sends Sir Frederick Macmillan the stories he would like collected as *A Changed Man, The Waiting Supper, and Other Tales*, TH's final volume of fiction.

22   Offers the rector of St Juliot assistance with the design of a new
     screen for the church.
27   Tells Sir George Douglas of the new collection of short stories –
     'mostly bad' – and asks him for his thoughts on 'the new ugly
     school of poetry' (*Letters*, IV, 300).

September
Louisa Harding, an early subject of TH's affection, buried at Stinsford.
TH's early 'The Place on the Map' appears in the *English Review*.
 3   (Wed) Reports himself 'just now over head & ears with un-
     interesting proof sheets' (*Letters*, IV, 302).
 6   Returns proofs of *A Changed Man* to the printers.
12   Sends Sir Frederick Macmillan the revised prefatory note to
     A Changed Man.
15   'Thoughts on the recent school of novel-writers. They forget in
     their insistence on life, and nothing but life, in a plain slice, that
     a story *must be worth the telling*, that a good deal of life is not
     worth any such thing, and that they must not occupy a reader's
     time with what he can get at first hand anywhere around him'
     (*Life*, p. 362).
27   'Ah, Are You Digging on My Grave' appears in the *Saturday
     Review*.

October
Agrees to become a member of the Society for Pure English. Writes
'Where They Lived'.
 4   (Sat) Explains to Sir Frederick Macmillan that he might at a
     future date like to reconstruct *The Poor Man and the Lady*, for
     which reason 'An Indiscretion in the Life of an Heiress', has not
     been included in *A Changed Man*. TH's interest in this project
     may have been stimulated by his re-encounter some time this
     year with Eliza Bright Nicholls, whom he found to be still
     unmarried.
 5   Tells Gosse that he has subscribed to *Poetry and Drama*, an an-
     thology mostly of Georgian poets.
 9   Agrees to let Fuller Maitland paint his portrait for Magdalene
     College, Cambridge. Returns to Harper Brothers the contract
     for *A Changed Man*.
14   Sends Harold St George Gray a copy of his pamphlet *Some
     Romano-British Relics Found at Max Gate, Dorchester*.

18 'Starlings on the Roof' appears in the *Nation*.
21 Attends the premiere of the film *Tess*.
22 Asks Florence Yolland to help identify the tombs of ELH's parents and grandparents in Plymouth.
24 *A Changed Man and Other Tales* published. TH, while not thinking very highly of the volume, is gratified at its favourable reception. Advises Sir James Murray on the meaning of the word 'tranter'.
29 Promises to send A. M. Broadley a copy of *A Changed Man*.

November
?1 (Sat) Arrives in Cambridge to be installed as an honorary fellow of Magdalene College. Greatly enjoys the ceremony and subsequent dinner.
5 Asks Sir Frederick Macmillan for advice in dealing with Tauchnitz over *A Changed Man*.
10 Thanks Macmillan for agreeing to act as agent in dealings with Tauchnitz.
13 Writes to Harrison, congratulating him on his *The Positive Evolution of Religion*, criticising Roman Catholicism severely, and agreeing that 'the times have a strange & disturbing colour just now' (*Letters*, IV, 319).
14 Thanks Mary Augusta Ward for sending a copy of her novel *The Coryston Family*, which he reports having finished reading in bed the previous evening at 1 a.m., and acclaims as her best work.
15 Thanks A. E. Housman for sending a copy of M. R. James's *Ghost Stories of an Antiquary* and *More Ghost Stories of an Antiquary*.
19 First performance by the Dorchester Debating and Dramatic Society of *The Woodlanders*. TH not present.
21 *The Three Wayfarers* opens at the Little Theatre in London.

December
'My Spirit Will Not Haunt the Mound' appears in *Poetry and Drama*, and 'The Telegram' in *Harper's Monthly Magazine*.
3 (Wed) Thanks Handley Moule for sending his *Memories of a Vicarage*, which is described as bringing back 'all sorts of submerged experience, dates, & faces of the past' (*Letters*, IV, 326).
7 Inquires of John Lane whether there is a well-printed volume of the complete poetical works of Hawker of Morwenstow.

10   Thanks Lane for sending Hawker's *Cornish Ballads and Other Poems*, commenting that 'Hawker, though bigoted and superstitious to a degree, had the imagination of a true poet, and I regret that I never met him' (*Letters*, IV, 328).
11   Letter on Anatole France (written 7 Dec) appears in *The Times*.
14   Sends Sir Frederick Macmillan a small correction for the Wessex Edition.
16   Sends Sir Frederick Macmillan an updated map for the Wessex Edition.
19   Letter on 'Performing Animals' appears in *The Times*.
20   'To Meet, or Otherwise' appears in the *Sphere*.
21   Sends Florence Henniker a pre-Christmas letter of news.

1914

Writes 'On the Doorstep' and 'Not Known'.

January
  3   (Sat) 'The Plaint of Certain Spectres', later retitled 'Spectres that Grieve', appears in the *Saturday Review*.
  9   Suggests cuts in the Dorchester Debating and Dramatic Society's version of *The Woodlanders*.
15   Advises the vicar of Stinsford on the date and possible method of preservation of the Stinsford font.
21   Agrees to the updating by Thomas Seccombe of Lionel Johnson's *The Art of Thomas Hardy*, but refuses to discuss his work with Seccombe, since 'The value, whatever that may have been, of Johnson's criticism and estimate lay in its detachment' (*Letters*, V, 5).
25   Typescript of 'Before and after Summer' sent to R. A. Scott-James for the *New Weekly*.
26   Declines invitation to a Pepys dinner at Magdalene College, Cambridge.
29   Writes to Florence Dugdale, 'the house is very solitary. But I keep well – missing you however, every minute' (*Letters*, V. 8).

February
  6   (Fri) Obtains a marriage licence.
10   Marries Florence Dugdale at St Andrew's Church, Enfield: 'Beyond the parties & the officiators there was not a soul present

but my brother & her father & sister. And although the church door stood wide open nobody walked in. It was a lovely morning, & the ceremony was over by 8.20!' (*Letters*, v, 10–11).

11 Writes to Dorothy Allhusen, Florence Henniker, Clodd, Cockerell and Gosse with news of the marriage. Cockerell is told, 'We thought it the wisest thing to do, seeing what a right hand Florence has become to me, & there is a sort of continuity in it, & not a break, she having known my first wife so very well' (*Letters*, v. 9). Many responses to letters of congratulation are sent in the following weeks.

March
21 (Sat) 'The Year's Awakening' appears in the *New Weekly*.
23 Tells Frederic Harrison, 'Our honeymoon – if it could be called such – was & is still being taken in slices, or phases, as I suppose I ought to say: three or four days in Devon; three days in London; &c, &c, between the prosiest of home doings in the way of seeing to repairs, the kitchen garden, getting in manure, & such like' (*Letters*, v, 21).

April
4 (Sat) 'Before and after Summer' appears in the *New Weekly*.
27 Agrees to attend a feast at St John's College, Cambridge. The *Life* reports of the subsequent occasion, 'the mellow radiance of the dark mahogany tables, curling tobacco smoke, and old red wine, charmed Hardy, inspite of his drinking very little, and not smoking at all' (*Life*, pp. 363–4).

May
'Channel Firing' appears in the *Fortnightly Review*, and 'How He Looked in at the Draper's', later retitled 'At the Draper's', in the *Saturday Review*.
14 (Thurs) Successfully invites Gordon Gifford to spend the Whitsun holiday at Max Gate.
25 The Commons pass Irish Home Rule Bill.

June
15 (Mon) Writes to Annie Watson, a relative of ELH's, trying to establish the whereabouts of the grave of ELH's grandmother.
28 Assassination of Archduke Franz Ferdinand of Austria and his wife by a Bosnian revolutionary. 'To Hardy as to ordinary

civilians the murder at Sarajevo was a lurid and striking tragedy, but carried no indication that it would much affect English life' (*Life*, p. 364).

July

15 (Wed) Agrees to Sir Frederick Macmillan's suggestion for a limited edition of the prose works, though hoping that the verse will also be included, and suggests the title Mellstock Edition. Also announces that he has enough poems to form a new volume of verse.

17 Tells Florence Henniker that he is planning to publish a volume of poems which will include verse written in commemoration of ELH, 'as the only amends I can make' (*Letters*, v, 37).

19 Suggests to Sir Frederick Macmillan *Satires of Circumstance, Lyrics and Reveries* as the title for the new volume of verse.

August

4 (Tues) Britain declares war on Germany. 'The whole news and what it involved burst upon Hardy's mind next morning, for though most people were saying the war would be over by Christmas he felt it might be a matter of years and untold disaster. . . . the contemplation of it led him to despair of the world's history thenceforward' (*Life*, pp. 365–6).

8 British troops land in France.

9 Comments to Sir Sydney Cockerell, 'Among the other ironies of the time is the fact that all the nations are praying to the same God' (*Letters*, v, 41).

10 Visited by the Cockerells at Max Gate. *Satires of Circumstance* sent to Macmillan.

15 FEH reports TH's reaction to the war to Sydney Cockerell: 'I think he feels the horror of it so keenly that he loses all interest in life' (Millgate, p. 498).

24 The allies begin to retreat from Mons.

28 Thanks Cockerell for agreeing to act as one of his literary executors.

September

5 (Sat) Writes 'Song of the Soldiers'.

9 This poem, later retitled 'Men Who March Away', appears in *The Times*. Though generally distrustful of his own country's imperialistic tendencies, TH appears to have decided that Ger-

many was chiefly to blame for the onset of war, and agrees to the government's request to writers to do what they can to support the British cause.

27 Agrees to assist Harley Granville Barker in adapting *The Dynasts* for the theatre, an offer which produces much correspondence in the ensuing weeks. The chief reason for TH's approval of the project seems to have been his desire to support a patriotic gesture.

28 Tells F. A. Duneka, 'You will know what a man of peace I am, & how ugly a thing war at its best is to me; but events proved to me with startling rapidity that there was no other course for us but to fight' (*Letters*, v, 52).

October
Writes 'England to Germany in 1914'.

7 (Tues) TH's letter 'Rheims Cathedral' appears in the *Manchester Guardian*.

11 TH's letter 'A Reply to Critics' appears in the *Manchester Guardian*.

18 Writes 'On the Belgian Expatriation'.

30 The first Battle of Ypres begins.

November

15 (Sun) Responds to a query from the parliamentary draftsman, Sir Courtenay Ilbert, about the militia ballot in the Napoleonic Wars.

17 *Satires of Circumstance* published. The *Life* observes that 'The "Lyrics and Reveries", which filled the far greater part of the volume, contained some of the tenderest and least satirical verse that ever came from his pen' (p. 367). Despite the volume's enormous literary merits, its publication had an unfortunate effect of suggesting to FEH her lack of success as a wife.

23 Sends Kate Gifford a copy of *Satires of Circumstance*, commenting, 'In later years an unfortunate mental aberration for which she [ELH] was not responsible altered her much, & made her cold in her correspondence with friends & relatives, but this was contrary to her real nature, & I myself quite disregard it in thinking of her' (*Letters*, v, 64).

25 First night of *The Dynasts* at the Kingsway Theatre. FEH attends. The run lasts for seventy-two performances. The Prologue and Epilogue specially composed for these performances by TH.

December
Writes 'An Appeal to America on Behalf of the Belgian Destitute'
and 'A Jingle on the Times'.
6   (Sun) Thanks Amy Lowell for sending a copy of her *Sword Blades
    and Poppy Seed*, on which he offers comments.
21   Sends Caleb Saleeby philosophical reflections on *The Dynasts*.
31   'A sad vigil, during which no bells were heard at Max Gate,
    brought in the first New Year of this unprecedented "breaking
    of nations".
        'It may be added here that the war destroyed all Hardy's
    belief in the gradual ennoblement of man' (*Life*, p. 368).

1915

'He seems to have been studying the *Principia Ethica* of Dr. G. E. Moore
early this year; and also the philosophy of Bergson' (*Life*, p. 369).
Writes 'In Time of "the Breaking of Nations"' and 'I Travel as a
Phantom Now'.

January
4   (Mon) 'An Appeal to America' appears in the *New York Times*.
7   Sends opinions on Dickens and Scott to Lady Hoare, judging
    Scott a more appealing poet than novelist, and describing *David
    Copperfield* as Dickens' best novel.
13   Writes to Gosse, again attacking the Georgian poets.
20   Thanks Virginia Woolf for high praise of the appreciation of her
    father in F. W. Maitland's *The Life and Letters of Leslie Stephen* and
    the poem 'The Schreckhorn', the latter appreciation of Stephen
    having recently been reprinted in *Satires of Circumstance*.

February
Writes 'The Pity of It'. 'A Hundred Years Since', never collected by
TH, appears in the *North American Review*.
2   (Tues) Sends Caleb Saleeby a detailed subjective critique of
    Bergson's *Creative Evolution*.
5   Sends off corrections for the reprint of *Satires of Circumstance*.
11   Asks Clodd for advice on share purchases.
23   Sends the rector of St Juliot sketches of details of St Juliot Church
    before its restoration.

24   Declines an invitation to reopen the Winchester Public Library.
     Agrees to sit for the sculptor Hamo Thornycroft.

March
'The Lizard', subsequently attributed to TH, appears in Florence
Dugdale's *The Book of Baby Pets*.

12   (Fri) Lavishly compliments William Watson on his sonnet 'To
     America, Concerning England': 'I think it one of the finest things
     – if not the very finest – you have ever written, & possibly any
     poet, both in craftsmanship & feeling' (*Letters*, v, 83).

16   Sends Caleb Saleeby further reflections on Bergson.

19   Asks Sir Evelyn Wood if he might assist Frank George's attempt
     to obtain a commission in the Dorset Regiment.

23   Sends Florence Henniker a proof of 'The Pity of It', and also his
     views on the blameworthiness of Germany in starting the war.
     Permits Edward Thomas to include work by TH in his *This
     England: An Anthology from Her Writers*.

April
Visited at Max Gate for the last time by Frank George. 'The Pity of It'
appears in the *Fortnightly Review*.

25   (Sun) Anglo-French forces land at Gallipoli.

May
7   (Fri) Suggests to Harold Child that he should regard 'my verse
     (including the D[ynasts]) as my *essential* writings, & my prose as
     my *accidental*, rather than the reverse: the fact being that I wrote
     prose only because I was obliged to' (*Letters*, v, 94). Sinking of
     the *Lusitania*.

14   'Have been reading a review of Henry James. It is remarkable
     that a writer who has no grain of poetry, or humour, or spon-
     taneity in his productions, can yet be a good novelist. Meredith
     has some poetry, and yet I can read James when I cannot look at
     Meredith' (*Life*, p. 370).

19   Writes to Sir Frederick Macmillan regarding royalty complica-
     tions of proposed filmings of some of the novels.

25   Explains to the surgeon Macleod Yearsley why he is not accom-
     panying FEH to London for an operation intended to cure her
     nasal catarrh.

26   Asks Constance Dugdale to send reports of her sister's progress.
     Asquith forms a coalition government.

June

10   (Thurs) Begins a two-day excursion into Devon, calling on Eden Phillpotts.

30   Sends Clodd birthday greetings, though remarking, 'whether you & I are going to wind up our earthly career under a cloud or not is at present a matter of conjecture' (*Letters*, v, 113).

July

Writes 'A Poet'.

2   (Fri) Discusses arrangements for *Selected Poems of Thomas Hardy* with Maurice Macmillan.

18   Thanks Habberton Lulham for sending a copy of his *The Other Side of Silence*, including the poem 'To Thomas Hardy'.

29   Advises Florence Henniker on professional architectural bodies.

August

6   (Fri) Fresh Allied landings at Suvla Bay, Gallipoli.

8   Sends manuscript of 'Cry of the Homeless' to Henry James for publication in *The Book of the Homeless*.

22   Frank George, whom TH had recently decided to make his heir, is killed in action in Gallipoli. 'He might say Militavi non sine gloria – short as his career has been' (*Life*, p. 371).

25   Thanks Galsworthy for sending his novel *The Freelands*, reporting that FEH is reading it aloud to him in the evenings.

September

2   (Thurs) Tells Florence Henniker, 'The death of a "cousin" does not seem a very harrowing matter as a rule, but he was such an intimate friend here, & Florence & I both were so attached to him, that his loss will affect our lives largely' (*Letters*, v, 121). 'Before Marching and After', TH's poem about George, written this month.

3   Brief biographical note about Frank George, written by TH, appears in *The Times*.

October

'Before Marching and After' appears in the *Fortnightly Review*.

4   (Mon) Sends Charles Gifford inquiries about ELH's family history.

6   Agrees to sign a letter congratulating Henry James on his naturalisation as a British citizen.
24 Sends Shorter 'The Dead and the Living One' for the *Sphere*.

November
7   (Sun) Asks Sir Frederick Macmillan's advice on a recent approach from A. E. Drinkwater about filming *The Dynasts*.
24 Death of Mary Hardy, a considerable blow to TH, who deeply
valued her company and admiration. 'Her character was a
somewhat unusual one, being remarkably unassertive, even
when she was in the right' (*Life*, p. 371). 'In the Garden' written
before the end of this year as a result of Mary's death.
26 Sends Lady Ilchester, whose guest he has been for a recent short
stay, a handwritten copy of 'Autumn in King's Hintock Park'.
29 Funeral of Mary Hardy at Stinsford Church. 'Buried her under
the yew-tree where the rest of us lie. As Mr. Cowley read the
words of the psalm "Dixi Custodiam" they reminded me strongly
of her nature, particularly when she was young: "I held my
tongue and spake nothing: I kept silence, yea, even from good
words." That was my poor Mary exactly. She never defended
herself; and that not from timidity, but indifference to opinion'
(*Life*, p. 371).

December
'Logs on the Hearth', 'Looking Across' and 'The Sun's Last Look on
the Country Girl', all inspired by Mary, written some time this
month.
2   (Thurs) Obituary of Mary by TH appears in the *Dorset County
Chronicle*.
5   Thanks Cockerell for his condolences, remarking, 'She was almost my only companion in childhood' (*Letters*, v, 135).
24 'The Oxen' appears in *The Times*.
25 'The Dead and the Living One', described as 'a war ballad of
some weirdness' (*Life*, p. 372), appears in the *Sphere*.

1916

Writes 'I Met a Man', 'To My Father's Violin', 'The Pedigree' and
'The Clock of the Years'. 'Cry of the Homeless' appears in *The Book
of the Homeless*.

January
10 (Mon) On behalf of the Society of Authors, congratulates Henry James on the award of the Order of Merit, and on his naturalisation.
19 In a letter to Hamo Thornycroft, congratulates his ward Siegfried Sassoon on 'To Victory'.
29 'In Time of "the Breaking of Nations"' appears in the *Saturday Review*.

February
'The Youth Who Carried a Light', written in 1915, appears in the *Aberdeen University Review*.
1 (Tues) Congratulates Harold Child on his *Thomas Hardy*, and invites him to stay at Max Gate.
6 Agrees to sit for portraits by William Rothenstein.
7 Sends Gosse various manuscripts and autograph letters for a Red Cross sale.
14 Writes 'To Shakespeare After Three Hundred Years'.
17 Sends Israel Gollancz 'To Shakespeare After Three Hundred Years' for inclusion in Gollancz's *A Book of Homage to Shakespeare*.
24 Asks Cockerell if he would be willing to be one of only two literary executors for TH, and suggests the financial terms. Again proposes release of *Selected Poems of Thomas Hardy* to Sir Frederick Macmillan.
28 Death of Henry James.

March
20 (Mon) Regrets being unable to attend the funeral of his cousin Augustus.
22 Accepts the terms proposed by Sir Frederick Macmillan for *Selected Poems*.
25 Congratulates Clodd somewhat lukewarmly on his lecture 'Gibbon and Christianity'.
31 Writes cordially to Galsworthy discussing philosophy and *The Dynasts*.

April
15 (Sat) Asks the Society of Authors for advice on the copyright of deceased authors.

17 Congratulates H. C. Duffin on his *Thomas Hardy: A Study of the Wessex Novels*. Cockerell arrives at Max Gate for a three-day stay.

24 The Easter Rising begins in Dublin, an event which confirms TH in his anti-Irish prejudice.

26 Offers Cockerell the use of a bath chair bought for ELH but little used by her.

28 Visited at Max Gate by George Bernard Shaw, J. B. Bury and their wives. The Irish rising much discussed by the guests.

30 Congratulates Hamo Thornycroft on his bust of TH, having seen a photograph of it.

May

6   (Sat) Invites Shorter to stay at Max Gate, but discourages him from further private printings of poems by TH, following advice from Cockerell.

17 Thanks Benjamin De Casseres for sending a copy of his *The Shadow-Eater*.

27 'The Wound' and 'A Merrymaking in Question' appear in the *Sphere*.

21 Sends Walter Hounsell, a local stonemason, instructions for his sister Mary's tomb.

22 Sends Sir Frederick Macmillan a photo of himself as a possible frontispiece for *Selected Poems*.

31 Battle of Jutland. The poem 'The Sea Fight', written some time later this year, commemorates the death of Captain C. I. Prowse in this battle.

June

Again serves as a Grand Juror at the Assizes. Revisits Riverside Villa, Sturminster Newton, for the first time since occupying the house, and perhaps as a result writes the Sturminster poems ('Overlooking the River Stour', 'The Musical Box' and 'On Sturminster Foot-Bridge') in *Moments of Vision*.

5   (Mon) Lord Kitchener and his staff drowned off Orkney.

22 First performance, in Weymouth, by the Dorchester Debating and Dramatic Society, of *Wessex Scenes from The Dynasts*. TH, responsible for the script, chiefly perhaps because of local loyalty, is not himself present.

July

1   (Sat) Commencement of the Battle of the Somme.
7   Refuses to sign a petition for the reprieve of Sir Roger Casement.
27 Thanks Henry Danielson for sending a copy of his book *The First Editions of the Writings of Thomas Hardy and Their Values*. Sends Maurice Macmillan suggestions for the title page of *Selected Poems*.

August

1   (Tues) Writes 'She, I, and They'.
13 Writes 'An Apostrophe to an Old Psalm Tune'. Sends J. W. Mackail thoughts on Shakespeare encouraged by a perusal of Mackail's recent British Academy Shakespeare lecture.
19 'In Time of Slaughter', later retitled 'When I Weekly Knew', and 'Quid Hic Agis' appear in the *Spectator*.

September

Makes another trip to Cornwall, accompanied by FEH, in the early part of this month. Much annoyed by the behaviour of the vicar at Tintagel, but appears to have begun planning *The Famous Tragedy of the Queen of Cornwall*.

8   (Fri) Writes 'The Marble Tablet' at St Juliot. 'The Monument-Maker' also suggested by this trip.
15 Thanks Masefield for sending his *Sonnets and Poems*. First use of tanks by the British on the Western front.

October

3   (Tues) *Selected Poems of Thomas Hardy*, a volume by which TH set great store, published.
11 Agrees to select and introduce the section to be devoted to Barnes in volume v of Thomas Humphry Ward's series *The English Poets*.
15 Thanks Galsworthy for sending a copy of his *A Sheaf*.
25 Suggests wording for a plaque to commemorate the royal associations of the Gloucester Hotel, Weymouth.

November

7   (Tues) Declines to become a member of the Council for Adult Suffrage: 'I have never taken any practical part in controversial

politics; & if I had it would now, alas, be time to give up'
(*Letters*, v, 186).

10 Visits German prisoners of war at a camp near Dorchester,
    subsequently arranging for them to receive translations of his
    works.

24 Despatches his Barnes contribution to Thomas Humphry Ward.

December

3 (Sun) Congratulates Sir Henry Newbolt on his *Tales of the Great
   War*.

6 First of three performances in Dorchester, by the Hardy Players,
   of *Wessex Scenes from The Dynasts*. Introductory speech for these
   performances supplied by TH.

7 Lloyd George succeeds Asquith as Prime Minister.

13 Agrees to Gosse's suggestion that he should become a member
    of the committee which organised the annual Red Cross sale of
    books and manuscripts, though doubting if he can make any
    positive contribution: 'I have not been in London *this year* – an
    unprecedented thing for one who was once half a Londoner'
    (*Letters*, v, 190).

20 Thanks T. J. Wise for sending his recently published Wordsworth
    bibliography, remarking, 'I consider myself a Faithful
    Wordsworthian, though not to the extent of those who follow
    him into the years when he became parochial & commonplace'
    (*Letters*, v, 192).

22 Congratulates Sir Arthur Quiller-Couch on his 'The Sacred Way'.

1917

January

1 (Mon) 'Am scarcely conscious of New Year's Day' (*Life*, p. 374).

3 Congratulates Arthur Symons on his *Figures of Several Centuries*.

6 'I find I wrote in 1888 that "Art is concerned with seemings
   only", which is true' (*Life*, p. 374). 'A New Year's Eve in War
   Time' appears in the *Sphere*.

11 In a letter to Alfred de Lafontaine, clarifies his involvement in
    the design and construction of Athelhampton Church.

18 Compliments Gosse on the extent of his work for the Red Cross.

February
Publication, in a privately printed pamphlet, of 'England to Germany in 1914'. 'I Met a Man' appears in the *Fortnightly Review*.
4   (Sun) Accepts the dedication of Sassoon's *The Old Huntsman and Other Poems*.
8   Regrets that he cannot attend a meeting of the Entente Committee, remarking that 'nothing effectual will be done in the cause of peace till the sentiment of *Patriotism* be freed from the narrow meaning attaching to it in the past . . . and be extended to the whole globe' (*Letters*, v, 202).
10   Reading Mackail's *Life of William Morris*.
23   Reports to Cockerell on alterations being made to the Max Gate garden by prisoners of war: 'Nothing has made me feel more sad about the war than the sight of these amiable young Germans in such a position through the machinations of some vile war-gang or other' (*Letters*, v, 203).

March
4   (Sun) Thanks Florence Henniker for her praise of *Selected Poems*, identifying 'When I Set Out for Lyonnesse' as his favourite: 'it has the qualities one should find in a lyric' (*Letters*, v, 204).
7   Sends off 'A Call to National Service' for use by the Ministry of National Service.
8   'February' Revolution in Russia.
12   'A Call to National Service' appears in *The Times*.

April
Writes 'A Backward Spring'.
6   (Fri) The United States declares war on Germany.
9   Battle of Arras begins.
11   Returns to the editor several early-nineteenth-century copies of the *Dorset County Chronicle* (borrowed but forgotten about), part of a process of reordering and destroying private papers begun around this time and eventuating in the production of an autobiography.
26   Congratulates Gosse on his new Swinburne biography.

May
15   (Tues) Sends a guarded response to a transatlantic inquiry about his favourites amongst his own poems.

18   Thanks Sassoon for sending *The Old Huntsman*, specifying the poems he has particularly admired in his reading of it so far.
20   Sends a letter of news to Florence Henniker.

June
5   (Tues) Congratulates Thornycroft on his knighthood.
7   Agrees to join a committee for the erection of a memorial to Shakespeare in Rome.
20   Declines an invitation from John Buchan to visit General Headquarters in France, in the company of J. M. Barrie and Sir Owen Seaman.
26   Gratefully accepts the dedication of Galsworthy's novel *Beyond*.

July
11   (Wed) 'Then and Now' appears in *The Times*.
15   Declines an invitation from Arthur Symons to write an appreciation of Jane Austen.
31   Battle of Passchendaele begins.

August
21   (Tues) Manuscript of *Moments of Vision* sent to Macmillan.
27   Thanks Sassoon for sending a reprint of 'To Any Dead Officer', revealing that he has already cut it out of the *Cambridge Magazine*.

September
FEH reports that she now has Hardy's notes on his early life up to the time he began work in London.
5   (Wed) Thanks Galsworthy for sending his *Beyond*.
15   Russian Republic proclaimed under Kerensky.
21   Sends Galsworthy his compliments on *Beyond*.

October
'The Fiddler's Story', later retitled 'The Country Wedding', and 'A Jingle on the Times' are published privately by FEH.
12   (Fri) Sends J. J. Foster an introductory note for his *Wessex Worthies*.
14   Recommends Foster's book to Newman Flower.
15   Returns to Thomas Humphry Ward the proofs of the Barnes section of *The English Poets*.

21 Sends an amusing letter of greeting to Sir Henry Newbolt, who has recently given a lecture on TH's poetry.

November
A three-day visit to the Plymouth neighbourhood, in search of Gifford memories and family history, made this month.
2 (Fri) A. J. Balfour declares that Britain favours the establishment of a national home for the Jews.
7 Lenin and Trotsky seize power in the 'October' Revolution.
10 'Often when Warring' published in the *Sphere*.
12 Congratulates Sir Frederick Macmillan on the appearance of *Moments of Vision*.
23 'I was a child till I was 16; a youth till I was 25; a young man till I was 40 or 50' (*Life*, p. 378).
24 'In Time of War and Tumults' appears in the *Sphere*.
25 Declines to write an article on the war for the *Graphic*.
30 *Moments of Vision* published by Macmillan. TH comments, 'I do not expect much notice will be taken of these poems: they mortify the human sense of self-importance by showing, or suggesting, that human beings are of no matter or appreciable value in this nonchalant universe' (*Life*, p. 378). FEH subsequently reports to Cockerell, 'I expect that the idea of the general reader will be that T. H.'s second marriage is a most disastrous one and that his sole wish is to find refuge in the grave with her with whom alone he found happiness. Well – all things end somewhere' (*Friends of a Lifetime*, p. 296).

December
10 (Mon) Corrections to be inserted should *Moments of Vision* be reprinted sent to Sir Frederick Macmillan.
19 Acknowledges receipt of John Drinkwater's *Tides*.
26 Sympathises with Sir Henry and Lady Hoare on the loss of their only son.
28 Thanks Sassoon for sending the anthology *Georgian Poetry 1916-1917*.
31 Sends New Year greetings to Sir Henry Newbolt, remarking, 'I don't know that I have ever parted from an old year with less reluctance than from this' (*Letters*, v, 239).

1918

Work on the *Life*, and the tidying-up operations associated with it, the chief literary task of this year. Writes 'The Woman I Met'.

January
Suffrage granted to all women over thirty in the United Kingdom.
2   (Wed) Attends a performance by women land-workers in the Corn Exchange, Dorchester.
3   Informs Sir Frederick Macmillan that he is prepared to allow three of his poems to be used in an anthology to be published in aid of the Humanitarian League.
4   In a letter to Galsworthy, criticises reviewers of *Moments of Vision*.
7   Commiserates with Shorter on the death of his wife, Dora Sigerson, who is probably commemorated in the poem 'How She Went to Ireland'.
23 Advises Isabel Smith how to maximise profit when the manuscript of *Far from the Madding Crowd* is auctioned for the benefit of the Red Cross.
24 'It is *the unwilling mind* that stultifies the contemporary criticism of poetry' (*Life*, p. 383).
25 'The reviewer often supposes that where Art is not visible it is unknown to the poet under criticism. Why does he not think of the art of concealing art?' (*Life*, p. 384).
28 Supplies Gosse with information for an article on TH's poems.
29 Reminds Hall Caine of the great age at which the classical tragedians wrote their best work.
31 Attends a charity performance in Dorchester of *The Mellstock Quire*.

February
2   (Sat) Reading closely Colvin's *Life* of Keats.
4   Offers Gosse further information on the history of his aversion to the 'jewelled line' in verse.
7   Sends a letter of miscellaneous news to Florence Henniker, including a castigation of critical appraisals of *Moments of Vision*, and his own views on the volume. Declines an invitation to lecture at the University of Chicago.
11 First mention in FEH's diary of her typing of the *Life*.

12   Agrees to become a vice-president of the Dorset County
      Museum.
18   Tells Gosse, 'last night I found that I had spent more years in
      verse-writing than at prose-writing!' (*Letters*, v, 253).
19   Authorises Maurice Macmillan to arrange the rights for a pro-
      jected (but never completed) film of *Jude the Obscure*.
24   FEH tells Cockerell, 'On looking through Colvin's *Keats* again,
      . . . T. H. came to the conclusion that the critical chapters were
      worthless – and that a poet may be much injured by over-
      criticism, that too much commenting and prying into motives
      etc., rub the bloom off the poetry' (*Friends of a Lifetime*, p. 297).
28   Sends Cockerell, now established almost as a member of the
      Max Gate household, a rare printing of *The Three Wayfarers*.

March
 3   (Sun) Declines offer from the *Evening News* for published
      reminiscences: 'I have considered the matter on previous occa-
      sions when the idea has been mooted to me, & have decided
      that I should not like to write any account of myself for publica-
      tion' (*Letters*, v. 257).

April
16   (Tues) Congratulates Gosse on his article 'Mr Hardy's Lyrical
      Poems' in the *Edinburgh Review*.
22   FEH notices that cycling to Bockhampton is now an effort for
      TH. TH himself made gloomy by the visit to his birthplace.

May
'Some sense of the neglect of poetry by the modern English may
have led him to write at this time:
      '"The poet is like one who enters and mounts a platform to give
an address as announced. He opens his page, looks around, and
finds the hall – *empty*."
      '" . . . My opinion is that a poet should express the emotion of all
the ages and the thought of his own"' (*Life*, p. 386).
 4   (Sat) Commiserates with Sir George Douglas on the loss of his
      mother.
 8   Adjudicates several food-profiteering cases at the Police Court
      in Dorchester, 'the only war-work I was capable of' (*Life*, p. 386).
20   Writes enthusiastically to Rendel Harris about his plan for an
      Anglo-American university at Plymouth.

27 The Germans launch an offensive on the Western front, leading
to many gains.

June
5   (Wed) Recommends Gosse's article to Florence Henniker.
10 Agrees to *The Woodlanders* and *The Return of the Native* appearing in braille.
20 Responds to Frederic Harrison's request for information on the
date at which hanging in chains ended.
25 Despatches to Alfred Pope the Foreword for Pope's *A Book of
Remembrance*.

July
6   (Sat) Sends Robert Pearce Edgcumbe news on developments in
Dorchester, and thanks him for introducing May O'Rourke,
subsequently to become TH's occasional secretary.
8   Thanks Sassoon for sending *Counter-Attack and Other Poems*.
10 Gratefully acknowledges receipt of a copy of Gray's *Poetical
Works* sent by Dorothy Allhusen.
18 The Allies launch a decisive counter-attack.
24 Answers a query from J. J. Foster on pictures by Thomas Beach.
30 Gratefully acknowledges the gift by Galsworthy of his *Five Tales*.

August
4   (Sun) Refuses to go to church because of opposition to new
services and new prayers. Relishing *Five Tales*, having abandoned Bennett's *Pretty Lady*. Tells FEH, 'It is unfortunate for the
case of present day poetry that a fashion for obscurity rages
among young poets, so that much good verse is lost by the
simple inability of readers to rack their brains to solve conun-
drums. They should remember Spencer's remark that the brain
power spent in ascertaining a meaning is so much lost to its
appreciation when it is ascertained' (*Friends of a Lifetime*, p. 299).
15 Tentatively forwards to Galsworthy, for publication in *Reveille*,
'The Whitewashed Wall': 'I cannot do patriotic poems very well
– seeing the other side too much' (*Letters*, v, 275).

September
Drafts an appeal for Dorothy Allhusen's canteens for French soldiers. 'The Sailor's Mother' appears in the *Anglo-Italian Review*.

3   (Tues) Sends FEH, away visiting relatives in London and
    Brighton, an account of events at Max Gate.
13 Gratefully acknowledges the gift by H. G. Wells of a copy of
    Joan and Peter.
21 Thanks Lord Northcliffe for the interest shown in his work.
27 Letter of news sent to Florence Henniker.

October
22 (Tues) British flu epidemic reaches its height.

November
'Appeal for Mrs. Allhusen's Canteens' privately printed. 'The Whitewashed Wall' appears in *Reveille*. TH's preface to the Barnes poems
in *The English Poets*, vol. v, finally published.
1   (Fri) Belatedly thanks Walter de la Mare, having found a
    favourable but ten-year-old review of *The Dynasts* while turning
    out papers.
6   TH's first meeting with Siegfried Sassoon, whose personality
    and poetry he is coming greatly to admire.
11 Armistice signed. TH's poem 'The Peace Peal' reflects on the
    event, but his overall lack of optimism seen in the failure to
    record the Armistice in the *Life*.
17 Gratefully accepts the dedication of the forthcoming anthology
    Georgian Poetry 1918–1919.

December
14 (Sat) Lloyd George and Bonar Law's coalition retains power in
    the General Election.
28 Sends a letter of miscellaneous news to Florence Henniker.
30 Sends New Year greetings to Sir Henry Newbolt, remarking
    'Well, it is all over now – at least I suppose so. I confess that I
    take a smaller interest in the human race since this outburst
    than I did before' (*Letters*, v, 289).

1919

January
10 (Fri) Commiserates with Harold Child on the death of his wife.
25 Records details of the execution of Mary Channing in Dorchester
    in 1705.

26 Thanks Amy Lowell for sending her *Can Grande's Castle.*
27 Invites H. G. Wells and Rebecca West, both currently staying in Weymouth, to visit Max Gate.

February
5   (Wed) Insists on recounting details of the execution of Mary Channing at a Max Gate tea party attended by Lady Ilchester and her fifteen-year-old daughter.
6   Asserts in a letter to Cockerell that Crabbe was one of the influences on his style, but not the most important. FEH tells Cockerell, 'The letter sorting is still going on – nineteen more years to do' (*Friends of a Lifetime*, p. 301).
11 Sends Harold Child a copy of *Moments of Vision* with corrections added by hand, and expresses his regret that critics have not taken more notice of 'Near Lanivet, 1872'.
15 Commiserates with Sir Arthur Quiller-Couch on the death of his only son.
18 FEH reports to Cockerell 'T. H. is very well. He seems to have grown so very much older though during the last few months, which is saddening at times. He forgets things that have happened only a day or two before, and people he has seen or heard from, though of course his memory of his early life is miraculous' (*Friends of a Lifetime*, p. 302).
22 Advises the vicar of Stinsford on how to reply to an inquiry about the 'original' William Dewey.

March
22 (Sat) In a letter to Sir Frederick Macmillan, suggests that the Wessex Edition should be brought up to date and that an edition of his complete poetical works in two volumes might be brought out.
23 Sends Cockerell best wishes for a speedy recovery from flu.

April
4   (Fri) 'According to the Mighty Working' appears in the *Athenaeum.*

May
2   (Fri) Goes to the Royal Academy private view, as part of a brief visit to London with FEH, accommodation being provided by J. M. Barrie at his flat in the Adelphi.

3   Attends the Royal Academy dinner, but is 'saddened to find
     how many of the guests and Academicians that he had been
     formerly accustomed to meet there had disappeared from the
     scene. He felt that he did not wish to go again, and, indeed, he
     never did' (*Life*, p. 388).
4   Visit the Gosses.
7   Tells Sir George Douglas, 'I have not been doing much – mainly
     destroying papers of the last 30 or 40 years, & they raise ghosts'
     (*Letters*, v, 303–4).

June
A Book of Remembrance, with a foreword by TH, issued.
2   (Mon) 'On his birthday in June he did what he had long in-
     tended to do – took his wife and sister to Salisbury by the old
     road which had been travelled by his and their forefathers in
     their journeys to London' (*Life*, p. 388).
5   Responds to Florence Henniker's birthday greetings with a la-
     ment that the condition of life appears unimproving.
12   Expresses pleasure at Sir Frederick Macmillan's announcement
     that the Mellstock Edition can now be proceeded with.
14   Alcock and Brown fly the Atlantic.
18   Sends Sir Frederick Macmillan alterations for *A Pair of Blue Eyes*
     in the Mellstock Edition. (This was to be the only novel for
     which he corrected the Mellstock Edition proofs.)
29   Sends birthday greetings to Clodd and thanks Handley Moule
     for sending a copy of the biographical notice of his father Henry,
     entitled, 'Doctrine, Manner of Life, Purpose', which he has at-
     tached to a collection of funeral sermons.

July
19   (Sat) Peace celebrations in Britain. Congratulates Sassoon on his
     Picture Show.
30   Sends a scathing letter to Robert Lynd, having discovered him
     to be the author of an anonymous review two years earlier.

August
29   (Fri) Sends J. C. Squire 'Going and Staying' for the first issue of
     the *London Mercury*.

September
5   (Fri) Sends Macmillan minor corrections for *The Dynasts*.

11   Congratulates Sir George Douglas on his recent article about Goethe.
19   Applies to hire a telephone.
22   Sends Gosse best wishes on his seventieth birthday.

October
Attend a piracy case at the Dorset Assizes.
10   (Fri) *Collected Poems*, containing all TH's printed poetry so far, published by Macmillan.
12   In a letter to Cockerell, confirms that the central incident of 'A Tradition of Eighteen Hundred and Four' is fictional.
13   Sends several letters of thanks for the 'Poets' Tribute', a bound anthology of manuscript poems sent as a birthday tribute by forty-three contemporary poets and delivered to Max Gate by Siegfried Sassoon.

November
The first two stanzas of 'Going and Staying' appear in the *London Mercury*. Early in the month, refuses to give autobiographical details to the literary critic Archie Whitfield: 'Speaking generally there is more autobiography in a hundred lines of Mr Hardy's poetry than in all the novels' (*Letters*, VII, 161).
18   (Tues) Visits his father's grave on his birthday.
22   Authorises a rise in the price of his books because of the increase in production costs since the war, and sends Sir Frederick Macmillan an errata slip for the *Collected Poems*.
24   'The Peace Peal (After Years of Silence)' appears in the *Graphic*.
28   Lady Astor becomes the first British woman MP.
30   FEH reveals to Sir Frederick Macmillan that TH has completed the narrative of the *Life* up to 1918.

December
The Mellstock Edition begins publication (completed 1920). 'By Mellstock Cross at the Year's End', later retitled 'By Henstridge Cross at the Year's End', appears in the *Fortnightly Review*.
2   (Tues) Makes a speech, containing several local reminiscences, at the opening of the Bockhampton Reading Room and Club, erected as a village war memorial. 'The room was erected almost on the very spot where had stood Robert Reason's shoemaking shop when Hardy was a boy, described in *Under the Greenwood Tree* as "Mr. Robert Penny's"' (*Life*, p. 394).

6   Advises A. E. Drinkwater on details of the projected production by the Oxford University Dramatic Society of *The Dynasts.*

11   Provisionally agrees to Charles Morgan's suggestion that he should travel to Oxford to see the OUDS production.

15   Congratulates Harold Child on his volume *The Yellow Rock and Other Poems of Love.*

18   Chided by FEH for mending twenty-year-old trousers with string and a packing-needle.

24   Claims to have seen a ghost in Stinsford churchyard after having laid a sprig of holly on his grandfather's grave.

25   Feeds Wessex (his dog) goose and plum pudding.

26   Declines an invitation to lecture at Yale.

27   Reading Inge's *Outspoken Essays.*

31   Sends New Year greetings, and reflections on Einstein, to J. McT. E. McTaggart.

1920

Writes 'A Wet August', 'If You Had Known', 'Our Old Friend Dualism' and 'A Philosophical Fantasy' (rewritten 1926).

January

'A Glimpse from the Train', later retitled 'Faintheart in a Railway Train', appears in the *London Mercury.*

6   (Tues) Sends Cockerell best wishes for a recovery from a temporary illness.

9   Thanks J. M. Murry for sending his *The Evolution of an Intellectual.*

15   Reading proofs of the Mellstock Edition of *A Pair of Blue Eyes.*

25   Insists that his presence at the OUDs presentation of *The Dynasts* should not be publicly acknowledged.

29   Compliments Sir Frederick Macmillan on the physical appearance of the Mellstock Edition.

31   Agrees to Sir Frederick Macmillan's suggestion that he should read the proofs of the verse volumes of the Mellstock Edition.

February

Dismayed by an attack on his pessimism by Frederic Harrison in the *Fortnightly.* Dissuaded by FEH from replying, but regards his friendship with Harrison as ended.

9 (Mon) Arrives in Oxford with FEH to attend the OUDS performance of *The Dynasts* and to receive an honorary DLitt. The *Life* (pp. 398–403) reprints an extensive account of the visit by Charles Morgan.

18 FEH declines to let TH be included in a forthcoming *Biographical Dictionary of Modern Rationalists*: 'He says he thinks he is rather an irrationalist than a rationalist, on account of his inconsistencies' (*Letters*, VII, 162).

28 Sends Florence Henniker a report of the Oxford trip.

March
7 (Sun) Responds in a friendly manner to John Slater's suggestion that he should be nominated as an honorary fellow of the Royal Institute of British Architects.

10 Ulster votes to accept the Home Rule Bill.

24 Death of Mary Augusta Ward.

April
3 (Sat) Sends condolences to Thomas Humphry Ward after the death of his wife.

15 Agrees to George Macmillan's proposal for an increase in the price of the Wessex Edition, and offers to send corrections for the forthcoming reprint.

18 Wessex Edition corrections sent off.

21 Last trip to London, attending the wedding of Harold Macmillan to Lady Dorothy Evelyn Cavendish at St Margaret's, Westminster, and signing as one of the witnesses. Stays (accompanied by FEH) with Barrie, attending a rehearsal of his play *Mary Rose*, and writing 'At a Rehearsal of One of J. M. B.'s Plays'.

29 Professes himself honoured by the RIBA accolade.

30 'The Maid of Keinton Mandeville', written in 1915 or 1916, appears in the *Athenaeum*.

May
4 (Tues) Offers to provide Harold Child with basic biographical facts for an article in celebration of TH's eightieth birthday.

11 Death of W. D. Howells.

14 Drives to Exeter with FEH and Kate Hardy, attending evensong in the cathedral: 'Felt I should prefer to be a cathedral organist to anything in the world' (*Life*, p. 404).

28 Sends a series of questions on American copyright to Sir Frederick Macmillan. Occupied during the spring and early summer with proofs of the Mellstock Edition.

June

Dora Sigerson Shorter's posthumous *A Dull Day* is published, with a prefatory note supplied by TH.

2 (Wed) TH's eightieth birthday. Receives a deputation from the Incorporated Society of Authors, and messages from the King, the Prime Minister, the Lord Mayor of London, and the Vice-Chancellor of Cambridge University. The *Life*, notwithstanding, contains several disillusioned birthday reflections on humanity's lack of moral advance.

4 Reports to Florence Henniker that he has had another letter from the King, thanking TH for the greetings on George V's own birthday.

8 In one of a large number of notes of thanks for birthday greetings, remarks to A. C. Benson 'I have decided that it was worth while to live to be eighty to discover what friends there were about me up & down the world, & my judgement against the desirability of being so long upon earth is therefore for a time at least suspended' (*Letters*, vi, 24).

30 Sends Clodd comments on the recent interest in spiritualism, comparing it to the interest in witchcraft of previous ages.

July

'At a House in Hampstead' written for *The John Keats Memorial Volume* (published in 1921). Spend some time driving Florence Henniker around Dorset, where she is thinking of buying a house.

17 (Sat) Answers a query from Howard Bliss about the manuscript of 'The Oxen'.

August

5 (Thurs) Thanks Florence Henniker for her visit, sending her a copy of *Two on a Tower*, and informing her that Max Gate is about to be visited by Robert Graves and his wife Nancy, a visit reported by Graves in *Goodbye to All That*.

8 Reading *Emma*, having finished *Persuasion* and *Northanger Abbey*.

12 Tells Clodd that he considers Dean Inge 'something of a trimmer' (*Letters*, vi, 36).

15 Sends the vicar of Stinsford's wife a design for the refurbishment of the church's Norman font.
23 Thanks G. Herbert Thring for sending an illuminated birthday address from the Incorporated Society of Authors.

September

Writes 'At Lulworth Cove a Century Back'.
1 (Wed) Designing a war-memorial tablet for the Dorchester Post Office.
2 Thanks Edmund Blunden for sending *The Waggoner, and Other Poems*.
6 Death of Evelyn Gifford, which gives rise to the poem 'Evelyn G. of Christminster'.
23 Returns to J. J. Foster the proof of *Wessex Worthies*.
25 Sends Sir Frederick Macmillan corrections to be embodied in the Medici Society's limited edition of TH's *Selected Poems*.
29 Sends a cheque towards the cost of reinstating the old Stinsford font.

October

6 (Wed) Signs an agreement covering Swedish translations of his novels.
26 Reports to J. M. Murry that he has just finished 'tearing up ill-written scraps' and listening to Florence reading aloud all six complete Jane Austen novels (*Letters*, VI, 43).
27 Writes to sympathise with Alfred Pope on the loss of his wife.
30 Declines to unveil the Dorchester Post Office war memorial.
31 Sends Florence Henniker whimsical speculation on what might have happened to Swithin after the end of *Two on a Tower*, adding, 'I suppose the bishop did find out the secret. Or perhaps he did not' (*Letters*, VI, 45).

November

11 (Thurs) Encourages Harold Child to publicise the Hardy Players' forthcoming performances of *The Return of the Native*, adapted by T. H. Tilley and including a version of the Mummers' Play specially prepared by TH. '"And There Was a Great Calm"', written this month, appears in the Armistice supplement of *The Times*.
16 The war memorial designed by TH for the Dorchester Post Office is unveiled. FEH, but not TH, present.

17   First of two evening performances of *The Return of the Native*, given by the Hardy Players in Dorchester.

28   Reports himself unable to send anything suitable for the periodical the *Dial*, though complimenting the magazine's inquirer, Ezra Pound: 'I am glad to get a letter from such an original thinker on poetry – and *in* poetry, I should add – as yourself: which very few people are nowadays, more's the pity' (*Letters*, VI, 47).

December

Tells an unidentified correspondent this month that he has no philosophy, 'merely what I have often explained to be only a confused heap of impressions, like those of a bewildered child at a conjuring show' (*Letters*, VI, 48).

3   (Fri) Thanks Pound for sending him his *Quia Pauper Amavi* and *Hugh Selwyn Mauberley*.

8   Declines an honorary vice-presidency of the Royal Society of St George.

9   Sends J. M. Murry 'At the Entering of the New Year' for publication in the *Athenaeum*.

13   Chides Alfred Noyes for suggesting that he sees the power behind the universe as an imbecile jester. In the course of a prolonged correspondence explains that he sees the cause behind the universe as without feeling or purpose, rather than as actively malign.

16   Advises Sir Henry Newbolt that it would be impracticable to think of producing the adaptation of *The Return of the Native* anywhere other than in Dorchester.

19   Refuses Ford Madox Ford's invitation to sign a petition about Ireland: 'I was faithful to Ireland for 30 years, but my views of late of that unhappy & senseless country have much changed' (*Letters*, VI, 53).

20   Further defines his beliefs in continued correspondence with Noyes: 'the said Cause is neither moral nor immoral, but *un*moral' (*Letters*, VI, 54).

21   Reports to Edward Clodd that the possession of a telephone 'makes the city seem curiously near us' (*Letters*, VI, 56).

22   Sends Christmas greetings to Florence Henniker. Thanks Eden Phillpotts for sending him his novel *Orphan Dinah*.

23   Thanks J. J. Foster for sending a copy of *Wessex Worthies*. Government of Ireland Act passed.

25 'On Christmas night the carol singers and mummers came to
    Max Gate as they had promised, the latter performing the *Play
    of Saint George,* just as he had seen it performed in his childhood'
    (*Life,* p. 411). The part of Eustacia Vye taken by a young local
    girl, Gertrude Bugler, to whom, FEH notes, TH has already lost
    his heart. 'She was for him, in one respect, the incarnation of the
    ideal daughter he had never had' (Millgate, p. 535).
26 FEH reports to Cockerell, 'He is now – this afternoon – writing
    a poem with great spirit: always a sign of well-being with him.
    Needless to say it is an intensely dismal poem' (*Friends of a
    Lifetime,* p. 307).
31 'At the Entering of the New Year' appears in the *Athenaeum.* 'The
    New Year found Hardy sitting up to hear the bells, which he
    had not done for some time' (*Life,* p. 412).

1921

Writes 'Xenophanes, the Monist of Colophon'.

January
3   (Mon) Sends a letter from Henry Mills Alden, and an apprecia-
    tion of his character, to his widow Ada, as an aid to her bio-
    graphy.
8   Encourages Madeleine Rolland to consider translating certain
    poems into French.
14 Supports the Revd Albert Cock's proposal for a Wessex Univer-
    sity. Thanks Lucien Wolf for sending a copy of his book *The
    Jewish Bogey.*
30 Sends letters from Handley Moule to his biographer, J. B.
    Harford. Congratulates Maurice and Helen Macmillan on the
    birth of a grandchild, Maurice.

February
Publication of J. J. Foster's *Wessex Worthies,* with an introductory note
by TH. Declines to write a preface to a Shakespeare play for a new
Oxford University Press edition.
5   (Sat) Writes unencouragingly to Gosse, having heard about the
    proposal to present TH with his portrait by Jacques-Emile
    Blanche, a portrait favoured by neither TH nor FEH.

7   Congratulates Galsworthy on his novel *In Chancery*, and wishes
     he could see California without having to travel there.
9   Helps Ethel Cowley, wife of the vicar of Stinsford, with the
     inscription on a monument in Stinsford Church. Informs Gosse
     of friends' strong dislike of the Blanche portrait.
23   'At a House in Hampstead' appears in *The John Keats Memorial
     Volume*.

March
14   (Mon) Sends Madeleine Rolland a full list of glosses for dialect
     terms in *Tess*.
18   Sends Pound limited criticism of *Quia Pauper Amavi* and *Hugh
     Selwyn Mauberley*: 'I gather that at least you do not care whether
     the many understand you or not' (*Letters*, vi, 77).
22   Approves Sidney Morgan's scenario for a film of *The Mayor of
     Casterbridge*, given its first showing later in the year.

April
'The Woman I Met' appears in the *London Mercury*.
5   (Tues) In a letter to J. H. Morgan, regrets the coal strike, and the
     Labour Party's support of it.
20   Thanks Lytton Strachey for sending a copy of his *Queen Victoria*,
     congratulating him on his excellent treatment of 'a most un-
     interesting woman' (*Letters*, vi, 84).
21   Thanks St John Ervine for informing him of the wish of a young
     literary group to present TH with a first edition of a Keats
     volume at his next birthday.

May
Writes 'Meditations on a Holiday' (originally dated 'April 21, 1921').
6   (Fri) Thanks Algernon Methuen for dedicating his *Anthology of
     Modern Verse* to TH, and for sending a copy.
11   Visited by J. M. Barrie. Death of Charles Moule, the last survivor
     of Henry Moule's seven sons.
18   Declines J. C. Squire's invitation to make the presentation of the
     Hawthornden Prize in London.
19   Writes a letter of condolence to Dorothy Bosanquet following
     the death of her father, Charles Moule.

June
3   (Fri) Thanks St John Ervine for the gift from the gathering of

young authors (including Graves, Joyce, Sassoon and Virginia Woolf) of a first edition of Keats's *Lamia, Isabella, the Eve of St Agnes, and Other Poems.*

6 Returns the proof of 'The Country Wedding' to Newman Flower.
9 Sees a performance of *The Mellstock Quire* by the Hardy Players in the castle ruins at Sturminster Newton. Afterwards visits his former Sturminster home at Riverside Villa, taking tea with the cast there, and insisting that Gertrude Bugler should sleep in the room in which he wrote *The Return of the Native.*
16 Visited by de la Mare, whom he takes to Stinsford the next day.
23 Permits Sir Henry Newbolt to use several of his poems in an anthology of English verse spanning six centuries.

July
2 (Sat) Reports to Florence Henniker a visit to the filming of *The Mayor* in Dorchester.
6 Refuses de la Mare's invitation to sign a petition against the government's Irish policy, also telling him that he had finished correcting the proof of a 'wretchedly bad poem [thought to be "Barthélémon at Vauxhall"], that nobody wanted me to write nobody wants to read & nobody will remember who reads it' (*Letters*, VI, 95).
21 Offers to assist Ruth Head with a selection from his works.
23 The maligned 'Barthélémon at Vauxhall' appears in *The Times.*
25 Pastes a passage from an article on Stravinksy into his 'Memoranda II' Notebook.

August
'The Two Houses' appears in the *Dial*. Declines an invitation to stay with J. M. Barrie at Stanway, Gloucestershire, FEH reporting that TH 'has discovered this year that he cannot go visiting any more – a person over 81 must stay at home' (*Letters*, VI, 96).
7 (Sun) Draws back from his offer of assistance to Ruth Head, though recommending *Selected Poems* for her verse selections. Also declines to offer suggestions to Ernest Rhys for an Everyman's Library anthology of short stories.
9 Thanks de la Mare for sending him his *Memoirs of a Midget*, on which he also sends congratulations.
29 Asks Sir Frederick Macmillan to suggest a fee for reproduction of two short stories in Ernest Rhys's anthology.

September
Sits for a portrait by W. W. Ouless at the end of this month and the beginning of the next.
1 (Fri) Attends the christening of Caroline Hanbury. 'To C. F. H.' written as a christening-present. TH's willingness to act as a godparent indicative of a greater conformity in matters of social and, more particularly, religious, observance, characteristic of his eighties.
22 Thanks Sassoon for sending a first edition of Rowe's *The Tragedy of Jane Shore*.
24 Refuses Roger Ingpen's invitation to write a sonnet about Shelley: 'I feel unable now to go back all of a sudden to old feelings on that greatest of all our lyrists' (*Letters*, vi, 101).

October
1 (Sat) Offers Harold Child factual help with brief queries regarding his articles on TH's poetry.
6 Agrees to sign an address marking Frederick Harrison's ninetieth birthday.
14 Visited by Masefield, who brings a scale model of a full-rigger ship, subsequently much valued, as a present for TH.
21 Congratulates Newbolt on the judiciousness of his selections from TH's work in his *English Anthology of Prose and Poetry*.
24 Thanks Galsworthy for sending his *To Let*, regretting that the Forsyte chronicles are now concluded.

November
8 (Tues) Tells Sir Frederick Macmillan that he now has enough material for a new volume of poems (later published as *Late Lyrics and Earlier*). Also suggests that *Collected Poems* and *The Dynasts* should be issued on thinner paper, and that both volumes in their present form should receive more publicity in America.
26 Returns the Stinsford parish registers, having transcribed several points of family history from them.

December
'Voices from Things Growing', written earlier this year, appears in the *London Mercury*. 'A December Rain-Scene', later retitled 'An Autumn Rain-Scene', appears in the *Fortnightly Review*.
6 (Tues) The Irish Peace Agreement establishes the Irish Free State, thus ending two years of violent unrest and hostility.

13 Thanks de la Mare for sending his *The Veil, and Other Poems*.
19 Sends a letter of miscellaneous news to Florence Henniker, including views on developments in Ireland and on the latest de la Mare volume: 'They are rather too obscure, I think: but many of them have his own peculiar beauty in them when you get to the bottom of their meaning' (*Letters*, VI, 110).
21 'The Haunting Fingers', later retitled 'Haunting Fingers', appears in the *New Republic*.

1922

January
Confined to bed for some of this month, and still afflicted in the early part of February by miscellaneous complaints, with cancer for a while feared. The 'Apology' to *Late Lyrics and Earlier* conceived during this illness, and intended as a riposte to his critics, as well as a justification of his views. 'An interesting point in this preface was his attitude towards religion. Through the years 1920 to 1925 Hardy was interested in conjectures on rationalizing the English Church . . . When the new Prayer Book appeared, however, his hopes were doomed to disappointment, . . . and from that time he lost all expectation of seeing the Church representative of modern thinking minds' (*Life*, p. 415).
9 (Mon) Thanks Siegfried Sassoon for acknowledging the gift of a privately printed copy of 'Haunting Fingers'.
23 Manuscript of *Late Lyrics and Earlier* sent to Sir Frederick Macmillan.
25 Expresses to Joseph Anthony a wish that 'An Ancient to Ancients' should appear in the April number of *Century Magazine*.
27 Tells J. C. Squire he should have included poems by Charlotte Mew in his *A Book of Women's Verse*, since the quality of her output is far greater than its quantity.

February
15 (Wed) Sends a draft of the 'Apology' to *Late Lyrics and Earlier* to Cockerell for his approval.
18 Thanks Cockerell for his minor amendments, and accepts his offer of help with the proofs.
23 Suggests to Sir Frederick Macmillan six poems from *Late Lyrics and Earlier* which might be given advance serial publication in America.

March

10 (Fri) Sends Cockerell a letter of miscellaneous comments on *Late Lyrics and Earlier*.

15 Accepts an honorary degree of Doctor of Laws from the University of St Andrews, though making clear that he cannot travel to have the degree conferred in person.

19 Thanks Harley Granville-Barker for sending a copy of his *The Exemplary Theatre*.

April

6 (Thurs) Corrected revise of *Late Lyrics and Earlier* sent to the printers.

12 Acknowledges himself a backsliding member of the Society for Pure English in a letter to its founder, Robert Bridges.

May

'The Children and Sir Nameless' appears in *Nash's and Pall Mall Magazine*.

2 (Tues) Thanks Harold Monro for sending his new volume of poems, *Real Property*.

11 Declines an invitation from Newman Flower to a private dinner party at the Savoy Hotel.

21 Acknowledges the arrival of Ruth Head's *Pages from the Works of Thomas Hardy*.

23 Publication of *Late Lyrics and Earlier*. The volume is reprinted twice this year.

24 Asks for complimentary copies of *Late Lyrics and Earlier* to be sent to Lytton Strachey and John Buchan.

26 Visits Stinsford and Higher Bockhampton. 'It was becoming increasingly painful to Hardy to visit this old home of his, and often when he left he said that he would go there no more' (*Life*, p. 415).

29 Explains to Florence Henniker why he has not sent her a copy of the new volume.

31 Thanks T. J. Wise for sending a copy of his catalogue *The Ashley Library*.

June

9 (Fri) Suggests 'The Oxen', 'When I Set Out for Lyonnesse' and 'In Time of "the Breaking of Nations"', for the Library of Little Manuscripts for the Dolls' House at Windsor Castle.

11 Thanks Edmund Blunden for sending *The Shepherd, and Other Poems of Peace and War*.

16 Directs Harold Monro to the 'Apology' to *Late Lyrics and Earlier* if he wishes to find out TH's views on the nature and function of poetry.

22 Discourages Vere H. Collins from publishing a translation of Frank Hedgcock's *Thomas Hardy, penseur et artiste*, largely on account of its biographical method and factual inaccuracies, 'the besetting fault of the writer being to go to the novels for facts in the author's life' (*Letters*, VI, 138).

24 Writes again to Collins saying that he cannot consider translation unless Hedgcock's biographical speculations are omitted.

29 Raises no objection to John Lane's proposed reissue of Lionel Johnson's *The Art of Thomas Hardy*.

July
Entertains several visitors this month, including Florence Henniker, Siegfried Sassoon, Edmund Blunden and E. M. Forster.

2 (Sun) Replies to an assurance from Vere H. Collins that the Hedgcock reprint will omit the offending biographical speculations. Inquires of the Incorporated Society of Authors whether their solicitors would be able to help in the drawing up of a will.

5 Writes to support the Duchess of Hamilton's efforts to ensure more humane methods of animal slaughter. Vere H. Collins writes to announce that he has decided to proceed no further with the Hedgcock translation.

11 Inquires why he has received no royalties from Harper Brothers for their Anniversary Edition of TH's works.

12 Clarifies his objections to Frank Hedgcock's book in a letter direct to the author.

17 Queries the wisdom of J. C. Squire's invitation to him to become Honorary President of the Architecture Club.

19 Sends further suggestions to Princess Marie Louise for the Library of Little Manuscripts.

August
Notes in 'Memoranda II', 'I am convinced that it is better for a writer to know a little bit of the world remarkably well than to know a great part of the world remarkably little' (*Personal Notebooks*, p. 60).

11 (Fri) Death of Judge Benjamin Fosset Lock, an early Dorchester

friend, commemorated in the subsequently written poem 'Nothing Matters Much'.

16   Declines to be interviewed by a young thesis-writer, asserting that such works 'should be based on published works alone of course' (*Letters*, VI, 151).

25   FEH reports to Cockerell that the *Life* is now finished 'so far as is possible' (Millgate, p. 544).

27   An article by FEH in the *Weekly Dispatch* comments on the happiness women can find in devotion to others. Her own devotion to TH, however, is increasingly tested.

September

11   (Mon) Takes a drive with Newman Flower and his family, accompanying Flower to the top of High Stoy.

17   Sends Samuel Chew an extensive list of corrections for the new edition of *Thomas Hardy: Poet and Novelist*.

18   Sends overdue annual subscription to the English Association.

25   Declines Stanley Galpin's invitation to express an opinion on the works of Dickens.

27   Suggests to Dorothy Allhusen the Tate and Brady version of Psalm 106, sung to the tune Wilton, as a hymn for use at her daughter's wedding.

October

Brief biographical notice of Horace Moule appears in the *London Mercury*.

12   (Thurs) Informs J. H. Morgan of some of the sources used for *The Dynasts*.

20   Sends Lady Grove comments on the reception of *Late Lyrics and Earlier*.

23   Bonar Law forms a Conservative ministry following the fall of Lloyd George's coalition.

25   Offers help with suggesting locations for the Goldwyn Pictures version of *Tess*.

28   Pleased to hear of Sir Frederick Macmillan's decision to print a new edition of the *Collected Poems* and also a thin-paper edition. 'The Later Autumn' (written in 1921) appears in the *Saturday Review*.

November

Marie Stopes begins actively to advocate birth control.

4   (Sat) Congratulates Robert Bridges on his publicised opposition
    to 'the woeful fogs of free verse worship' (*Letters*, VI, 165). An
    extract from Bridges' article on free verse in the *London Mercury*
    is pasted into the 'Memoranda II' Notebook.
11 Declines Lucy Clifford's invitation to write a preface for the
    reissue of her first novel, *Mrs Keith's Crime*.
14 Accepts with pleasure a proposal for his election to an honorary
    fellowship of Queen's College, Oxford.
15 Votes against Labour in the municipal election. First perform-
    ance, in Dorchester, by the Hardy Players, of T. H. Tilley's
    dramatisation of *Desperate Remedies*.
22 Asks Sir Frederick Macmillan for advice on what to do with
    requests to sign copies of his work.
27 'E's death-day, ten years ago. Went with F. and tidied her tomb
    and carried flowers for her and the other two tombs' (*Life*, p. 418).
    TH's steadfast commemoration of anniversaries connected with
    ELH, so often forgotten in her lifetime, begins to become a
    burden to FEH.
28 Asks to see proofs of the *Late Lyrics and Earlier* section of the new
    edition of *Collected Poems*.
29 Suggests to the Mayor of Dorchester that a pavement be built
    along the Wareham Road into Dorchester, as part of a scheme
    for finding useful labour for the unemployed.

December
30 (Sat) Agrees to serve as a governor of the Dorchester Grammar
    School for a further term of three years.
31 Writes 'The Absolute Explains'.

1923

January
6   (Sat) Writes 'On the Portrait of a Woman about to be Hanged'
    (Edith Jessie Thompson, hanged at Holloway on the 9th).
8   Thanks Hamo Thornycroft for sending a photograph of the
    proposed redevelopment of the Charing Cross area, giving re-
    collections of his years there.
10 Agrees to Sir Frederick Macmillan's suggestion for a cheap
    edition of four TH novels for the Indian market, and asks him to

send no further review copies to the *Spectator*, its reviews of TH's works having become so unfavourable.

11 Sends 'On the Portrait of a Woman about to be Hanged' to the *London Mercury*, partly as a protest against the recent execution of Edith Jessie Thompson.

17 Sends Harold Monro 'The Church and the Wedding' for the *Chapbook*.

21 Commiserates with Austin Harrison on the death of his father, Frederic Harrison, and with J. M. Murry on the death of his wife, the writer Katherine Mansfield.

24 Sends Harold Monro a revision for 'The Church and the Wedding'.

February

Sends 'The Faithful Swallow' to Queen's College, Oxford, for a (never-produced) *Miscellany*. 'On the Portrait of a Woman about to be Hanged' appears in the *London Mercury*.

9 (Fri) Declines an invitation from Ernest Rhys for one of his novels to appear in the Everyman series.

12 Congratulates the Revd E. J. Bodington on the literary part of a recent lecture about TH, but criticises the biographical content.

22 Returns proof for 'The Church and the Wedding', with another correction.

26 Copies into the 'Memoranda II' Notebook an old note: 'A story (rather than a poem) might be written in the first person, in which "I" am supposed to live through the centuries, in my ancestors, as one person, the particular line of descent chosen being that in which *qualities* are continuous' (*Personal Notebooks*, p. 69).

March

'The Church and the Wedding' appears in the *Chapbook*.

7 (Wed) Sends an appreciative letter of criticism to Amy Lowell.

22 Thanks St John Ervine for sending his book *Some Impressions of My Elders*.

25 Thanks H. G. Wells admiringly for his *Men like Gods*: 'I don't know at all how you can manage to keep so fresh, & at such a high level, so continuously' (*Letters*, VI, 1 $\ulcorner\urcorner$).

April

Finishes rough draft of *The Famous Tragedy of the Queen of Cornwall*. First meeting with T. E. Lawrence.

3   (Tues) Advises Masefield on the desirability of collected editions of an author's work.

4   Death of Florence Henniker: 'the empty place she left in the ranks of Hardy's trusted friends and comfortable correspondents was never to be filled' (Millgate, p. 547).

May

20   (Sun) Informs Virginia Woolf that he will not be able to contribute to the *Nation and Athenaeum*, which her husband has just begun to edit.

June

3   (Sun) Visited by the Granville-Barkers and Beerbohms.

7   Asks Macleod Yearsley if he would examine a gland on FEH's neck and give an opinion on the desirability of an operation.

10   'Relativity. That things and events always were, are, and will be (*e.g.* Emma, Mother and Father are living still in the past)' (*Life*, p. 419).

16   Thanks J. C. Squire for sending *American Poems and Others*, a volume dedicated to TH.

21   Visits the battleship *Queen Elizabeth* off Portland.

24   Asks if they might call in on Masefield on a visit to Oxford.

25   Leave for a two-night visit to Queen's College, Oxford, the last time TH sleeps away from Max Gate. Stops made *en route* at Salisbury and at Fawley, Berkshire: 'Here some of Hardy's ancestors were buried, and he searched fruitlessly for their graves in the little churchyard' (*Life*, p. 420). The *Life* gives an account of the Oxford visit by Godfrey Elton, and concludes, 'This occasion was an outstanding one during the last years of his life' (p. 422).

July

2   (Mon) The British Matrimonial Causes Act gives women equality in divorce suits.

9   Thanks Harley Granville-Barker for his thorough comments on *The Queen of Cornwall*.

18   Advises his sister Kate on good vantage points for the Prince of Wales's visit to Dorchester and Max Gate.

20   Entertains the Prince of Wales at Max Gate: 'the main characteristic of the visit was its easy informality' (*Life*, p. 422).

August

11   (Sat) Visited at Max Gate by the American novelist Hamlin Garland.

22   Visited by H. G. Wells and Rebecca West.

25   Grants Clive Holland permission to take photos at Max Gate, but declines any form of press interview.

27   Thanks Ernest Brennecke for sending the typescript of his *Thomas Hardy's Universe: A Study of a Poet's Mind*, but declines to comment on it or to grant an interview for any practical purpose.

30   Sends Sir Frederick Macmillan the manuscript of *The Queen of Cornwall*.

September

10   (Mon) Approves specimen pages of *The Queen of Cornwall*, and agrees to the drawing-up of a new consolidated agreement with Macmillan.

21   Meets Augustus John, who paints TH's portrait later this autumn.

22   Asks Sir Frederick Macmillan to confirm that there is no immediate chance of his family relinquishing control of their publishing-business, and returns the consolidated agreement with a few minor alterations.

23   Death of Lord Morley.

October

2   (Tues) Returns proofs of *The Queen of Cornwall* to Macmillan.

4   Approves proofs of the drawings and a dummy volume of *The Queen of Cornwall*.

18   Declines Ford Madox Ford's invitation to contribute to the *Transatlantic Review*.

November

'The Missed Train' appears in the *Owl*.

8   (Thurs) Writes 'The Best She Could'.

11   Sends Harold Child a detailed letter about *The Queen of Cornwall*, inviting him to attend a rehearsal or performance.

12   Agrees with Clodd on the indispensability of people meeting together at least once a week in the cause of some religion.

15   *The Queen of Cornwall* published by Macmillan. TH congratulates Sir Frederick Macmillan on the appearance of the volume.

17   Thanks Alfred Noyes for his review of *The Queen of Cornwall*,

'53 years in contemplation, 800 lines in result, alas!' (*Letters*, VI, 224).

28 First performance, by the Hardy Players, of *The Queen of Cornwall*. 'Naturally a poetic drama did not make a wide appeal. However, the performance, and particularly the rehearsals, gave Hardy considerable pleasure' (*Life*, p. 423).

December

7 (Fri) Death of Sir Frederick Treves. 'Because of the early association and the love which they both bore to the county, there was a strong link between these two Dorset men' (*Life*, p. 423).

9 Sends Cockerell a letter received from Swinburne about *Jude*.

30 George Bernard Shaw and T. E. Lawrence lunch at Max Gate.

1924

Writes 'A Popular Personage at Home'.

January

2 (Wed) Attends the funeral of Sir Frederick Treves, and burial of his ashes.

3 Thanks Charlotte Mew for her acknowledgement of his part in securing her a Civil List pension.

5 'In the Evening', written in memory of Sir Frederick Treves, appears in *The Times*.

9 Photograph of Augustus John's portrait of TH appears in *The Times*, on the occasion of its presentation to the Fitzwilliam Museum.

13 Sends George Dewar 'Xenophanes, the Monist of Colophon' for publication in the *Nineteenth Century and After*.

22 Writes 'Compassion' for the Royal Society for the Prevention of Cruelty to Animals.

24 Ramsay MacDonald forms the first Labour Government.

27 Thanks St John Ervine for the gift of *The Lady of Belmont*.

February

4 (Mon) The composer Rutland Boughton visits Max Gate, TH subsequently claiming to like him more than any person he has ever met, though never approving of his Communist sympathies.

12   Seeks Sir Frederick Macmillan's permission for Boughton to make a music drama based on *The Queen of Cornwall*, and welcomes Macmillan's decision to bring out a pocket edition of *The Dynasts*, with *The Queen of Cornwall* added at the back.
15   Advises John Drinkwater on the possibility of bringing out a selection of Barnes's poetry.
20   Sends Sir Frederick Macmillan revised copy for the pocket edition of *The Queen of Cornwall*.
23   Thanks Eden Phillpotts for sending a copy of his novel *Cheat-the-boys*.

March
'Xenophanes, the Monist of Colophon' appears in the *Nineteenth Century and After*. Sends to Macmillan 'The Son's Portrait'.
 8   (Sat) Asks George Macmillan to allow C. W. Faulkner and Co. to use 'The Oxen' for a Christmas card.
20   Tells Sir Frederick Macmillan that he has a further accumulation of poems – though not yet enough for a volume – and asks him to arrange publication for some of them in American magazines.
23   Sends Sir Frederick Macmillan seven poems which might be so used.
28   Thanks J. M. Murry for his defence of TH and attack on George Moore in a recent review, making no secret of his dislike for Moore: 'Somebody once called him a putrid literary hermaphrodite, which I thought funny, but it may have been an exaggeration' (*Letters*, vi, 243).

April
 5   (Sat) Sends 'Compassion' to the RSPCA for use in its centenary celebrations.
26   FEH unable to persuade TH to read *Wuthering Heights*, which he claims never to have read in full because of what he considers its unrelieved ugliness.

May
 6   (Tues) Responds to queries from Rutland Boughton.
12   Specifies ways in which he is happy for his works to be used in raising money for the Dorset County Nursing Association.

June

2 (Mon) 'Among the many letters which arrived on . . . the 84th anniversary of his birth, was one from a son of the Baptist minister, Mr. Perkins, whom, in his youth, Hardy had so respected. . . . More than sixty years had elapsed since Hardy had had any contact with this friend of his youth, and for a little while he was strongly tempted to get into touch with him again. However, too wide a gulf lay between and, as might have been told in one of his poems, the gesture was never made and the days slipped on into oblivion' (*Life*, p. 424).

3 Thanks J. C. Squire for his broadcast birthday lecture 'An Appreciation of the Life and Work of Thomas Hardy'.

6 Thanks Virginia Woolf for sending a copy of Leslie Stephen's *Some Early Impressions*.

16 'Compassion' appears in *The Times*. 'Although not one of his most successful efforts, as he was never happy when writing to order, it served to demonstrate the poet's passionate hatred of injustice and barbarity' (*Life*, p. 425).

17 Accepts an offer from the Balliol Players, an Oxford University dramatic group, to present an abridgement in translation of the *Oresteia* in the garden at Max Gate.

19 Acknowledges birthday greetings from the Revd William Perkins.

21 Sends Ernest Brennecke a delayed critique of his book, suggesting that the influence of Schopenhauer has been exaggerated, and that of Darwin, Huxley, Spencer, Comte, Hume and Mill undervalued.

27 Agrees to sign a letter to *The Times* proposing that a memorial to Byron should be set up in Westminster Abbey to mark the centenary of his death. The Dean of Westminster's subsequent rejection prompts the poem 'A Refusal'.

July

1 (Tues) The Balliol Players perform their version of *The Oresteia* on the lawn at Max Gate.

5 Sends C. E. S. Chambers 'A Bird-Scene at a Rural Dwelling' as a contribution to *Chambers's Journal* intended to mark the diamond jubilee of TH's first appearance in the magazine.

12 Thanks Sir Frederick Macmillan for sending a copy of his *The Net Book Agreement*.

August
Sits for a bust by Serge Youriévitch. Writes 'A Refusal'.
3   (Sun) Sympathises with Sir Sidney Colvin on the death of his
     wife. Death of Conrad.
6   Entertain Sassoon and T. E. Lawrence to tea. The typescript of
     the *Life* originally commented, 'Hardy was devoted to this world-
     famous soldier, and their not infrequent meetings during the
     last few years of Hardy's life were a source of great interest to
     both' (*Personal Notebooks*, pp. 279–80).
24 States the terms on which he will allow the Hardy Players to
     stage his adaptation of *Tess*.
28 Attend a performance of Boughton's *The Queen of Cornwall* at the
     Glastonbury Festival.

September
6   (Sat) Tells Sir Frederick Macmillan that 'The Midnight Revel' is
     available to be offered as a Christmas poem to an American
     magazine.
12 Waives any fee for the Glastonbury presentation of *The Queen of
     Cornwall*.
17 FEH is advised by a surgeon to have a potentially cancerous
     lump removed from her neck.
19 Thanks Sir Frederick Macmillan for presenting the year's
     royalty accounts.
24 Accepts John Drinkwater's proposal that his next volume of
     verse, *From an Unknown Isle*, should be dedicated to him.
25 Suggests modified terms to Boughton. Thanks Lady Ottoline
     Morrell for sending a photo of TH taken on a recent visit to
     Max Gate.
27 Reports to A. C. Benson, 'I am close to the spots of my childish
     memories (though far from my middle-age scenes), & I revive
     them very often by going to "a slope of green access" about a
     mile from here, finding no pain in so doing' (*Letters*, VI, 276).
30 FEH undergoes a cancer operation.

October
1   (Wed) Offers J. C. Squire either or both of 'Waiting Both' and
     'An East-End Curate' for the *London Mercury*.
3   Advises Hermann Lea to accept Macmillan's idea of producing
     Thomas Hardy's Wessex in a smaller format.

5   Sends a letter of domestic news to FEH.

6   Confirms in a letter to FEH that Henry Hardy will collect her from London by car.

9   FEH's arrival at Max Gate, after worrying delays, occasions the poem 'Nobody Comes'.

15 Congratulates J. B. Priestley on his *Figures in Modern Literature*.

22 Declines to write an article on Conrad for the *Nouvelle revue française*.

28 Two-volume pocket edition of *The Dynasts* with *The Queen of Cornwall* published.

29 General Election, resulting in a large majority for the Conservative Party.

November

'The Last Leaf' appears in *Nash's and Pall Mall Magazine*, and 'Waiting Both' and 'An East-End Curate' appear in the *London Mercury*.

2   (Sun) Sends Sybil Thorndike a copy of the dramatisation of *Tess* to study, inviting her husband Hugh Casson to come to see one of the Dorchester performances.

13 Invites Harold Child to attend a dress rehearsal of *Tess*.

18 Agrees to let Masefield stage *The Queen of Cornwall* in the theatre in the grounds of his house at Boar's Hill, Oxford, but regrets that he cannot attend a performance: 'alas, I am getting to be a mere vegetable in point of immobility' (*Letters*, VI, 287).

26 First performance, in Dorchester, of *Tess*. TH's affection for Gertrude Bugler by now the cause of local gossip.

29 Tells Sir Johnston Forbes-Robertson that the first claim for acting Tess on the London stage must be Gertrude Bugler's, and the second Sybil Thorndike's: thereafter, Sir Johnston's wife might be able to claim the part. Informs Sir Frederick Macmillan that he does not wish the dramatisation of *Tess* published.

December

'The Midnight Revel', later retitled 'The Paphian Ball' appears in *McCall's Magazine*; 'The Portrait', later retitled 'Family Portraits', appears in *Nash's and Pall Mall Magazine*.

1   (Mon) Thanks J. H. Morgan for sending his *John, Viscount Morley*, also including his own condemnation of the religious views of Gladstone.

2   Sends Gertrude Bugler a manuscript chant in addition to two presentation copies of his novels.

3   Asks Harley Granville-Barker to come to see a performance of
    Tess in Weymouth, in order to advise on whether the play
    would need adaptation for Sybil Thorndike.
4   Agrees to Sir Frederick Macmillan's suggestion that there should
    be an illustrated edition of *Tess*, also suggesting that the artist
    should come to see Gertrude Bugler take the title part in Wey-
    mouth, since she is 'the very incarnation of her' (*Letters*, VI, 292).
6   'Winter Night in Woodland' appears in *Country Life* and 'A Bird-
    Scene at a Rural Dwelling' in *Chambers's Journal*.
9   Sends Harold Child a list of his works for the stage and other
    bibliographical amendments for the new edition of Child's
    Thomas Hardy.
11 Attends both performances of *Tess* in Weymouth, helpfully
    slipping a wedding-ring onto Gertrude Bugler's finger just be-
    fore the marriage scene.
13 Tells the theatrical manager Frederick Harrison that for Gertrude
    Bugler to take part in London matinee performances is unlikely
    to offend Sybil Thorndike, whose interest in playing Tess has
    not been confirmed.
16 In affectionate terms, communicates to Gertrude Bugler the
    substance of his letter to Harrison.
19 Asks J. M. Barrie to advise what terms author and principal
    lady should expect of Harrison.
24 Thanks J. W. Mackail for sending a lecture on *The Pilgrim's
    Progress*, adding recollections of the extraordinary effect that
    the book had on him in childhood.
25 Writes 'Christmas: 1924' around this date.
26 Thanks A. C. Benson for sending his *Selected Poems*.
31 'Sat up and heard Big Ben and the London church bells by
    wireless ring in the New Year' (*Life*, p. 427).

1925

Writes 'The Lady in the Furs' and 'A Placid Man's Epitaph'.

January
'Vagrant's Song' appears in *Nash's and Pall Mall Magazine*.
6   (Tues) Tells the theatrical agents Curtis Brown that he is not
    eager to see *Tess* acted on the professional stage.

9   Turns down the performance fee offered by Masefield for putting on *The Queen of Cornwall*.
10 Cockerell, arriving at Max Gate, detects a new atmosphere of strain caused by TH's continuing infatuation with Gertrude Bugler.
12 Fails to acknowledge FEH's birthday.
23 Tells the theatrical agent R. Golding Bright that *The Queen of Cornwall* is available for stage performance and film production.

February
'The Absolute Explains' appears in the *Nineteenth Century and After*.
1   (Sun) Makes arrangements for receiving the French journalist Frédéric Lefèvre at Max Gate.
3   Gives permission for St John Ervine to make his own dramatisation of *Tess* if he wishes.
4   Declines, on account of failing eyesight, J. C. Squire's invitation to him to be one of the judges for a new literary prize.
7   Writes to Gertrude Bugler having heard of her decision not to act the part of Tess in London, the result of a private and deeply felt intervention by FEH. Writes to sympathise with Annie Lane following the death of her husband John Lane.
9   Sends St John Ervine the text of the *Tess* dramatisation.
19 Tells St John Ervine that he has decided against major revisions of his dramatisation of *Tess*, rendering further help from Ervine superfluous.
28 'No Bell-Ringing' privately published by FEH in a limited edition.

March
6   (Fri) Thanks Amy Lowell for sending a copy of her *John Keats*, praising the book's skill and industry.
21 Sends Sir George Forrest a description of Anne Loveday from *The Trumpet-Major*, confirming that it was written with Anne Procter in mind.
23 The University of Bristol offers TH an honorary degree.

April
1   (Wed) Advises the publisher C. Borlase Childs not to accept Ernest Brennecke's *The Life of Thomas Hardy*, which has recently appeared in the United States.

4   Seeks help from Sir Frederick Macmillan in ensuring that
     Brennecke's book does not find an English publisher.
15   Congratulates Sassoon on his *Lingual Exercises for Advanced
     Vocabularians*, terming it an advance on Sassoon's previous
     poetry.
18   Perturbed by the behaviour of his dog Wessex towards the
     secretary of the Society of Dorset Men in London, William
     Watkins. Watkins dies hours afterwards.
26   Tells the Duchess of Hamilton that he thinks all animal-protec-
     tion societies should make it their object to campaign for public
     slaughterhouses.

May
'Freed the Fret of Thinking' appears in the *Adelphi*.
5   (Tues) Writes to sympathise with Dorothy Allhusen following
     the death of her husband, remarking, 'I am losing nearly all my
     friends' (*Letters*, vi, 324).
14   Death of Rider Haggard.
26   *The Times* publishes a letter suggesting a Thomas Hardy Chair
     of Literature at a Wessex University.
27   Agrees to receive a deputation from the University of Bristol to
     present him with an honorary degree.

June
'Circus-Rider to Ringmaster' appears in *Harper's Monthly Magazine*.
1   (Mon) Thanks John Drinkwater for his recently published poem
     'To Thomas Hardy'.
12   Tells R. Golding Bright that he is withdrawing the dramatisa-
     tion of *Tess* from offer to theatrical agents, at any rate for the
     time being.
13   'Coming Up Oxford Street: Evening' appears in the *Nation and
     Athenaeum*.

July
15   (Wed) Deputation from Bristol University confers an honorary
     degree on TH at Max Gate.
21   Sends Philip Ridgeway, anxious to produce *Tess* at a London
     theatre, four desirable characteristics of any actress selected to
     play Tess.
23   Tells R. Golding Bright that he has decided to let Ridgeway

produce the play, asks Harold Child whether he might be able to review it, and sends Ridgeway suggestions for casting. Tells George Macmillan that he now has enough material for another volume of poems.

29   Manuscript of the new volume, at this stage titled *Poems Imaginative and Incidental*, sent off to Macmillan.

August

'The Turnip-Hoer' appears in *Cassell's Magazine*.

3   (Mon) Suggests to Ridgeway that he might invite Gertude Bugler to play Tess.
18   Agrees to see Ridgeway and some members of the cast on 23 August.
20   FEH takes steps to ensure that there will be no more Hardy plays in Dorchester.
25   Tells Sir Frederick Macmillan that he would like *Poems Imaginative and Incidental* to be retitled *Human Shows, Far Phantasies, Songs, and Trifles*, a suggestion to which Macmillan agrees.

September

'Epitaph on a Pessimist' and 'Cynic's Epitaph' appear in the *London Mercury*. 'A Popular Personage at Home' appears in the *Flying Carpet*.

7   (Mon) First performance of *Tess* at the Barnes Theatre.
10   Encourages the transference of *Tess* to a West End theatre.
12   Forwards the remainder of the *Human Shows* proofs to Cockerell for correction.
13   Thanks St John Ervine for his generous review of *Tess*, also sending him a handwritten copy of the poem 'Donaghadee'.
21   Agrees to allow *John o' London's Weekly* to run a second serialisation of *Tess*, with a fee of £1000, one third to be payable to Macmillan.
25   Sends the Mayor of Dudley an inscription for the town war memorial.
26   Thanks Sir Frederick Macmillan for sending the royalty accounts up to 30 June, the total being just over £4,400 for the year.
28   Thanks Cockerell for his comments on and attention to the proofs of *Human Shows*, remarking, 'I don't expect much from it: indeed I am weary of my own writing, & imagine other people are too by this time' (*Letters*, VI, 359).

October
8 (Thurs) Sends Sir Frederick Macmillan corrections for the Wessex Edition volume containing *Late Lyrics and Earlier* and *The Queen of Cornwall*.
17 Approves minor alterations to the dramatisation of *Tess* suggested by the leading lady of the Barnes production, Gwen Ffrangcon-Davies.
20 Thanks Granville-Barker for sending generous observations on the Barnes production of *Tess*, though doubting whether the 'gentler and more clinging quality given to the character by Miss F. D. . . . is consistent with the smouldering ancestral fire in Tess's nature that broke out in the murder' (*Letters*, VI, 362).
30 Thanks Herbert Grimsditch for sending his *Character and Environment in the Novels of Thomas Hardy*, though suggesting that attention might better have been given to the poems.

November
'A Leader of Fashion' appears in the *Adelphi*.
2 (Mon) *Tess* transfers to the Garrick Theatre.
7 Congratulates the *Saturday Review* on its seventieth anniversary, claiming to have purchased the *Review* since the age of two, and hence to be among its earliest readers living.
20 *Human Shows, Far Phantasies, Songs and Trifles* published. First printing almost immediately sold out, and corrections immediately sent by TH for a second. Tells R. Golding Bright that he and Macmillan would be prepared to allow a film version of 'Romantic Adventures of a Milkmaid' (never in fact produced).

December
6 (Sun) Private performance of *Tess* given at Max Gate.
9 Sends the printers, R. & R. Clarke, two further minor corrections for *Human Shows*.
19 Tells Harley Granville-Barker that he feels that *The Madras House* would have been better cast as a novel. Death of Sir Hamo Thornycroft.
31 Asks not to be reconsidered for election as a governor of Dorchester Grammar School.

1926

Rewrites 'A Philosophical Fantasy' and 'Christmas in the Elgin Room'.

January

4 (Mon) Approves Vivien Gribble's illustrations for a new limited edition of *Tess*, and signifies his intention of adding a footnote to the 'Apology' to *Late Lyrics and Earlier* when it appears in the Wessex Edition.

9 Dissuades Sir Frederick Macmillan from publishing a revised edition of F. O. Saxelby's *A Thomas Hardy Dictionary*, giving his low opinion of the book.

20 Thanks Lady Pinney for sending details about Martha Browne, recalling her public execution: 'I remember what a fine figure she showed against the sky as she hung in the misty rain, & how the tight black silk gown set off her shape as she wheeled half-round & back' (*Letters*, VII, 5).

February

16 (Tues) Declines to become a patron of the Westminster Abbey Special Choir.

23 Advises the vicar of Stinsford, the Revd H. G. B. Cowley, on the restoration of the church bells, offering to make a financial contribution towards any expense incurred.

24 Explains to Sir Frederick Macmillan the meaning of the phrase 'green malt in floor' in *Tess*.

27 Sends H. G. B. Cowley information on similarities between 'Mellstock' and Stinsford, for use in the church appeal.

March

1 (Mon) Agrees to support an application for a memorial to Blake in St Paul's Cathedral. Thanks J. C. Squire for sending him his *Poems in One Volume*, and specifies his favourites in it.

2 Agrees to a Czech translation of *Tess*.

14 'The Newspaper Soliloquizes', later retitled 'The Aged Newspaper Soloquizes', appears in the *Observer*.

21 Thanks T. J. Wise for sending the latest volume of his catalogue of the Ashley Library.

April

3 (Sat) Thanks Sir Frederick Macmillan for sending good news of sales of the signed limited edition of *Tess*, and suggests that the proposed similar edition of *The Dynasts* should also be illustrated.

13 Returns the approved text of the Stinsford bell appeal.

16 Gracefully declines to give Marie Stopes an opinion on the

censor's refusal of her play *Vectia*, though criticising the play's improbability: 'I cannot conceive a young woman not an imbecile who has been married three years being in such crass ignorance of physiology, especially with a young man just through the party-wall ready to teach her' (*Letters*, VI, 16–17).

18 FEH reports to Maurice Macmillan that TH is revising the *Life*: 'This may be wise, or the reverse. However, he is greatly interested' (Millgate, p. 561).

19 Sends a portrait of himself by Strang to Queen's College, Oxford.

22 Thanks Theodore Maynard for sending an article about TH's poetry, and comments, 'you may discover as you get older that the harshness you say you notice in some of his poems is deliberate, as a reaction from the smooth alliterations of the Victorian poets' (*Letters*, VI, 18).

24 Answers a query from General J. H. Morgan about the source for 'The Peasant's Confession'.

27 In a letter to Roy McKay, recommends abridgement of the creeds and other parts of the liturgy.

May
3 (Mon) Beginning of the ten-day General Strike.
7 Sends Dorothy Allhusen several quotations which might serve as epitaphs for her recently deceased daughter.
22 In a letter to Arthur Hind, indulges in humorous obfuscation regarding the original of 'Little Hintock'.

June
2 (Wed) 'He Never Expected Much' written at about this date.
3 Asks the Curator of the Dorset County Museum to caution the porter against making any statements about TH's personality to reporters. Also annoyed at this time by an article by Robert Thurston Hopkins in the *Westminster Gazette*, over which he takes legal action.
19 Answers a query about his attendance at King's College, London, from the current Principal.
22 First performance, at Keble College, Oxford, of a version of *The Three Wayfarers* revised by TH.
24 Sends Daniel Macmillan corrections 'of a very trifling kind' for *The Dynasts* (*Letters*, VII, 31).

29 Receive the Balliol Players to perform *Hippolytus* on the Max Gate lawn.

July
3 (Sat) Resigns from the committee of the Dorset County Library, suggesting, successfully, that FEH should take his place.
5 Sketched by Alfred Aaran Wolmark.
9 Authorises Rutland Boughton to proceed with separate publication of songs from *The Queen of Cornwall*.
15 Asks Sir Frederick Macmillan to arrange terms for the reserialisation of *The Mayor* in *John o' London's Weekly*.

August
8 (Sun) Thanks J. B. Priestley for sending a copy of his *George Meredith*, pronouncing himself 'much interested in the bright writing of one in whom I had already fancied I discerned a coming force in letters' (*Letters*, VII, 38).
29 Thanks Galsworthy for sending his novel *The Silver Spoon*, which he subsequently acknowledges as 'One of the very best you have done' (*Letters*, VII, 42).

September
5 (Sun) Thanks H. G. Wells for sending a copy of a limited signed issue of *The World of William Clissold*.
8 John Drinkwater's dramatisation of *The Mayor* opens at the Barnes Theatre.
9 Authorises St John Ervine to begin a dramatisation of *Jude*.
20 *The Mayor* given an afternoon performance at Weymouth to enable TH to see it. Considerable ovation.

October
Acknowledges a legacy of £30 from the writer William Stebbing.

November
'During this month . . . his friend Colonel T. E. Lawrence called to say good-bye, before starting for India. Hardy was much affected by this parting, as T. E. Lawrence was one of his most valued friends' (*Life*, p. 434). Lawrence's *Seven Pillars of Wisdom* appears this year.
1 (Mon) '"Went with Mr. Hanbury to Bockhampton and looked at fencing, trees, etc., with a view to tidying and secluding the Hardy house."

'That was his last visit to the place of his birth. It was always a matter of regret to him if he saw this abode in a state of neglect, or the garden uncherished' (*Life*, p. 433).

10   Asks Sir Frederick Macmillan to ensure that revisions and additions to the Wessex Edition prefaces are added to the Uniform and Pocket Editions.

23   Declines an invitation to a dinner at King's College, London: 'I am getting more and more every year like a vegetable that will not bear transplanting' (*Letters*, VII, 50).

December
2   (Thurs) Authorises a Czech translation of *Jude*.
4   'The Lady in the Christmas Furs', later retitled 'The Lady in the Furs', appears in the *Saturday Review*.
5   Death of Monet.
23   Welcomes carol-singers to Max Gate.
27   Wessex put to sleep after thirteen years at Max Gate. 'Faithful. Unflinching' inscribed on his gravestone in the Max Gate pets' cemetery – though the dog was perhaps more unflinching in his approach to many guests and postmen than several such visitors would have wished. The poem 'Dead "Wessex" the Dog to the Household' expresses TH's considerable sense of loss, whilst FEH comments to Cockerell, 'Of course he was merely a dog, and not a good dog always, but *thousands* (actually thousands) of afternoons and evenings I would have been alone but for him, and had always him to speak to' (*Friends of a Lifetime*, p. 314).

1927

Writes 'He Resolves to Say No More'.

January
'A Philosophical Fantasy' appears in the *Fortnightly Review*. 'Hardy liked the year to open with a poem of this type from him in some leading review or newspaper' (*Life*, p. 436).
29   (Sat) Thanks Sir Frederick Macmillan for sending a royalty cheque for over £5000.

February

18 (Fri) Suggests to Sir Frederick Macmillan that his *Selected Poems* should be brought up to date by the inclusion of some more recently published poems.

24 Congratulates Newman Flower on acquiring the publishing-house of Cassell.

March

24 (Thurs) Asks Sir Frederick Macmillan to send a copy of *The Dynasts* to a German critic intending a study of TH's novels, in order to increase knowledge of the work in Germany.

April

15 (Fri) Writes 'Unkept Good Fridays'.

May

8 (Sun) Asks to add an additional quotation, from *Aeneid* VI, to the title page of *The Dynasts*.

13 'Black Friday', with collapse of the German economy.

20 Gives Sotheby's permission to auction a letter to Geneviève Smith, though expressing surprise at the proposal.

June

2 (Thurs) TH's eighty-seventh birthday. Visit the Granville-Barkers in Devonshire for part of the day. 'At the end of the day he seemed in a sad mood, and his wife sought to amuse him by a forecast of small festivities she had planned for his ninetieth birthday, which she assured him would be a great occasion. With a flash of gaiety he replied that he intended to spend that day in bed' (*Life*, p. 437).

July

6 (Wed) The Balliol Players perform *Iphigenia in Aulis* on the Max Gate lawn.

16 Agrees to put his mind to a reminiscence of George Meredith.

21 Lays the foundation stone of the new Dorchester Grammar School. Speech subsequently printed in the *Dorset County Chronicle* and *The Times* (also in *Life*, pp. 437–9).

August

Writes 'Seeing the Moon Rise'. Visit Bath. 'Hardy walked about and

looked long and silently at various places that seemed to have an interest for him. He seemed like a ghost revisiting scenes of a long-dead past (*Life*, p. 440).
6   (Sat) Accepts the dedication of Holst's *Egdon Heath* and invites him to call for lunch.
9   Visited by Holst, with whom they drive to Puddletown.
25   'Yuletide in a Younger World' appears as the first of the *Ariel Poems*.

September
Prepares a new edition of *Selected Poems*, entitled *Chosen Poems*.

Poems
21   (Wed) Suggests to Louis Untermeyer poems which might be included in a revised version of his *Modern British Poetry*.
27   Agrees to Sir Frederick Macmillan's suggestion for a one-volume edition of the short stories. Makes his last entry in the 'Memoranda II' Notebook.
29   Congratulates Edmund Gosse on his recovery from typhoid.

October
12   (Wed) Informs W. M. Meredith that he has finished the reminiscence of his father, and regrets that it is not of a higher quality.

November
4   (Fri) Visits the family graves at Stinsford, and his brother's house at Talbothays, the last of a series of regular weekend visits to his family extending back over forty years.
17   Thinking and speaking a great deal about H. R. Bastow, but does not agree to FEH's suggestion for trying to get back in contact with him.
21   'G. M.: A Reminiscence' privately printed by FEH, anticipating its appearance in the *Nineteenth Century and After*, February 1928.
27   'The fifteenth anniversary of the death of Emma Lavinia Hardy; Thursday was the anniversary of the death of Mary, his elder sister. For two or three days he has been wearing a black hat as a token of mourning, and carries a black walking-stick that belonged to his first wife, all strangely moving' (*Life*, pp. 443–4). Writing for much of the day, and working on the poem 'An Unkindly May'.
28   'Speaking about ambition T. said to-day that he had done all

that he meant to do, but he did not know whether it had been worth doing.

'His only ambition, so far as he could remember, was to have some poem or poems in a good anthology like the Golden Treasury' (*Life*, p. 444).

30   Reports himself reading with interest Granville-Barker's Preface to *King Lear*.

December
Sends 'A Gentleman's Second-Hand Suit' to Harper Brothers.

3   (Sat) Clarifies for Sir Frederick Macmillan negotiations with Harper Brothers for an edition of 'The Romantic Adventures of a Milkmaid'. 'Lying Awake' appears in the *Saturday Review*.

11   'An illness, which at the commencement did not seem to be serious, began on December 11. On the morning of that day he sat at the writing-table in his study, and felt totally unable to work. This, he said, was the first time that such a thing had happened to him' (*Life*, p. 444).

24   'Christmas in the Elgin Room' appears in *The Times*.

25   TH unable to come downstairs for the first time during the course of this illness. Tells Gosse, 'I am in bed on my back, living on butter-broth & beef tea, the servants being much concerned at my not being able to eat any Christmas pudding, though I am rather relieved' (*Letters*, VII, 89).

26   'He said that he had been thinking of the Nativity and of the Massacre of the Innocents, and his wife read to him the gospel accounts, and also articles in the *Encyclopaedia Biblica*. He remarked that there was not a grain of evidence that the gospel story was true in any detail' (*Life*, p. 445).

1928

January
10   (Tues) Slight recovery, enabling him to insist on making out a cheque to the Incorporated Society of Authors. In the evening asks to have Browning's 'Rabbi Ben Ezra' read to him.

11   Asks to be read a stanza from the *Rubáiyát of Omar Khayyám*. Composes and dictates waspish epigrams on George Moore and G. K. Chesterton. Dies shortly after 9 p.m. after a heart

attack. Cockerell opens the will and begins to plan a more public funeral than TH envisaged.

12   'The dawn of the following day rose in almost unparalleled splendour. Flaming and magnificent the sky stretched its banners over the dark pines that stood sentinel around' (*Life*, p. 446). The Dean of Westminster, in response to lobbying arranged by Cockerell and Barrie, gives permission for TH to be buried in Westminster Abbey. Fulsome obituary tributes appear, *The Times* for example declaring that English literature has been deprived of its most eminent figure. The heart removed from TH's body.

13   The body sent to Woking for cremation.

16   Three services take place at 2 p.m. TH's ashes interred in Poets' Corner, Westminster Abbey; his heart in the grave of his first wife at Stinsford. A local memorial service takes place in St Peter's, Dorchester.

TH was assembling his final volume of poetry, *Winter Words*, at the time of his death, with a view to publishing it on his birthday, 2 June. Serial rights for fifty of the poems are sold by FEH and Cockerell to the *Daily Telegraph*, where they appear at irregular intervals between 19 March and 26 September (for details see Purdy, pp. 252–61). The volume itself is published on 2 October. The *Life*, published as the work of FEH, appears in two volumes: *Early Life* (published 2 Nov) and *Later Years* (published 29 Apr 1930). 'Old Mrs Chundle', never printed in TH's lifetime, appears in the *Ladies Home Journal*, February 1929. TH survived by his brother Henry (died in 1928), by FEH (died 17 October 1937), and by his sister Kate (died 1940, the hundredth anniversary of TH's birth).

Principal Sources Consulted

The Hardy Memorial Collection in the Dorset County Museum: marginalia and datings in TH's copies of the Bible, the Book of Common Prayer and Keble's *Christian Year*.

Gatrell, Simon, *Hardy the Creator: A Textual Biography* (Oxford, 1988).
Gittings, Robert, *The Older Hardy* (London, 1978).
———,*Young Thomas Hardy* (London, 1975).
Gittings, Robert, and Manton, Jo, *The Second Mrs Hardy* (London, 1979).
Hardy, Emma, *Diaries*, ed. Richard H. Taylor (Ashington, Northumberland, 1985).
'Hardy, Florence Emily', *The Life of Thomas Hardy* (London, 1962).
Hardy, Thomas, *Collected Letters*, ed. Richard Little Purdy and Michael Millgate, 7 vols (Oxford, 1978–88).
———, *Literary Notebooks*, ed. Lennart A. Björk, 2 vols (London, 1985).
———, *The Personal Notebooks*, ed. Richard H. Taylor (London, 1978).
———, *The Variorum Edition of the Complete Poems*, ed. James Gibson (London, 1979).
Hassall, Arthur, *A Handbook of European History* (London, 1897).
Meynell, Viola (ed.), *Friends of a Lifetime: Letters to Sydney Carlyle Cockerell* (London, 1940).
Millgate, Michael, *Thomas Hardy: A Biography* (Oxford, 1982).
Nicholl, John, *Tables of European History, Literature, Science, and Art* (Glasgow, 1888).
Pinion, F. B., *A Hardy Companion* (London, 1968, repr. 1974).
Purdy, Richard Little, *Thomas Hardy: A Bibliographical Study* (London, 1954).
Steinberg, S. H., *Historical Tables*, 10th edn (London, 1979).
Williams, Neville, *Chronology of the Modern World: 1763 to the Present Time* (London, 1966).

Index